New Critical Thinking

New Critical Thinking
Criticism to Come

Edited by Julian Wolfreys

EDINBURGH
University Press

Edinburgh University Press is one of the leading university presses in the UK. We publish academic books and journals in our selected subject areas across the humanities and social sciences, combining cutting-edge scholarship with high editorial and production values to produce academic works of lasting importance. For more information visit our website: edinburghuniversitypress.com

Edinburgh University Press Ltd
The Tun – Holyrood Road, 12(2f) Jackson's Entry, Edinburgh EH8 8PJ

Typeset in 10/12 Adobe Sabon by
IDSUK (DataConnection) Ltd, and
printed and bound in Great Britain by
CPI Group (UK) Ltd, Croydon CR0 4YY

A CIP record for this book is available from the British Library

ISBN 978 0 7486 9966 7 (hardback)
ISBN 978 0 7486 9967 4 (webready PDF)
ISBN 978 0 7486 9964 3 (paperback)
ISBN 978 0 7486 9965 0 (epub)

Contents

Contributors

Christine Berberich is a Senior Lecturer in Twentieth-Century and Contemporary English Literature at the University of Portsmouth. Her research specialism focuses on English national identity and its creation on the one hand, and on post-memorial Holocaust writing on the other. Her publications include the book *The Image of the English Gentleman in 20th Century Literature: Englishness and Nostalgia* (Ashgate, 2007), the co-edited collections *These Englands: A Conversation on National Identity* (Manchester University Press, 2011), *Land & Identity: Theory, Memory & Practice* (Rodopi, 2012) and *Affective Landscapes in Literature, Art and Everyday Life* (Ashgate, 2015), the edited collection *The Bloomsbury Introduction to Popular Fiction* (Bloomsbury Academic, 2014), as well as essays and articles on authors as diverse as Ian Fleming, W. G. Sebald, Julian Barnes, Rachel Seiffert and Uwe Timm. She is, with Neil Campbell, series editor of *Place, Memory, Affect* with Rowman & Littlefield. Currently she is working on an edited collection dedicated to *Trauma & Memory: The Holocaust in Contemporary Culture* and has started planning a monograph on Perpetrator Fictions.

Catherine Bernard is Professor of English Literature and Art History at Paris Diderot University. She has published extensively on contemporary art (Cy Twombly, Andy Warhol, Rachel Whiteread, but also Gillian Wearing and Sam Taylor-Wood) as well as recent English fiction (Martin Amis, Peter Ackroyd, Pat Barker and John Lanchester). Among her recent publications, one may mention 'Deller, Wallinger, Wearing: Towards an Ethics of Visual Interpellation', in Jean-Michel Ganteau and Christine Reynier (eds), *Ethics of Alterity, Confrontation and Responsibility in 19th to 21st Centuries British Art* (Presses universitaires de la Méditerranée, 2015). Her research has also turned to Virginia Woolf, the Bloomsbury Group and, more widely, modernist aesthetics. She has co-edited several volumes of articles on Woolf and is the author of a critical study of *Mrs Dalloway* (Gallimard, 2006).

She has also published a critical edition and translation of *Flush* (Gallimard, 2012) and a translation and critical edition of a selection of Woolf's essays (Gallimard, 2015). She is currently working towards a monograph on the body politic(s) of contemporary British literature and visual arts to be published in 2017.

Mary Ann Caws is Distinguished Professor of English, French and Comparative Literature at the Graduate School of the City University of New York. An expert on surrealism and modern English and French literature, who works on the interrelations of visual and literary texts, her recent publications include *Undoing Art*, with Michel Delville (Luca Sossella Editore, 2016), *Glorieuses modernistes: art, écriture et modernité au féminin*, with Anne Reynes-Delobel (Presses universitaires de Liège, 2016) and *Miracles and Reason: The Life and Work of Blaise Pascal* (Reaktion Books, 2017).

Páraic Finnerty is Reader in English and American Literature at the University of Portsmouth. He is the author of *Emily Dickinson's Shakespeare* (University of Massachusetts Press, 2006) and co-author of *Victorian Celebrity Culture and Tennyson's Circle* (Palgrave Macmillan, 2013). His scholarly essays have appeared in *Literature & History*, *Prose Studies*, *Comparative American Studies*, *Critical Survey*, *Genders*, *Symbiosis: A Journal of Transatlantic Literary and Cultural Relations* and the *Emily Dickinson Journal*. His next book, *Dickinson and Her British Contemporaries: Victorian Poetry in Nineteenth-Century America*, is forthcoming from Edinburgh University Press.

Anton Froeyman is a post-doctoral researcher at the department of Philosophy and Moral Sciences at Ghent University. He has MAs in history and philosophy, and a PhD in philosophy. His research is about the crossroads between history, ethics and experience. He has published articles in (among others) *History and Theory*, Rethinking History, *Historical Methods* and *Journal of the Philosophy of History*. He has also published a book, *History, Ethics and the Recognition of the Other* (Routledge, 2015), in which he argues for a Levinasian view on the writing of history.

J. Hillis Miller is UCI Distinguished Research Professor of Comparative Literature and English Emeritus at the University of California at Irvine. He has published many books and essays on nineteenth- and twentieth-century literature and on literary theory, including *Communities in Fiction* (Fordham University Press, 2015); *Twilight of the Anthropocene Idols*, co-authored with Tom Cohen and Claire Colebrook (Open Humanities Press, 2016); and *An Innocent Abroad: Lectures in China* (Northwestern University Press, 2015), which gathers fifteen of the more than thirty lectures Miller gave at various universities in China between 1988 and 2012. Miller is a Fellow of the American Academy of Arts and Sciences and a member of the American Philosophical Society.

Kelly Oliver is W. Alton Jones Professor of Philosophy at Vanderbilt University. She is the author of over a hundred articles, fourteen scholarly books and ten edited volumes. Her authored books include, most recently, *Hunting Girls: Sexual Violence from The Hunger Games to Campus Rape* (Columbia University Press, 2016) and *Earth and World: Philosophy After the Apollo Missions* (Columbia University Press, 2015). Earlier works include *Technologies of Life and Death: From Cloning to Capital Punishment* (Fordham University Press, 2013), *Knock Me Up, Knock Me Down: Images of Pregnancy in Hollywood Film* (Columbia University Press, 2012), *Animal Lessons: How They Teach Us to Be Human* (Columbia University Press, 2009), *Women as Weapons of War: Iraq, Sex, and the Media* (Columbia University Press, 2007), *The Colonization of Psychic Space: A Psychoanalytic Theory of Oppression* (University of Minnesota Press, 2004), *Noir Anxiety: Race, Sex, and Maternity in Film Noir* (University of Minnesota Press, 2002) and perhaps her best-known work, *Witnessing: Beyond Recognition* (University of Minnesota Press, 2001). She has published in *The New York Times*, and has been interviewed on ABC television news, CSPAN, various radio programmes and the Canadian Broadcasting network. Her work has been translated into seven languages. Most recently, she has published two novels in the *Cowgirl Philosophy Mystery Series*.

Sarah Pardon studied Comparative Modern Literature at Ghent University and Literary Studies at the Catholic University of Louvain. She worked as a PhD Fellow of the Research Foundation Flanders (FWO) at the Department of Literary Theory of Ghent University. Her research revolves around the intersection of fact and fiction in representations of the past. She foregrounds the effects of dramatic irony and historical experience in the process of reading as two key notions to help us understand our relation with the past. She currently works as an editor for an academic publishing house.

Jean-Michel Rabaté is Professor of English and Comparative Literature at the University of Pennsylvania since 1992, a curator of Slought Foundation, an editor of the *Journal of Modern Literature* and a Fellow of the American Academy of Arts and Sciences. He has authored or edited more than thirty-five books on modernism, psychoanalysis and philosophy. Recent books include *Think, Pig! Beckett at the Limits of the Human* (Fordham University Press, 2016), *The Pathos of Distance* (Bloomsbury, 2016) and *Les Guerres de Derrida* (Presses de l'Université de Montréal, 2016).

Tone Selboe is Professor of Comparative Literature at the University of Oslo. Her most recent articles in English include 'Emotional Mapping in Jean Rhys' *Good Morning, Midnight*' (2014), 'Hungry and Alone: The Topography of Everyday Life in Knut Hamsun and August Strindberg' (2015) and 'Virginia Woolf and the Perception of Things' (forthcoming). Her latest book is *Hva er en roman* (Universitetsforlaget, 2015).

Monika Szuba is Lecturer in English Literature at the University of Gdańsk. Her research covers twentieth-century and twenty-first century Scottish and English poetry and prose, with a particular interest in ecocriticism informed by phenomenology. She is co-editor of the *between.pomiędzy* series published by the University of Gdańsk Press.

Julian Wolfreys is Professor of English and Director of the Centre for Studies in Literature at the University of Portsmouth. He is the author and editor of numerous books, including *Victorian Hauntings: Spectrality, Gothic, The Uncanny, and Literature* (Palgrave Macmillan, 2001), *Derrida: A Guide for the Perplexed* (Continuum, 2007), *Literature, in Theory: Tropes, Subjectivities, Responses, and Responsibilities* (Continuum, 2010) and *Dickens's London: Perception, Subjectivity, and Phenomenal Urban Multiplicity* (Edinburgh University Press, 2015). He is also the author of *Silent Music*, a novel (Triarchy Press, 2014). His most recent publications are two collections of poetry, *Draping the Sky for a Snowfall* (Triarchy Press, 2016) and *The Grand European Bestiary/Wielki bestiariusz europejski*, translated by Monika Szuba (Wydawnictwo Maski, 2016), and *Haunted Experience: Being, Loss, Memory* (Triarchy Press, 2016).

Introduction: New Critical Thinking – To Read so as to Become Acquainted

Julian Wolfreys

> . . . knowledge imposes a pattern, and falsifies,
> For the pattern is new in every moment
> And every moment is a new and shocking
> Valuation of all we have been.
>
> T. S. Eliot, *Four Quartets* (2015: 179)

> To be really mediaeval one should have no body. To be really modern
> one should have no soul.
>
> Oscar Wilde, *An Ideal Husband* (2009: 109)

> The 'modern' (*das 'Moderne'*) . . . is as varied in its meaning as the
> different aspects of one and the same kaleidoscope.
>
> Walter Benjamin, *The Arcades Project* (1999: 545)

The title of the present volume might mislead you. Consider: a book appears to make a claim to offer the reader something 'new'. Is there, any more, any new critical thinking? Have we not thought everything we are likely to think in the humanities already? Or are the chapters of this collection 'new' in the sense of being 'inexperienced' or 'unaccustomed'? The answer to these questions is not a direct one. The very baldness of the title, which is also a boldness bordering on hubris (imagine, someone claims to have identified new thinking, finally we can do away with all the old thoughts), leaves open the door to all manner of ungovernable thoughts and suppositions on the part of the reader as to the contents, while equally leaving the editor hostage to fortune or accusations of recklessness.

It is the case though that if you can't judge a book by its cover, you certainly should not do so by its title. Or at least, you should not let the title do your reading for you. The title in question signifies a much more modest purpose, even as it recognises the validity of T. S. Eliot's observation in the *Four Quartets*. The essays gathered here are new in a few senses. Taking existing ideas, critical forms, approaches to criticism, they seek to introduce new perspectives, shifting the patterns and requiring valuation. They search for ways of making received wisdom a little unfamiliar or strange, so that the reader might take a new look at what he or she thought was known already. They offer the possibility of taking that which already exists and, in beginning to think once more, as if for a first time, about what is known, or believed to be known critically, about history, culture, ethics, textuality, art, poetry, film, photography, and so forth, and so imagine the experience of a reading that takes place *as if for the first time*. Far from being formulaic, predictable, programmed the contributors to *New Critical Thinking* invent critical thinking in a transformed and transformative manner, reinvigorating critical thinking in the process.

Why are transformative and reinvigorating processes necessary, or, at least, useful? In universities literary theory and critical thinking courses retread, year after year well-established, now canonical texts. This is a perfectly legitimate way to proceed of course, and has proved very successful. Foucault continues to appear every year, as do various other proper names, as privileged signifiers for ways of thinking, standing for those considered to be foundational thinkers; and of course, in some senses, they are; although this in itself plays, often unthinkingly and uncritically, and in a not very new way on metaphysical notions of origin, source, and so forth. Equally, there are those approaches to critical thinking that orbit around, or depart from large conceptual planets and constellations: postcolonialism, gender studies, ecocriticism, to name but three. Again, to point to this continuing trend is not to be critical of it. It is of course necessary to begin the education of undergraduates new to critical thinking, its modalities and interests, in some way, and the continuing employment of the two models I have briefly acknowledged are as good as their continued usage suggests.

Perhaps the problem though, if indeed there is one, is not with such approaches, but with thinking itself within the limits of the institution. The university today is a business; it always has been in some sense, but the nakedness of the market-driven model is more apparent than ever in the first quarter of the twenty-first century, and everything appears to need to justify itself in gestures of outward-facing accessibility and marketability, as well as being able to process its students, as efficaciously as possible, in order to justify a self-replicating machinic function we can define as business as usual. We need just enough thought, and we need that thought to be packaged in particular ways. Literary theory, literary criticism, critical thinking, critical theory – all have had, at what I am sure someone somewhere has described as the coalface of higher education, their thinking done for them and settled into the ebbs and flows of just enough fashionableness as the market will bear.

Now, it might be nice to dream of some genuinely 'new' critical thinking, but there is nothing that is absolutely new. If something 'new' were to emerge, this cannot be anticipated, programmed or determined ahead of the event. Critical thinking is not an experiment where the outcome is posited and a way of proceeding is sought so as to arrive at the desired goal. Going back to those modest definitions of the new, particularly that definition that stresses seeing or experiencing what already exists in a different manner, the motivation is to move, in however small a way, from *thought* to *thinking*, from product to process. Believing that it is better to travel hopefully, etc., the present collection of essays endeavours to foreground the ongoing and continuous necessity of acts of critical reading, engagement and exploration.

This brings me to the subtitle of this volume: *Criticism to Come*. Some readers will recognise what is now a familiar critical locution, 'to come'. It is a phrase, a translation, that in recent years has been taken up, from the work of Jacques Derrida and the distinction made by Derrida between two different French expressions of the future: *futur/e* and *l'avenir*. The context of the remark is a voice-over by Derrida near the beginning of the documentary *Derrida* (2002), though in *Politique de l'amitié* (1994) Derrida had already played on the 'à venir' that haunts, and so deconstructs 'l'avenir'. In the film, the disembodied voice of Jacques Derrida comes – and returns – unexpectedly, over an initially blurry image of water, followed by railway tracks, the crossing of a river, some buildings, in the background of which are cranes; then we cross water once more:

> In general, I try and distinguish between what one calls the Future [*futur/e*] and 'l'avenir' [the 'to come']. The future is that which – tomorrow, later, next century – will be. There is a future which is predictable, programmed, scheduled, foreseeable. But there is a future, l'avenir (to come) which refers to someone who comes whose arrival is totally unexpected. For me, that is the real future. That which is totally unpredictable. The Other who comes without my being able to anticipate their arrival. So if there is any real future, beyond the other known future, it is l'avenir in that it is the coming of the Other when I am completely unable to foresee their arrival. (*Derrida* 2002)

Derrida speaks French (with the occasional English word, 'unpredictable', 'to come'); subtitles appear in English. More than one language, therefore, and certainly three texts, four if one includes the soundtrack (and one must) by Ryuichi Sakamoto. With the landscape in motion, the developing sound of the music, the movement of the subtitles and the ongoing voice, the audience/auditor/reader finds him- or herself involved in an intermedial space that does not come to rest, edit following edit, as word follows word, note, note.

My decision as editor to choose the distinction in Derrida's thinking of the future, his differentiation between an authentic and programmed future, was not governed by the sense that, if critical thinking has the chance to be new, to find the unfamiliar, the unexpected, and so to begin to see from a position or positions, perspectives, other than those that are carefully programmed, it would have to be a critical thinking that was irreducibly more than one thinking, that it was not to be knowingly or consciously governed by schools, names, and so forth. The only chance of any new critical thinking was in the to come. The essays in this volume thus engage in a thinking, in multiple acts of thinking that do not strive for novelty, for making grand claims. Instead, they work patiently at thinking, at critical interventions, the hope of which is that something may always come, something unexpected may return, as if arriving for a first time, from another place, in turning to particular texts, wherein a different turn is taken, and thinking meets this unpredictable future. In this, critical thinking might, it is hoped, lead to other ways of thinking that are not simply governed or dictated by business as usual.

There is too another sense of the 'new': modern, a word the contemporaneity of which seems never quite on time, signifying as it does in Latin 'just now'. This 'just now' signals a complex temporality that undoes from within any present moment as a myth of stable identification or reflection. However you are reading this, on a screen, on paper, there is already a challenging plurality, having to do with acts of reading, writing, pedagogy and critical thinking, underneath all of which is an implicit question articulated by Robert Gibbs in an article titled 'Time and Pages': '[a]s the humanities change, what is the changing interpretation of the future? Or how can we open a question about what kinds of futures are possible in the humanities to come?' (Gibbs 2015: 241–2) Critical thinking implicitly engages with such questions, not as questions to be answered, but as the everyday work of thinking in the face of what Gibbs calls, in the context of university time scales, an 'accelerated temporality of technology and capitalism' (2015: 242). Critical thinking, 'new' or 'modern' critical thinking, it seems, under the accelerated, and constantly accelerating temporality in which universities willingly collude to (often very much) greater or lesser extents, is caught in a dilemma. Thinking takes time, but there is no time to think, time is not allowed for thinking, and the time of the university is such that it holds – or attempts to hold – sovereign sway over thinking by dictating its pace so that the 'new' is not the 'just now' but something not yet thought, yet desired with a somewhat febrile near-immediacy. Universities, no longer content with departments or schools, establish centres, presuming the centre has a function in solving a problem that is larger than the discipline associated with the centre. The Centre is charged with a demand for innovation, for a product that is capable of being commercialised (Gibbs 2015: 242). The modern is too old, too out of date. It must no longer be merely new, no longer simply just now, but a future, which, increasingly, within the sovereign (a)reason of the university, is guaranteed and always already about to arrive.

Had the present volume been called *Modern Critical Thinking*, this would have been no less ambiguous, no less equivocal than the idea of the 'new' though it might have got everyone, from the contributors to the editors off the hook of coming up with novelty. Imagine it (it's easy): a novelty that can be described as modern because it has happened; no longer new, it still remains, recently enough, to be termed in a somewhat old-fashioned manner, 'modern'. How would one distinguish the 'modern', 'modernity'? Would one wish to? Would there not be a question of defending such a choice, the defence requiring a greater vigour than 'new'? And would 'modern' be opposed to something, not 'old' exactly, but perhaps 'classical'? Modern, new-fangled critical thinking. More than modern, supra-modern. In a sense, thinking of the critical kind, as opposed to an uncritical thinking (which might just as well be non-thinking) is always 'modern', always just not-quite on time, always slightly behind the times and the experiences, the perceptions, apprehensions, that the thinking seeks to accommodate; hence its being just now, rather than now. For the humanities, and this is a particular crisis long in the making, is always the somewhat spectral site of what remains, in the grip of a hauntological accommodation. The humanities is a dwelling, giving place to dwelling on ghosts. Indeed, the humanities, in embracing what, for convenience's sake we shall call 'literary theory' as a powerful and transitional force in its critical thinking, has been 'remarkably modern', to use a phrase of Oscar Wilde's.

The humanities are, and have been just like Mabel: 'a little too modern, perhaps. Nothing is so dangerous as being too modern. One is apt to grow old-fashioned quite suddenly' (Wilde 2009: II, i). With its will-to-commercialisation, a kind of naked and somewhat venal greed, the university (in some parts of the world) has taken on the guise of Lady Markby; but unlike Mabel, the humanities has spent so much time trying to give itself relevance that it is no longer pretty, the one thing that would have kept it fashionable. The desire to 'make it new' on the one hand, and the fervour of modernity on the other has instituted a 'moment of crisis' (Gibbs 2015: 243), which has in fact stalled any proper temporality for critical thinking. Caught in a stasis of constantly renewing, we find ourselves in the midst of a strange aporetic experience. Yet, this aporia is perhaps the very space where critical thinking might take place – and I would argue does in the essays in this collection – against the accelerated temporalities on the one hand of the recent history of the humanities and on the other hand the pedal to the metal mentality of the 'modern' university. That's a good thing too, the pause, the gap, between the event and the thinking of the event. In the space, there is the possibility of reflection as a beginning, and, with that, the arrival (the hope of the arrival) of that which can always come, that which is to come, though never as a certainty. Critical thinking of the right sort (something I think akin to good reading) allows for the indirect revelation of a deconstruction (if there is such a thing) in the process of authorised thinking. Too much in the humanities has served to reinforce the exclusions and contradictions in humanist discourse, while serving to blur the lines between a liberal humanist unreflective philosophy and the ethos of a neo-liberal marketplace. Thinking has delivered itself over into the service of universal goals 'too much on the basis of an unstable present – one of totality [and of totalisation, of teleological thinking, of goals and aims, that have in their construction] . . . a presumption of [strategic] universality', hiding the violence of its operations (Gibbs 2015: 269). To the contrary, a true critical thinking, one that revels in the just now, with the reflection of a sustained glance opens the door, suspends the moment, extends the duration, to welcome whatever might arrive. 'New', 'modern' critical thinking is just this, it has at least these possibilities: the suspended step, the invention of a duration, necessary to the task of thinking but not known ahead of the task.

I am playing with questions of time, I'm playing for time with this gesture of the 'new', and its uneasy companion, the 'modern'. Both, I want to suggest, have about them something of the trace. Something in each suggests a pause, but also something that remains. The deliberate strategy of the reductive term, which says everything and nothing, everything and all the rest, is intended as a solicitation to thinking, and with that, an opening onto a thinking of the 'infinitely calculable' (as, in this volume, J. Hillis Miller says Derrida says, of the meanings of *reste*). That there is always the idea of the 'new', in every return to what is known, there remains in the infinitely calculable, the incalculable itself as the chance of an iteration beyond, an iterability to come.

This is, I have the feeling, precisely just the chance of reading, a reading not avoiding reading in being dictated by a model of critical process. Good reading, reading that chances on the new, is always a process, described by Heidegger as *denkende Erfahrung* – thinking experience. Experience emerges from the act of thinking. There takes place the emergence of a reading between a text, a work of art, a concept such as 'the ethical', in which reading an insight might come to arrive as intellectual experience. The good reader grasps a situation through a process of cognition, which is experiential, belonging to a discontinuous process, one of blindness and insight, the experience unveiling the 'just now' through this temporality that is most singularly the temporality of reading. Reading as the modern, never quite on time, opens itself to the remains of the new, that temporally, within the space of its inscription, countersigns, and so opens that which remains as a trace 'just now', while placing itself anew in order to invite what remains, whatever remains, to come. Critical thinking should thus pause (and all good critical thinking does), gathering what remains, and demonstrating a hospitality to what might come, through a challenge, implicit or explicit to the unstable present. What is, I would argue, new precisely in these essays, is a hospitality, a welcome to thinking, a welcome to be thought by every reader. The essays that make this volume *New Critical Thinking* take responsibility for thinking itself, giving place to a calling as 'the Responsibility, which exceeds all responsibilities' of the institution (Steinnes 2008: 117). It is only by putting into question that critical thinking makes possible that it becomes possible to think of a future that cannot be imagined, and it is only in a genuine openness to the question, the idea of question, that critical thinking might appear, contrary to an orthodoxy where a 'given order of things . . . [expresses] pretentions to a mastery over the order of things in the name of knowledge' (Peim 2013: 174). New Critical Thinking, as a single idea is unrealisable but necessary, it does not refer to a given state of affairs; instead it names the hope of a promise, and takes responsibility for where we are just now. As these essays might serve to illuminate for you, a new critical thinking, non-homogeneous, never reducible to an itself in itself, is a process of welcoming and working with all that haunts, being 'open to rupture in the name of both critique and creativity', to which in turn there is an ethical dimension. Critical thinking takes place therefore in suspension, in acts of reading that are acts of waiting, reflecting and dwelling, without hope, without expectation. It does so with a certain urgency in the face of present demands, having the courage often to resist such demands, 'in the name of a certain emancipatory and *messianic* affirmation, a certain experience of the promise that one can try to liberate from any dogmatics' (Derrida 1994: 89). In the present state of higher education, having no hope is better than false hope:

> Open waiting for the event as justice this hospitality is absolute
> only if it keeps watch over its own universality. The messianic in its
> revolutionary forms (and the messianic is always revolutionary, it
> has to be) would be urgency, imminence, but irreducible paradox, a
> waiting without horizon of expectation. (Derrida 1994: 168)

One expression, if not exactly a form of being open and waiting, is the act of turning. In contradistinction to the turn made because one's route is planned or as a result of some 'autopilot' such as a GPS system, is that turn that takes place as part of not knowing where the turn leads, virtually or really, as Mary Ann Caws argues. The first of three chapters that comprise the principal section of the volume, 'Turnings and Re-Turnings' initiates a sustained critical thinking on subjectivity, the natural world and its representation. In her essay, Caws investigates various types of turn; not just the linguistic turn or the philosophical turn, or any turn of events or serious paradigm shift, but rather – in keeping with the modesty of the notion of the new that informs this volume – she considers a modest and often merely metaphoric or visual bend in something as everyday as a road. Taking as an example, she reflects on Nicolas de Staël's *Road in the Vaucluse*, which leads off the canvas into or onto somewhere else. One does not know where one is or one will go, or be led. Thus the critical voice takes a road less travelled, we might suggest, in order to see where the turn, and with it a rumination on the turn as the gesture of being open and investing critically in the open, the unexpected, first visual, then verbal and imaginative, might lead, taking in various literary turnings, including those in Virginia Woolf's novels.

Another aspect of being open, and awaiting the event, the to-come that cannot be seen is explored by Monika Szuba, in '"Peering into the dark machinery": Modernity, Perception and the Self in John Burnside's Poetry'. Szuba attempts to draw out that which is 'not-yet-seen' and the limits of what can be known. The chapter reads various aspects of exteriority and interiority in John Burnside's poems. It argues that the particular preoccupation with surfaces in Burnside's work foregrounds the tension between the visible and the invisible, the outside and the inside, presence and absence. Peering, in order to pierce the invisible, gazing in the hope of seeing 'the not-yet-seen', Burnside's speakers attempt to probe the condition of modern being. The increasingly insistent self-gaze is an attempt to understand oneself, to grasp a sense of self. Further, gazing upon himself, the poetic subject self-reflexively looks into the nature of selfhood. The self becomes an object of obsessive introspection or reflexive action. Inheritor of a dualistic vision of the self, the speaker emphasises the discontinuity between body and mind, demonstrating persistent mindedness, yet striving to reach beyond. This self-mirroring is thus an attempt to obtain a more profound self-knowledge through immediacy of experience. Scepticism towards hyperrationality accompanies a possibility of a nondualistic, embodied understanding of subjectivity. As the unfulfilled promise made by modern science to explain the world is sensed ever more acutely, in his writing Burnside often demonstrates the influence of progress on the individual. Despite the advances of modern technology, the limits of knowledge – and knowability – are deeply experienced by Burnside's speakers. The poet challenges the incontestability of facts and the certainty of vision. The latter proves to be an insufficient method of knowing, and only foregrounds the sense that reality constitutes merely a confusing collection of dispersed and unintelligible signs.

Following Szuba's interrogation of subjectivity in the world of Burnside's poetry, in 'Modernity's Sylvan Subjectivity, from Gainsborough to Gallaccio' Catherine Bernard examines how, from Jean-Jacques Rousseau to J. W. Goethe, William Wordsworth or John Clare, the sylvan world is perceived as the locus of reflexiveness and introspection. The definition of modern subjectivity, she argues, is symmetrically associated with the aestheticisation of nature. The rational instrumentalisation of the forest world and the rise of modern phenomenology may thus be seen as the two symmetrical facets of the birth of the modern subject: rational and sensitive, disciplined and expansive. Thus, in this light, Bernard suggests, the rational instrumentalisation of the forest world and the rise of modern phenomenology may thus be seen as the two symmetrical facets of the birth of the modern subject: rational and sensitive, disciplined and expansive.

Yet, she avers, the symmetry may be deceptive. The chapter thus aims to explore the sylvan imagination of modernity from a longer view in order to take a new turn, and open up what is not yet seen. Focusing both on visual arts (from Eugène Delacroix or Thomas Gainsborough, to contemporary installation artist Anya Gallaccio), it explores modernity's conflicted relation to the forest. As much as fetishes inscribed with man's nostalgic yearning for a lost relation with nature, trees should be read as both allegories of modernity and lived sites of phenomenological experience. In these paradoxical 'quasi-objects', as defined by Michel Serres and Bruno Latour, is thus crystallised the paradoxical economy of modernity's experimental/experiential reason, a reason that is both self-divided and dialectical.

From matters of subjectivity and phenomenological perception addressed in the first essays of *New Critical Thinking*, what follows addresses history and historicity, and from there to questions of ethics; in truth, the divide is not clean, good reading and critical thinking refusing to remain politely in methodological boundaries. Thus in formal terms, the presentation of chapters is not divided into sections. It is important to read between and across the collection.

To think historicity, to engage with the past in a meaningful manner beyond some arid contextualising exercise, critical discourse has to remember the subject's experience of the past. It also has to read, and read through, the aesthetic experience of history's texts, where reading and critical discourse might take into account what Sarah Pardon calls, in her examination of texts concerning the assassination of John F. Kennedy, the beginning and end, the limits, of the mediation process of reading historical representations.

Starting from Keith Jenkins's concern about why we still write, study and theorise about history if we have arrived at the realisation that it is a linguistic reconstruction much like any other type of text, Pardon argues that we first need to move away from a discussion about the multiple interpretations of the word 'fiction'. Instead, she insists, we need to emphasise that both history writing and fiction are equally concerned with evoking images of the past in our minds (concerns that will be addressed in a different manner also in Christine Berberich's chapter). From this, Pardon treats the representation of historical figures such as Kennedy or Lee Harvey Oswald as historical experiences that each ask for their own set of formal representations, similar in both fictional and factual texts. It is not, she continues by averring, just the ontological status of a text that determines the choice of representation. The need for an authentic experience of a historical figure also influences the selection of formal representations that critical readers would find credible in both fictional and factual representations. Her aim is thus to show through the reading of the reading process how we can begin anew to analyse the actualisation of an absent past.

With such ideas in mind, Páraic Finnerty examines Emily Dickinson's representations of past experiences and her exploration of forgetfulness in the context of Frank Ankersmit's ideas about the role forgetting plays in humanity's experience of the past. For Ankersmit, historical writing stems from and attempts to remedy humanity's separation from the past and its desire for access to this foreclosed realm. The division between the past and present becomes most pronounced and undeniable at moments of social and political upheaval, when a past identity, life and worldview must be collectively abandoned or forgotten as a response to such dramatic rupture or transformation. What is forgotten becomes experienced in its absence, associated with a mythic world that is forever lost, and sublimely encountered as an epistemological and conceptual challenge to a current worldview. Finnerty's essay uses Ankersmit's ideas to offer a new way of understanding much-discussed features of Dickinson's work, especially her preoccupation with past events and experiences, loss and memory, and, most strikingly, her couching of these in imagery and language associated with the sublime and in relation to psychological self-division and incomprehensible states. These elements of her writing along with her recurring figurations of death, violence and revolution are indicators of what Ankersmit terms sublime historical experience. They are markers of her position as a poet writing in the aftermath of the American Revolution and during a shift within her Anglo-American culture involving the loss of a former identity centred on religious belief, and the designation of a new secular and sceptical identity in terms of that which has been forgotten and renounced.

Knowledge of the past from philosophical perspectives is also the focus of Anton Froeyman's 'Reading Microhistory: Three Layers of Meaning'. Drawing also on Frank Ankersmit's philosophy of history, and the epistemological challenges Ankersmit issues to the orthodoxies of certain Anglo-American historicisms, Froeyman argues that, analysed from a cognitive point of view, if microhistories have a contribution to our knowledge of the past in the same sense as physics contributes to our knowledge of physical reality, they only do so in a very limited and at best derivative sense. He then contests that what is primarily at stake is the creation of a feeling of being there, or of historical experience. In the third part of his analysis, Froeyman suggests that this feeling is not there just for its own sake, but also for ethical reasons, in a double way. First, microhistorians promote an emancipating agenda with respect to their contemporaries. Second, they also are driven by a sense of ethical commitment, of responsibility towards the past itself. Revitalising the past is not just relevant for our time, it also creates a sense of historical justice, which fits in a view of ethics as an ethics of recognition and representation.

The sense of an ethical commitment and, with that, the feeling of historical experience pervades Christine Berberich's discussion of Holocaust Fiction, 'Writing Fiction, Making History: Historical Narrative and the Process of Creating History'. Almost seventy years on from the end of the Second World War, she argues, the Holocaust still holds considerable cultural capital. Even though the numbers of actual survivors of the atrocities are now inexorably diminishing, new publications on the Holocaust appear almost every month. In lieu of survivor accounts, the ethically troublesome genre of Holocaust Fiction is gaining ever more ground. Occupying the grey zone between memoir and fiction, Holocaust *faction* is also getting increasingly popular. As such, critics and readers have seen the appearance of works of fiction enhanced by factual research on the one hand, and works of factual research more problematically manipulated by fiction on the other as writers try to engage with the Holocaust from ever-changing and challenging perspectives.

One of these perspectives is that of the perpetrator – a topic long shunned but now increasingly coming to the fore. Apart from the biographical accounts of children and grandchildren of the *real* perpetrators, there is now fiction about imagined perpetrators (Jonathan Littell's vastly influential though no less troubling *The Kindly Ones*, for example) as well as imagined narratives about 'real' perpetrators. Berberich's chapter offers a critical discussion of the narrative strategies employed by Patrick Modiano's *The Search Warrant* (1997) Laurent Binet's *HHhH* (2009). Both texts offer 'factional/fictional' writing on the Holocaust and its aftermaths that challenge traditional history writing. Both Modiano and Binet interweave their historical narratives with highly self-reflexive accounts about their own research, their writing strategies and their concerns about the 'veracity' of the history they present. In his account, Binet focuses on the Czechoslovakian assassins of Reinhard Heydrich whose story, however, is constantly overshadowed by that of their 'victim', Heydrich himself. A story about resistance heroes is thus turned, problematically, into a story foregrounding the perpetrator.

If ethical thinking is as inescapable and difficult as it is necessary, in the regard one turns to the past or towards the other, then an ethics within the limits of a mere humanism, then the question of witnessing and attestation, seen already in a number of ways in this volume – through the interrogation of subjectivity, through the interrogation of the experience and memory of the past, and through the reflection on forms of identity – must turn to environment, through what Kelly Oliver in this volume calls a response ethics in 'Witnessing, Recognition and Response Ethics'. While she agrees that the ideal of mutual recognition is admirable, Oliver's central argument is that in practice, recognition is experienced as conferred by the very groups and institutions responsible for withholding it in the first place. In other words, recognition is distributed according to an axis of power that is part and parcel of systems of dominance and oppression. Taking up more recent attempts to link recognition to vulnerability rather than to self-consciousness, Oliver both challenges the concept of vulnerability as exclusive to, or constitutive of, humanity, on the one hand, while criticising the concept for levelling differences in degrees of vulnerability, on the other. In this regard, vulnerability, she contests, could be seen as the flip side of political recognition. Some people or animals are given political recognition while others are made vulnerable.

In the second part of her chapter, Oliver proposes witnessing, grounded in response ethics, as a supplement to recognition models of political and ethical subjectivity. In conclusion, she relates witnessing and response ethics to an ethics of earth grounded on our shared bond to our singular home, planet earth. Rather than start with our recognition of ourselves as self-conscious human beings, or recognition of our shared vulnerability as human beings, she asks what happens when we see ourselves as earthlings who exist by virtue of our ability to respond to the call of others, including our environments. Moving beyond the humanism of most theories of mutual recognition of either self-consciousness or vulnerability, Oliver argues for a response ethics grounded on our singular shared bond to the earth. Witnessing as ongoing address and response between earthlings and their environments cannot be reduced to recognition, mutual or otherwise.

Underpinning all the essays commented on thus far are, implicitly, ideas of the modern, a modernity irreducible to a single definition but seen, received, understood and felt. The final section of *New Critical Thinking: Criticism to Come* considers aspects of the modern and modernity, through matters of gendered identity in the context of the modern city, new ontologies and challenges to reading afford through formal experiment, the question of the subject's engagement with radical textualities, and the experiment with the self that the proper name puts into play. In each case, with the four chapters of this section, there is the reading of an experience of expropriation, or of a certain give and take between expropriation and exappropriation (as I explore in my essay on Derrida and experiment).

In 'A Norwegian Abroad: Camilla Collett's Travelogues from Berlin and Paris', Tone Selboe concerns herself with the gendered experience of a woman on the streets of Berlin and Paris. Camilla Collett spent the latter part of the nineteenth century travelling in Europe. She was an observant commentator of a wide range of topics, from the French Revolution to urban planning and city life in Paris and Berlin. In essays and travelogues she compares what she observes abroad with conditions in the Norwegian capital, Kristiania (later Oslo). Thus, Selboe suggests that while Collett was part of a particular European, modern context, she came at the same time, through the reflection that the travelogues afforded, to be intensely concerned with the question of national identity and *Bildung*. Focusing on Collett's travelogues from Berlin and Paris, with a special emphasis on her discussion of life on streets and in parks, and the possibility for women walking the streets alone, Selboe explores Collett's experience of the self as other through a reading of how daily life in Berlin and Paris is compared, by Camilla Collett, with the dreariness of Kristiania, her texts being striking examples of how a writer from the margins of Europe is in dialogue with the contemporary European scene.

In many ways, if Collett comes as the outsider from central Europe, a European other exploring the cultural identity of a cosmopolitan modernity, while reflecting on the gendered, marginal self, Alfred Jarry is the very apotheosis of that urban modernity. Jean-Michel Rabaté illustrates through a reading of 'Alfred Jarry's Nietzschean Modernism' how Jarry, a radical Nietzschean with anarchist leanings, was a living bridge between late symbolism and futurism. More than his plays (the Ubu cycle), his novels, too rarely discussed, serve for Rabaté to exemplify the inception of French modernism – this modernism being defined by Rabaté as the splicing of the old and the new in a context defined by stylistic experimentation, sexual explicitness, and the creation of a new ontology in which humans and machines exchange their properties.

The clinamen is that figure of the unpredictable swerve, first identified and so named by Lucretius. It figures as the 'discursive necessity of play in the canon'. It is the 'play of canonicity' (Barker 1989: 72) – or what Jarry termed *la bête imprévue* – an interest shared, albeit in very different ways, between Nietzsche, Jarry and Jacques Derrida. The clinamen is just this turn, this opening, the 'radical beast' of an unexpected event, giving on to invention, which opens thinking to itself. After Jarry's publications, there is arguably no more radical a 'beast' textually speaking than Jacques Derrida's *Glas*, a text of which it might best be said that we are very far from beginning to think towards it, much less with it. The very question of a reading is called into doubt on opening the book, as J. Hillis Miller confesses in his essay, which attempts to 'read' the first page of Jacques Derrida's *Glas*. At the same time Miller seeks to report as best he can what actually goes on when he makes this effort of reading. He tries to exemplify in detail his claim that what goes on in reading is much stranger and more complex that one might think, recalling an intricate series of events that took place when he first received *Glas* in the mail and opened it, reading first the single-sheet insert and then looking at the cover, the title page and, finally, the first page of the text proper. In Miller's case, at least, in addition to trying to make sense of the words on the page, all sorts of somatic and affective responses were involved, as well as a constant unsuccessful attempt to create a coherent mental image based not only on the way the words are arranged on the page (in two columns), but also on the bewildering complexity of what the words say.

One might suggest that Miller's essay is an experiment in thinking reading, or just reading; or just thinking in the face of a text that appears from the get-go, experimental, inventive. Reading must needs be inventive also, it must acquaint itself as if for a first time with what takes place when one thinks (one reads) and when one (thinks one) reads. Reading of the good kind is, like a true critical thinking, an experience, an encounter, harbouring the possibility for an event, for something to come. It is thus an invention, a searching after something already there. It is also an act of becoming acquainted. Experiment and experience are close relations of course, both having to do with acquaintanceship, of making something known. To acquaint is to make known, but there is a question perhaps as to whether this is a conscious act or whether that which makes itself known in acts of reading and thinking is that which arrives out of an unexpected turn, where something is invented (found) through this experience of and experiment in a critical reading.

In the final essay in the collection, I ask the question of whether Jacques Derrida experiments. Specifically I question whether there is an experiment taking place in Derrida's texts in the proper name, in his call to, response to, experience of, the proper name. At the same time as pursuing this reading, I suggest that critical thinking should always be, after a fashion, a small experiment, especially around that experimentation and experience of the proper name. In the experience of a critical thinking various modalities of experience arise: response, avoidance, engagement, and so forth. I examine certain of these experiences (experiences of reading and non-reading, thinking and non-thinking) in the name of Jacques Derrida, turning to consider, beyond naming, citation, reference, allusion, calling, bearing witness, leading in conclusion to a realisation of the experience in the name of the name that might stand in for the possibilities of a new critical thinking itself, as that which always strives to exceed and escape systematisation, totalisation, so that what is to come, what remains to come in the name of a critical thinking is something that speaks through the experience of what Derrida, with reference to the proper name, calls 'a universal pronoun, but of so singular a universality that it always remains precisely singular' (Derrida 1984: 281). Or in other words, a true critical thinking, always new, always remaining to become acquainted with, so singular is its universality.

WORKS CITED

Barker, Stephen (1989), 'Canon-Fodder: Nietzsche, Jarry, Derrida (The Play of Discourse and the Discourse of Play)', *Journal of Dramatic Theory and Criticism*, 4: 1 (Fall), 69–83.

Benjamin, Walter (1999), *The Arcades Project*, trans. Howard Eiland and Kevin McLaughlin, Cambridge, MA: Harvard University Press.

Derrida, documentary, directed by Kirby Dick and Amy Ziering Kofman. USA: Jane Doe Films, 2002.

Derrida, Jacques (1984), *Margins of Philosophy*, trans. Alan Bass, Chicago: University of Chicago Press.

Derrida, Jacques (1994), *Politiques de l'amitié*, Paris: Galilée.

Eliot, T. S. (2015), 'East Coker', from *Four Quartets*, in *The Poems of T. S. Eliot Vol. I*, ed. Christopher Ricks and Jim McCue, London: Faber & Faber, pp. 177–211.

Gibbs, Robert (2015), 'Of Time and Pages', *College Literature*, 42: 2 (Spring), 241–79.

Peim, Nick (2013), 'Education, Schooling, Derrida's Marx and Democracy: Some Fundamental Questions', *Studies in Philosophy & Education*, 32: 2 (March), 171–87.

Steinnes, Jenny (2008), 'Transformative Teaching: Restoring the Teacher, under Erasure', *Educational Philosophy and Theory*, 41: 2 (August), 114–25.

Wilde, Oscar (2009), *An Ideal Husband*, ed. Russell Jackson, London: Methuen.

CHAPTER I

Turnings and Re-Turnings

Mary Ann Caws

I'd like to investigate various types of turn, not just the linguistic turn or the philosophical turn or any turn of events or serious paradigm shift, rather a modest and often merely metaphoric or visual bend in something as everyday as a road. As an example, I would take Nicolas de Staël's *Road in the Vaucluse*, which leads off the canvas into or onto somewhere else. Part of the point is not knowing where, another part is my acquaintance with the region and still another is my obsession with this particular turning. I'd like to see where such a rumination, first an example of the visual, then a meditation on things verbal and imaginative, might lead.

Here is my initial thought: that modernism now is not so much about meanings but more about, or at least as much about, what something turns and points to. Turnings call for a turning into, turnings involve a going back incessantly more than going forward. I am fascinated by re-turnings, inturnings and turning aside, as in the so celebrated and celebratory theatre asides. Modernism is, as I see it, about learning by turning, not by just going straight ahead.

So let me take further examples than the visual de Staël that began my rumination. First, because it is so intensely visual (see Luchino Visconti's brilliant film), let me take the gorgeous and haunting visage and figure of Tadzio, from Thomas Mann's *Death in Venice* (1963). We are looking at Tadzio in his striped linen suit with red breast-knot, walking on the shore by the sea, where he is visible and takes all the space:

> He paced there, divided by an expanse of water from the shore, from
> his mates by his moody pride, a remote and isolated figure, with
> floating locks, out there in sea and wind, against the misty inane.
> Once more he paused to look: with a sudden recollection, or by an
> impulse, *he turned from the waist up, in an exquisite movement, one
> hand resting on his hip, and looked over his shoulder at the shore* . . .
> (Mann 1963: 74; my emphasis)

And Aschenbach looks on, simply qualified as 'the watcher', as he sits, rests his head and then lifts his head, 'as if it were to Tadzio's gaze . . .':

> It seemed to him the pale and lovely Summoner out there smiled at him and beckoned; as though, with the hand he lifted from his hip, he pointed outward as he hovered on before into an immensity of richest expectation. And, as so often before, he rose to follow. (Mann 1963: 75)

It gives you a gulp in the chest, this turning. In the magnificent filmed version, you see Tadzio half-turn, as in a pose of *contrapposto*, just like the famous Ballthrower, as does every pose in a counterpose.

A RETURNING TO MEMORY

This turn deserves the other to which we often refer, since Virginia Woolf always is on every modernist menu, and we have with us a great Woolf specialist, Catherine Bernard, with whom I have so enjoyed speaking before, in the French Association of Virginia Woolf scholars. Here, from *To the Lighthouse*, is that grand passage of the children's rhyme, 'Luriana Lurilee', which works, as Andre Gerard (2014) points out, as a homage to the love between Mr and Mrs Ramsay or Leonard and Virginia:

> As if a dialogue, her unspoken thoughts: '*And all the lives we ever lived and all the lives to be are full of trees and changing leaves.*' The words seem to be spoken by her own voice, outside her self . . . what had been in her mind the whole evening while she said different things. She knew that everyone at the table was listening to the voice saying:
>
> > I wonder if it seems to you,
> > Luriana, Lurilee
>
> . . . then Augustus Carmichael had risen, and stood chanting:
>
> > *To see the Kings go riding by*
> > *Over lawn and daisy lea*
> > *With their palm leaves and cedar sheaves,*
> > *Luriana, Lurilee,*
>
> and as she passed him he turned slightly towards her repeating the last words:
>
> > *Luriana, Lurilee*
> > come out and climb the garden path,
> > Luriana Lurilee.
> > The china rose is all bloom and buzzin with the yellow bee.

. . . She knew, without looking round, that every one at the table was listening to the voice saying:

> I wonder if it seems to you, Luriana, Lurilee . . .

But the voice stopped. She looked round. She made herself get up. Augustus Carmichael had risen and, holding his table napkin so that it looked like a long white robe he stood chanting:

> To see the Kings go riding by . . .

And as she passed him, he turned slightly toward her, repeating the last words:

> Luriana, lurilee

And bowed to her as if he did her homage. . . . she returned his bow and passed through the door . . .

It was necessary to carry everything a step further . . . It changed, it shaped itself differently: it had become, she knew, flinging one last look at it over her shoulder, already the past. (Woolf 1981: 110–11)

This is the famous look over the shoulder, so the turn, implied, does not have to be even mentioned, it is present.

My own implication here is that the turn, as the returning, scarcely needs emphasis: in modernist writings we know so well, it is simply there. Like Clarissa, it is there and we could end upon it.

Andre Gerard (2014) has commented on this passage, which Leonard Woolf knew as 'A Garden Song' by Charles Isaac Elton, and which he noted down in his copy of Aristotle's *Nicomachean Ethics* and recited to Virginia, before it appeared in Vita Sackville-West and Harold Nicolson's 1946 anthology *Another World Than This*. The Vita and Harold version has the line 'Till you sleep in a humble heap' whereas the Woolf version reads 'Till you sleep in a bramble heap' – significant because the word bramble appears several times in *To the Lighthouse* (Gerard 2014). So, Gerard posits, this is a communion between Leonard and Virginia. He also points out the 'waving leaves' in the anthology and the 'changing leaves' in Virginia's recitation . . . no less significant:

> Come out and climb the garden-path, Luriana Lurillee
> The China-rose is all abloom and buzzing with the yellow bee,
> We'll swing you on the cedar-bough, Luriana Lurillee
>
> I wonder if it seems to you, Luriana Lurillee,
> That all the lives we ever lived and all the lives to be
> Are full of trees and waving leaves, Luriana Lurillee.
> . . .

Swing, swing on the cedar-bough, Luriana Lurillee,
Till you sleep in a *bramble* heap or under the gloomy churchyard-tree
And then fly back to swing on a bough, Luriana Lurillee. (Woolf
1981: 110; my emphasis)

Mrs Ramsay continues to murmur this unforgettable unknown poem, which
is actually 'A Garden Song':

all the lives we ever lived
and all the lives to be
are full of trees and changing leaves (Woolf 1981: 110)

In the original, it seems that in Leonard's copy, it reads 'waving leaves'. That
it should be 'changing' in *To the Lighthouse* as opposed to 'waving' seems
equally important, in such a novel of change and loss and recovering and
vision, but that is not my point here (see McBee n.d.).

I wonder if it seems to you
Luriana Lurilee
That all the lives we ever lived
And all the lives to be,
Are full of trees and waving leaves,
Luriana Lurilee.   (Woolf 1981: 111)

Then Mrs Ramsay reads from a book on the table:

She did not know at first what the words meant at all

Steer, hither steer your winged pines, all beaten Mariners

she read . . . '*Nor praise the deep vermillion in the rose*,' she read
and so reading she was ascending, she felt, on to the top, on to the
summit. . . . she held it in her hands, beautiful and reasonable, clear
and complete . . . the sonnet. (Woolf 1981: 119, 121)

This is of course Shakespeare's Sonnet 98 'From you have I been absent in the
spring', and as she reads, Mr Ramsay finds her astonishingly beautiful:

Yet seem'd it winter still, and, you away,
As with your shadow I with these did play,
she finished.
    'Well?' she said, echoing his smile dreaming, looking up from
    her book.
        As with your shadow I with these did play,

she murmured, putting the book on the table. (Woolf 1981: 121)

But there is a further turn, in the boat at the end, and this turn takes upon itself to overcome the so mournful words that Mr Ramsay is fond of, is used to, quoting:

> Mr. Ramsay had seen himself walking on the terrace, alone . . . Sitting in the boat, he bowed, he crouched himself, acting instantly his part – the part of a desolate man, widowed, bereft . . . and said gently and mournfully,
>
> > But I beneath a rougher sea
> > Was whelmed in deeper gulfs than he . . .
>
> Cam half started on her seat. . . . The movement roused her father: and he shuddered and broke off, exclaiming: 'Look! Look!' so urgently that James also turned his head to look over his shoulder at the island. They all looked. They looked at the island. (Woolf 1981: 166)

And now it is explicit, near the end of this valuable book, this turn made by James, whose trip it was supposed to be in the beginning, to that lighthouse by which we, so many of us, measure our voyage and our glance and our seeing: this is our look also.

Most urgently, and lastly, we recognise Mr Ramsay's reciting, repeatedly, these lines:

> *We perished . . . each alone*
> *. . .*
> *But I beneath rougher sea* (Woolf 1981: 165–6)

Of course, this is part of something longer, from William Cowper's 1799 poem 'The Castaway':

> No voice divine the storm allayed,
> No light propitious shone,
> When, snatched from all effectual aid,
> We perished, each alone:
> But I beneath a rougher sea,
> And whelmed in deeper gulfs than he. (Cowper 2016)

And the point is not, here, our recognition or not, but his 'usual spams of repentance or shyness' in reciting it, and then after again murmuring 'But I beneath a rougher sea' he is heard – as he means to be, sighing and saying,

> gently and mournfully,
>
> > *But I beneath a rougher sea*
> > *Was whelmed in deeper gulfs than he* (Woolf 1981: 166)

But finally, when Mr Ramsay was about:

James and Cam were afraid, to burst out:

> *But I beneath a rougher sea*

and if he did, they could not bear it; they would shriek aloud; they could not endure another explosion of the passion that boiled in him . . . But at last he said, triumphantly, 'Well done!' (Woolf 1981: 206)

Even as we all hear the lines, we all feel triumphant in his not sighing and not saying them, unexpected as is his silence now, and his compliment. It seems to me that every time we reread *To the Lighthouse*, this nonspeaking of what we continue to hear increases its power, so that the entire recitation, memory and final unspeaking lets us have all our own visions, not just Lily alone.

Echoing through *The Waves* of 1931 are not just the 'waving leaves' of that same 'Garden Song' shortened into *The Waves*, but also the lines from Shelley's 'Ode to the West Wind', instantly recognisable by many, in its blowing through Louis's mind in its sorrowful sweep.

As for that last act that cannot be finished, *Between the Acts* (1941), it will have to start on a nursery rhyme:

> *The King is in his counting house*
> *Counting out his money*
> *The Queen is in her parlour* (Woolf 1940: 115)

And then the tune starts over, and does not come to an end:

> *The King is in his counting house*
> *Counting out his money*
> *The Queen is in her parlour*
> *Eating . . .*

Suddenly the tune stopped. The tune changed . . .
The tune changed; snapped; broke; jagged. (Woolf 1940: 122)

We can all finish, because each of us in the reading audience remembers, remembers. That is of course what we have always returned towards. And so it is in us that the resolution is made, that each of us makes, for all of us – which is real sharing, between the author and the audience. This is, after all, the point. While we wait for what the Queen is eating, we know it's bread and honey and then it doesn't come upon rereading and we know Mrs. Ramsay will be finished between parentheses, we see a prediction of her disappearance, and she will not be returning.

But the reassurance of what everyone knows is what we return to, and this one ends as it should:

> *Happy and glorious,*
> *Long to reign over us,*
> *God save the King.* (Woolf 1940: 195)

The King is no longer in his counting house but on the throne, and we have, all of us, moved on from a nursery rhyme to a hymn recited by a whole country. So it has gone from Macaulay and Milton and Shelley and Shakespeare – what we may remember or not, from the learned and ultra learned, in Virginia Woolf's first novel *The Voyage Out* (1915), through a shared poem Leonard had said to Virginia, all the way to the unresolved nursery rhyme in *Between the Acts*, those most well-known verses we find in our memories and therefore for which we can and must complete the resolution in our own selves. We have finally to turn to resolving what is incomplete.

Of course, we can look up 'my home is at Windsor, close to the Inn', and can be ironically amused by how many hotels want to put us up as we are researching the lines, if we feel ironic in that moment. But the point I want to make is not that. It is not a point about irony, but about life, not always the same thing. It is this: wherever we might be, in our counting houses and in our parlours, and whatever childhood or grown-up memory it might bring back, we probably have to listen to the incompletion, and manage to complete it from our own selves, turning towards it, and towards our own remembering. It sounds and reads as if it were indeed about our own lives, learning not to wait for the honey, as if it were to be about going on with it.

ALWAYS TO END WITH

I want to end on, very simply, Marcel Proust's *Search*, as we refer to it in English: here is the passage from the third volume, or *Time Regained*, translated by C. K. Scott-Moncrieff and Terence Kilmartin. Here, the end is near, and we should indeed end upon this point:

> The mind has landscapes which it is allowed to contemplate only for
> a certain space of time. In my life I had been like a painter climbing a
> road high above a lake, a view of which is denied to him by a curtain
> of rocks and trees. Suddenly through a gap in the curtain he sees the
> lake, its whole expanse is before him, he takes up his brushes. But
> already the night is at hand, the night which will put an end to his
> painting and which no dawn will follow. (Proust 1981: 1092)

So this landscape is the final one to which we turn, and – though we are not painters, most of us, but only writers, and as such, deeply moved by the way

Proust is ending his work, not as the cathedral it is, but as the most modest of objects, such as one made with Françoise, constructing something towards which we finally turn, in utter simplicity:

> And . . . I thought that at my big deal table, under the eyes of Françoise . . . I should work beside her and in a way almost as she worked herself . . . and, pinning here and there an extra page, I should construct my book, I dare not say ambitiously like a cathedral, but quite simply like a dress. (Proust 1981: 1090)

WORKS CITED

Cowper, William (2016), 'The Castaway (1799)', in Robert J. DeMaria, Jr. (ed.), *British Literature: An Anthology 1640–1789*, 4th edn, Chichester: John Wiley & Sons, p. 1027, reprinted in Kim Provost McBee (n.d.), 'Poetry in *To The Lighthouse*', available at <http://www.uah.edu/woolf/lighthouse_poems.pdf> (last accessed 19 December 2016).

Death in Venice, film, directed by Luchino Visconti. Italy: Warner Bros., 1971.

Gerard, Andre (2014), 'Blog #129: Charles Elton's "A Garden Song" and To the Lighthouse Brambles', 13 January, available at <http://patremoirpress.com/blog/?p=1236> (last accessed 19 December 2016).

McBee, Kim Provost (n.d.), 'Poetry in *To The Lighthouse*', available at <http://www.uah.edu/woolf/lighthouse_poems.pdf> (last accessed 19 December 2016)

Mann, Thomas (1963), *Death in Venice*, trans. H. T. Lowe-Porter, New York: Vintage.

Proust, Marcel (1981), *Remembrance of Things Past*, vol. 3 of *In Search of Lost Time*, trans. Charles Kenneth Scott-Moncrieff, Terence Kilmartin and Andreas Mayor, New York: Random House.

Sackville-West, Vita and Harold Nicolson (1946), *Another World Than This*, London: Michael Joseph.

Woolf, Virginia (1940), *Between the Acts*, New York: Mariner.

Woolf, Virginia (1981), *To the Lighthouse*, London: Harvester Wheatsheaf.

CHAPTER 2

'Peering into the dark machinery': Modernity, Perception and the Self in John Burnside's Poetry

Monika Szuba

The promise made by modern science to explain the world has been countered with the limits of knowledge, sensed ever more acutely now that its grand project seems to have gone awry. A collection of dispersed and unintelligible signs, reality remains as unreadable as before. Any knowledge (including self-knowledge) is marked by uncertainty, instability and undecidability. The self has become an object of introspection, driven by a very modern sense of insecurity and fluidity. Qualities emerging after meticulous self-scrutiny are liquidity, indeterminacy and impermanence, as Zygmunt Bauman (2000) writes. The modern subject's increasingly insistent self-gaze is an attempt to grasp a sense of self. Gazing upon him- or herself, the subject narcissistically – and hopefully – looks into the nature of selfhood. But this reflective consciousness may come at a price of flesh. As the modern subject gazes and peers (and processes), he or she becomes more and more disconnected from his or her corporeality. The discontinuity between body and mind results in persistent mindedness. Technological progress has introduced new practices of representation, removing any immediacy of experience, making the divide between presence and absence more fuzzy, underlining spaces in between.

One of the consequences of modernity is also a divide between the natural and human world (a paradoxical turn of phrase as it seems to imply that what is natural is necessarily inhuman and what is human is unnatural), which has governed Western intellectual life since the seventeenth century. This separation constitutes the foundation of the image of modern Western man. The priority given to science and the rising importance of technology in the life of Europeans have led to the dire effects of industrialisation. This has allowed both science and the humanities to make their own claims for absolute truth. As a result, anthropocentrism has become more pronounced than ever.

Considering the above, I would like to examine the problems of perception, (self-)knowledge and mortality in John Burnside's poetic work in the context of a larger identity of Europeanness. Engaging with the European heritage, his poems anatomise the Western mind and body. Persistent self-mirroring reveals aspects of the visible and the invisible, surface and depth. I would like to argue that Burnside's writing reflects a considerable preoccupation with surfaces: ice ('Pieter Brueghel: Winter Landscape with Skaters and Bird Trap 1565'), glass ('Joseph Wright of Derby: *An Experiment on a Bird in the Air Pump, 1768*'), mirrors ('The Myth of Narcissus') and skin ('*De Humani Corporis Fabrica* (after Vesalius)'). Slippery and smooth, hard or soft, fragile and brittle, surfaces separate, reflect, refract, invite. The urge to know what is beyond the immediate impression, the mere facade, brings a tension between the outside and inside, between exteriority and interiority. Explored by means of senses, any surface is tantalising only with depth that it hides beneath. The poet's preoccupation with surfaces may bring to mind Georges Poulet's essay, 'The Phenomenology of Reading' (1969), and his consideration of the 'inner' life of things that only the literary can reveal.

For the purposes of this chapter I have selected four ekphrastic poems that will illustrate my discussion. I wish to see how, by incorporating Pieter Brueghel, Vesalius and Joseph Wright of Derby among others, Burnside constructs a bridge between a sixteenth-century vision of man and a contemporary one, reinforcing continuity, but at the same time challenging these images and posing timely questions. I would like to examine various spaces depicted in these texts: the space of mind, body and natural world. I would like to see how these poems (three of them relating to visual works from the sixteenth century and one from the eighteenth century) aim at reaching under the skin of the modern man represented in Burnside's poetry:

1. 'Pieter Brueghel: Winter Landscape with Skaters and Bird Trap 1565' (from *Black Cat Bone*)
2. 'Joseph Wright of Derby: *An Experiment on a Bird in the Air Pump, 1768*' (from *All One Breath*)
3. 'The Myth of Narcissus' (from *The Good Neighbour*)
4. '*De Humani Corporis Fabrica* (after Vesalius)' (from *The Good Neighbour*).

'PIETER BRUEGHEL: WINTER LANDSCAPE WITH SKATERS AND BIRD TRAP 1565'

'Just now' (from Latin *modernus, modo*): this meaning of the word 'modern' is at the centre of Burnside's poem 'Pieter Brueghel: Winter Landscape with Skaters and Bird Trap 1565', which comes from the collection *Black Cat Bone* (Burnside 2007: 59–60). If we look at the painting, we notice how, consumed with the activity, human figures give in entirely to what is just now, as if diving into the surface of things. The brittleness of these tiny skaters and their scattered movements reinforce the impression of momentariness and fleetingness. Concerned with this present moment, the skaters are suspended between past and future, forgetful of the experiences, oblivious of the consequences. The bird trap in the foreground offers an allegory of human life, the entrapment of being. The freedom of skaters in the background, their carefree activity, which seems to provide a momentary release from the everyday, is in stark contrast with the lurking danger, hidden from their sight. The juxtaposition of the free, unfettered movement of the skaters and the ensnarement awaiting birds is quite striking. The realisation of the viewers – we know something the skaters seem not to cognise – imparts knowledge of the inevitable. The skaters do not see the bird trap: their sight does not reach that far, they are separated from knowledge. However, the perspective of the viewer of the painting – and the poetic subject – allows for detachment. The distance also enables a comprehension inaccessible to the skaters. Due to the time perspective, the viewer/reader may have an insight into their precarious situation that is not available for those involved. The speaker of the poem comments on their activity, relating the contrast between the momentary freedom of skaters and the ensnarement of their lives in the second stanza:

> this is their escape
> from hardship,
> but each has his private hurt, her secret dread (Burnside 2007: 59)

Each of them is temporarily released from the trap, 'momentarily involved / in nothing but the present'. The movement lifts them from their daily lives – releases them – and helps to focus on what is happening just now. One man skates away from 'the loveless matron he's had to endure / for decades'; one woman, 'never released from the fear', is afraid that her husband will beat her 'as he's beaten her for years'. This immersion in the present – the self-abandonment – lasts but a brief moment, in which they become enmeshed in the present, just for an instant: an 'infinitely short space of time'. They enjoy themselves innocently, 'unaware of any / danger', like these starlings, fieldfares and redwings (Burnside 2007: 60). The bird-like figures of skaters, their arms spread like wings (birds frequently appear in Burnside's poems, e.g. 'Kestrel', 'Peregrine', 'Geese', 'Joseph Wright of Derby: *An Experiment on a Bird in the Air Pump*, 1768', a sign of the importance of birds in human understanding, a demonstration of how they live within us, how significant they are for us), the human silhouettes are as big as the bird figures. Burnside imagines that the skaters, tied to a mundane, humdrum existence, are hankering after freedom represented by birds. Yet, the reference to birds emphasises the irony that governs their lives, as in the light of the trap seen in the foreground, their freedom is illusory and fleeting.

The poem's epigraph comes from the inscription on Breughel's painting: 'Learn from this picture how we journey in the world. Slithering as we go, the foolish and the wise.' 'Lubricitas vitae humanae' suggests the slippery surface, the precariousness of human life. The sense of transitoriness pervades both the visual and poetic image. The fragility of ice brings to mind the provisionality of existence, its fickleness, interspersed with brief and uncertain moments of oblivion. The citation also juxtaposes implicitly the happy moment of brief oblivion with that greater oblivion of death. The skaters seem unreflexive and carefree; one of them experiences 'thoughtless grace', the moment takes him back to childhood, representing an idyllic time: 'to glide free / in the very eye of heaven'. And 'it could be simple – paradise foreseen – / but': the final word ending any illusion of paradise, the following lines ('thorns and briars', 'rope' and 'snakes') suggest the opposite: hell, pain, finality.

The looming vision of the snare is there, present: the skaters, resembling birds, circle dangerously close to the trap with their illusory existence and petty problems. Focusing on being in the present, however fugitive it might be, the skaters continue with the shadow self at their back. The poem leaves us with 'other to his other' as we read in the last stanza of the poem:

> It seems a fable and perhaps it is:
> we live in peril, die from happenstance,
> a casual slip, a fault line in the ice;
> but surely it's the other thought that matters,
> the sense that, now and then, there's still a chance
> a man might slide towards an old
> belonging, momentarily involved
> in nothing but the present, skating out
> towards a white
> horizon, fair
> and gifted with the grace
> to skate forever, slithering as he goes,
> but hazarding a guess that someone else
> is close beside him, other to his other. (Burnside 2007: 60)

He senses a shadow, a companion moving 'towards an old / belonging'. A possibility in the form of another self brings a shudder of strangeness at the brief realisation of alterity. Yet, the nagging sense of not belonging can be shed for an instant, just now. Acutely aware of this condition, the modern man in Burnside's poem cannot fully shake the sense of precariousness. He experiences a yearning to transcend his life in a moment of elation, to free himself from the commonplace and the habitual, to slough off the only life that he knows in the hope of a renewed self. Behind that there is perhaps a pervading sense of transience.

'JOSEPH WRIGHT OF DERBY: *AN EXPERIMENT ON A BIRD IN THE AIR PUMP*, 1768'

The next poem also features a bird, but this time it is given a central position and is in effect entrapped. The poem, 'Joseph Wright of Derby: *An Experiment on a Bird in the Air Pump*, 1768' (Burnside 2014: 26–8), coming from Burnside's latest collection *All One Breath*, focuses on the moment in social history of modern Europe that brought scientific advances, inevitably changing people's understanding of the world. Particularly, the laws of nature had to be considered and reconsidered. The pneumatical engines, or air pumps, were 'all the rage', demonstrating the nature of air and its force of life-support. People gathered for a show to watch small animals die of hypoxia. Usually conducted by a natural philosopher, the shows instructed and entertained, part of 'modernity's project of the technological domination of nature' (Zimmerman 1994, qtd in Westling 2014: 149).

Burnside's poem depicts animal experimentation, which results in unnecessary suffering of the bird, serving as mere visual pleasure, reifying it. Similarly, by offering a representation of suffering, the painting performs a similar function. In this, Burnside also provides a comment as the painting does the same, offering a critique of representation. Suffering is applied in a more sophisticated manner thanks to the power of technology. From the perspective of 250 years we can see that technological advances have actually enabled efficacy and sophistication in killing, making it more efficient and/or more cruel. The distance the machine offers in the act of ending a life makes the act 'clean', saving the hands from becoming dirty, creating an illusion of the removal of the responsibility, helping the perpetrator not to think about the death of the other.

The text demonstrates the attitude of modern Europeans to nature and to elementary things such as life and death, breath and self. Combining light and dark, the chiaroscuro can serve as a representation of modern science versus traditional values and beliefs. Memento mori creeps in once more, but this time it is technologically enhanced. The painting shows a candlelit scene; the viewers lean in a reverential attitude around an air pump. Inside a bird is fighting for breath. The image is visually arresting, demonstrating admiration of scientific advances and hope to understand and grasp reality. The use of chiaroscuro and the arrangement of figures reminds us of Caravaggio and his *Nativity with St Francis and St Lawrence* (1609). The reverence demonstrated by the witnesses of the experiment in Joseph Wright of Derby's painting points us back to the religious scene, simultaneously suggesting a secularisation that has taken place. Not a newborn Jesus, but a dying parrot: the reversal demonstrates a new direction in the development of the industrial era, its secular, perhaps even cynical inclinations.

Studied empirically in the seventeenth and eighteenth centuries, the properties of air, including the power of vacuum, fascinate. Space devoid of matter, the void – even if seen in operation – is difficult to comprehend. What the spectators are witnessing is an empty space that kills. One might say, *horror vacui*, nature abhors a vacuum. Some viewers in the painting are demonstrably fascinated by death, searching for answers to final questions, the primal source of life (air/breath). The pump enables 'amateurs' to play 'god for an hour'. Modern science ushered in more sophisticated scientific experiments – but what is so special about killing a bird with a sleight of hand, technologically supported magic? As Francis Bacon argues in *Novum Organum Scientiarum* (1620): 'Man is Nature's agent and interpreter; he does and understands only as much as he has observed of the order of nature in fact or by inference; he does not know and cannot do more' (Bacon 2000: 33). And so the modern man believes that the desire to possess knowledge entitles him in his doings and explains his actions.

The experiments with the pneumatical engine performed by Robert Boyle in 1660, who tested the reliance on air in the survival of small creatures (birds, mice, eels, snails and flies), are one of many examples of the disturbed relationship between birds and modern men. Boyle is the implied figure in the poem, presented as a 'showman' (the word is employed twice: in lines 3 and 42), who 'brings a touch of theatre to the lives / of squires and merchants'. Indeed, he is a theatrical figure, perhaps a bit blasé, his eyes 'incurious', as if he has seen it all. He has assumed a vantage point of a coolly disinterested spectator, for whom death is 'one more / instance of casual slaughter'. Science is depicted as showmanship, the experiment as a staged act, 'the game of life and death', a dramatic gesture and a slick move. His shows are routine: 'whenever he peddles his trade, / it's always the same'. The first-person voice (rendered in italics) leaves no doubt as to the possibilities of revival or resurrection. The conclusion is equally unsentimental: placed *in vacuo*, living creatures die. They perish bodily deprived of air, but there is another implication here as they die figuratively when everything is reduced to 'fact', and data.

There is a stark contrast between his casualness and the audience's reactions ranging from fascination to terror to rapture. All of them watch with close attention to the spectacle unfolding in front of their eyes (part of the society of the spectacle (Debord 2000), they are gathered for a show; what they experience indirectly is a mere representation). The participants in the experiment reveal a growing distance in the relationship between nature and culture, the former reified and turned into mere natural objects. It is as if the void behind the glass represented a different dimension, in which animals ceased to be living beings and instead became things. Or perhaps the spectacle of the pneumatic engine seems to fascinate 'squires and merchants' exactly because the bird is like them, breathes like them, which makes the show all the more riveting. The participatory present tense of the poem brings us closer to the picture, draws us into the scene. The speaker bridges the then and now, ambiguating the showman's role. We are drawn in much like the contemporary audience even though we experience the scene from the temporal and spatial distance.

The final gaze is directed out of the room, unseen by the gathered people, who are transfixed by the show and oblivious to – or perhaps ignorant of – the world outside (and the world in general): 'the moon is full tonight / . . . though nobody here can know / the world it illuminates'. The unknowability of the world is impossible to transcend, even with the support of technology. The poem ends with the following words:

> and the silence that follows a kill, when everything stops,
> that held breath over the land
> till the dead move on. (Burnside 2014: 28)

It touches upon one of the most fundamental elements of modernity, namely, the drive for knowledge, the urge to pierce the surface in order to reach the essence of things (whatever it is). It involves collecting empirical evidence: scientific observation, measuring, calculating, labelling. The result might be disenchantment, as the sociologist and philosopher Max Weber calls it: 'the knowledge or belief that . . . there are no mysterious incalculable forces that come into play, but rather that one can, in principle, master all things by calculation' (Weber 1946, qtd in Macfarlane 2015: 24). 'Wonder', associated with enchantment and unknowing, has been draining from the modern experience, replaced with disenchantment, which is a 'function of the rise of rationalism' (2015: 24). What follows is that 'In modernity mastery usurped mystery' (2015: 25).

'THE MYTH OF NARCISSUS' (CARAVAGGIO, *NARCISSUS*, 1599)

The introspective and reflective subjectivity, the hallmark of modernity, produces a rational attitude towards the inner self and the world. The next poem, coming from the 2005 collection *The Good Neighbour* (Burnside 2005: 50–4), 'The Myth of Narcissus' (Book III of Ovid's *Metamorphoses*, 2004), undertakes a recurrent theme in Burnside's writing (for instance, in *A Summer of Drowning* (2012), one of the characters, Ryvold, quotes Leon Battista Alberti's study, *Della pittura, On Painting* (2013), to discuss Narcissus).

The poem's epigraph is a citation from Yamamoto Tsunemoto: 'Our bodies are given life from the midst of nothingness', introducing the doubleness of existence and inexistence, form and emptiness. Narcissus emerges from nothing: his self appears with his reflection. The tension between presence and absence is foregrounded, provoking the questions: what is there before the look, what is the nothingness before form, the nonexistence before matter? Is the real above or beneath the surface? The inside appears outside, or as Poulet (1969) argues, we are inside it, it is inside us: 'the shadows glide like fish' (Burnside 2005: 50) (compare the skaters in Pieter Brueghel), where the shadows are 'ebbs of nothingness' (2005: 51). The poem opens with a dualistic vision of the world: a sap and a shadow, 'where friend or foe / is all there ever is / to make a world' (2005: 50). The effect is reinforced by the repetitions, which usher in the absent Echo and remind us about the reflection. Narcissus's gaze is directed to the surface of his potential self, which will be 'the perfect body':

and he is here, who may be all

reflection:
        here, in the not-yet-seen,
    in the unenchanted. (Burnside 2005: 51)

Waiting for the enchantment to be lifted, and a spell to be unsung, Narcissus remains watchful, expectant, one could perhaps say on tenterhooks, as if stretched on a frame. The repetition of the word 'here' foregrounds – grounds – his being (although the poem belongs to the section of the volume entitled 'There') as if stretching and fixing it. The present imperfect body is *there* 'for hurt and sin'.

What Narcissus notices on the surface surprises him, as 'what he sees is not the animal / he half-expected' (Burnside 2005: 52). His animal-nature dissolves in the reflection: 'what he sees / is something like the future he has gathered' (2005: 52). The dyadic specularity of his identity is reinforced by the glassy surface of the water. What he sees is his potential self, or 'something like' (Burnside favours lack of precision, vagueness of feeling, perception and language; compare *Something Like Happy*, 2013) Further in the poem the words: 'rising to find the surface / and bleeding through' (2005: 54) suggest an emergent thing, becoming, accompanied by pain. The ability to cross over or pass through foregrounds a transcendental notion of the self. 'A new form' emerges, an idea finds its way to the surface. It fetches loss as the employment of the word 'forfeit' suggests: we abandon the body, we slough it off, going beyond. Further we read:

    the presence left unnamed, unrecognised,
    the blue scent flowing through, the emptiness
    that wanders in the current
                    shaped
                            and lost
    by looking:
                proven
                    immaterial. (Burnside 2005: 50)

The word 'still' is repeated (2005: 51), meaning both unmoving and incessant, and also in the present, existing. The present – the 'here' – gliding on the surface of time in a form of a continuous return, in the iterability of 'here' and 'still' is spread in front of our eyes, stretched as if on a canvas, even though 'left unnamed, unrecognised', 'immaterial'. Both these concepts – here and now – constitute an iterable motif in Burnside's poem. It may be applied to images. The viewer is always at the surface of a painting, in its here and now, a situation which creates a tension between the 'here and now' of the representation and what is understood historically in the depths of reflection on the part of the modern viewing subject. Narcissus continues his existence in a self-contained world. His gaze is reflected from the surface and bounces back to him:

> the look
> that turns back on the self
> and makes it whole (Burnside 2005: 51)

Narcissus, a representative of the modern man, displays an obsession with selfhood whose main characteristics are instability and uncertainty. He may become complete when he fully (i.e. bodily) perceives himself and 'perception is not the achievement of a mind in a body but rather of a whole organism in its exploratory movement through the world' (Westling 2014: 7). Yet, gazing at his own reflection, Narcissus remains still, unmoving. Marshall McLuhan suggests that Narcissus does not recognise himself:

> The Greek myth of Narcissus is directly concerned with a fact of human experience, as the word Narcissus indicates. It is from the Greek word narcosis, or numbness. The youth Narcissus mistook his own reflection in the water for another person. This extension of himself by mirror numbed his perceptions until he became the servomechanism of his own extended or repeated image. The nymph Echo tried to win his love with fragments of his own speech, but in vain. He was numb. He had adapted to his extension of himself and had become a closed system. (McLuhan 1999: 41)

Immobile, he becomes numb; having lost his speech, he becomes dumb – he is all sight, the other senses have deserted him (or perhaps he has shed them all). He just gazes, riveted, rooted, vanishing slowly into absence. There is a powerful sense of loss of physicality as the world disappears into a heap of broken images. His self-sensed self is disembodied, vacuous. He faces a realisation that knowable reality transcends his awareness, transporting himself into the mercurial self on a shimmering surface, losing his grounding, exchanging his palpable being for a virtual one. He sees himself seeing, he catches a glimpse of self-realisation. But trapped in the mirror stage (Lacan 1977), he finds his self only with the assistance of a mirror, an object placed outside himself. His identity is only definable with the aid of something external.

Narcissus's gaze bounces off the surface and returns to him, initiating a process of disembodiment, as his self-perception moves to his reflected, virtual self. In *Realist Magic, Objects, Ontology, Causality*, Timothy Morton cites 'an ontological insight . . . engraved onto the passenger side wing mirrors of every American car' (Morton 2013: 32): 'objects in mirror are closer than they appear'. Indeed, for Narcissus, his reflected self seems closer than himself. The words 'That *self* is metaphor' (Burnside 2005: 53) offer a concept of identity as a representation of something else, designating a distant ideal.

'DE HUMANI CORPORIS FABRICA (AFTER VESALIUS)' (1543)

In the final poem that I would like to discuss we get under the skin. '*De Humani Corporis Fabrica* (after Vesalius)' from *The Good Neighbour* (Burnside 2005: 4–7) refers to *De humani corporis fabrica libri septem*, or *The Fabric of the Human Body*, an Early Modern anatomical atlas published in 1543, which explores different systems of the body, combining modern science and anatomy. Scientific enquiry is represented in the form of artful woodcut illustrations painstakingly depicting the human body.

The Latin word *fabrica*, meaning 'the manner of construction' or 'workmanship', 'skilful production', can also signify simply 'craft' or 'art'. Employing the title of the anatomic atlas, Burnside thus continues its idea of the body as an artful construction, a work of art (is there an artist behind it?). What follows is the idea of orderly nature, with no hint of contingency. The priority of close, direct observation results in meticulous visual rendering but the impossibility of a verbal one, creating once again a dichotomy between surface and depth, visible and invisible. The first words of the poem, 'I know the names of almost / nothing', signal a recurrent concern in Burnside's writing: language is insufficient. 'I know' – the first words of the poem – is countered by 'nothing'; the 'names' are not there. The poetic subject does not know himself – or the world, for that matter. Labelling and naming mark the limits of his knowledge. He foregrounds his ignorance, repeating: 'I have no words', as if his word-hoard was empty, as if he were speechless. At times the known words are emptied of their meaning, signifiers missing their signifieds: 'or else I know the names / but not the function' – the distance between the two impossible to abolish.

The above lines echo Michel de Montaigne's (1993) question 'What do I know?' (*Que sais-je?*, people are unable to attain true certainty) and Jacques Derrida's 'Qui suis-je?' ('Who am I (following)?', *être* or *suivre* (Derrida 2008)). In a constant pursuit of self-knowledge, the modern man reaches under the skin to find there – yes, what? Perhaps the intransgressible limits of self-knowledge, another proof of the unintelligibility of oneself. Transcending the boundary of skin does not bring many answers. The unreadability of the self is stressed by the impassable limits. Reaching beneath the surface does not remove doubts, crossing the barrier does not eliminate the distance. In an attempt to understand, the speaker tries to pierce the outer layer, to 'peer into the dark machinery / of savage grace' (Burnside 2005: 6). But as we peer inside, things appear paradoxically covered. The use of the word 'machinery' suggests its mechanical function (in the seventeenth century the word 'machinery' had theatrical connotations as 'devices for creating stage effects'). A mechanistic vision of the body as the vessel for spirit – 'Hydraulics for the soul' (2005: 5) – emphasises the body's function, which is down-to-earth and mundane (but indispensable). What is under the skin presents an obscure vision of things, reflecting the fallibility of language since – whatever it is – is not named or not recognised (labelling does not help). Language fails us, repeatedly, irrevocably. As in 'The Myth of Narcissus', the body is a mere imitation of an ideal form:

> as if I had been asked to paraphrase
> this body with the body I possessed:
> hydraulics for a soul
> > cheese-wire for nerves
> a ruff of butcher's meat
> > in place of thought. (Burnside 2005: 5)

The body replaces the mind, meat replaces thought. This is one of the two references to meat in the poem, the second one in lines 41–3: 'ribbed and charred / like something barbecued' (Burnside 2005: 5). How can we talk about the modern triumph of rationalist concepts of mind and intellect? The empiricists' advocacy of matter designed for thought?

Apart from the representations of the human body in the anatomical atlas the poem contains a reference to George Stubbs, an engraving from *The Anatomy of the Horse*. This foregrounds the affinity of humans and animals: both Cartesian machines, complex and alike under the skin. For Descartes (1988) animals were mere machines, devoid of a reflective cogito. We do not know for certain whether the horse or any other animal has consciousness. Stripping it of its skin, reaching beyond the surface will not render an answer. And thus once again the problem of surface and depth resurfaces. Peering under the skin's surface does not reveal more than raw flesh. The closeness is further emphasised in the ending of the poem: 'the living flesh / revealing and erasing what it knows / on secret charts / of watermark / and vellum' (Burnside 2005: 7) – the last word of the poem is 'vellum', or parchment made from animal (calf) skin. Our creaturely nature cannot be ignored as it brings an embodied 'knowing'. The kind of knowledge coming from embodiment, from the chiasmus of the flesh, to use Merleau-Ponty's term, is there before rational thought.

There is also a soul – or as Burnside prefers to call it these days, a spirit: a choice, which, as he explains, is an attempt

> to replace the idea of the duality, which suggests two separate things,
> with an idea of the binary, where the two things complement each
> other. What is interesting is the play between these imaginary forces
> that you might think of as spirit and matter. There is no such thing
> as matter separate from spirit, or spirit separate from matter. (Dósa
> 2009: 119)

The essence of the living things is there – 'the single eye exposed: / a window into primal emptiness' (Burnside 2005: 5) – with the preposition 'into' standing between the outside and the inside, surface and depth, the visible and the invisible, presence and absence.

CONCLUSION: AN ATTEMPT AT

Peering to pierce 'the not-yet-seen', Burnside's poetic subjects attempt to probe the condition of the modern subject. Is humanity really 'the apex of creation' (Westling 2014: 6) as Descartes wanted? The triumph of technology, which has brought machines mastering nature, does not seem to have the power to enchant any more. Disconnected from the natural world by dualistic logic for the past three centuries, just now the modern man needs to access intuitive knowledge that comes from the phenomenological alertness to the moment in time. Burnside proposes to abolish the view of the natural, in which the human and the animal are separated, the former absent from his bodily reality. Oscillating between exteriority and interiority, Burnside sees a possibility of a nondualistic, embodied understanding of subjectivity. He reminds us that in the material frame we are grounded – our bodies provide this grounding – as we experience our selves enmeshed in the world. Just now, the unstable function of the self, a shimmering mirror-image, could be deepened. Perhaps a non-narcissistic inter-subjectivity is on the horizon: thanks to kinship – 'kinship of flesh with flesh' ('Ports', in Burnside 2000: 5) – there is a possibility to erase dichotomies and entrenched views in the hope of attaining an ideal form within a larger living system, the mesh of interconnections (Morton 2011), 'this very knot of relations' (Merleau-Ponty 2012: lxxxv).

WORKS CITED

Alberti, Leon Battista (2013), *On Painting*, trans. Rocco Sinisgalli, Cambridge: Cambridge University Press.

Bacon, Francis (2000), *The New Organon*, trans. Michael Silverthorne, Cambridge: Cambridge University Press.

Bauman, Zygmunt (2000), *Liquid Modernity*, Cambridge: Polity Press.

Burnside, John (2000), *The Asylum Dance*, London: Jonathan Cape.

Burnside, John (2005), *The Good Neighbour*, London: Jonathan Cape.

Burnside, John (2007), *Black Cat Bone*, London: Jonathan Cape.

Burnside, John (2012), *A Summer of Drowning*, London: Vintage.

Burnside, John (2013), *Something Like Happy*, London: Jonathan Cape.

Burnside, John (2014), *All One Breath*, London: Jonathan Cape.

Debord, Guy (2000), *The Society of the Spectacle*, trans. Fredy Perlman, Detroit: Black & Red.

Derrida, Jacques (2008), *The Animal That Therefore I Am*, trans. David Wills, New York: Fordham University Press.

Descartes, René (1988), *Selected Philosophical Writings*, trans. John Cottingham, Robert Stoothoff and Dugald Murdoch, Cambridge: Cambridge University Press.

Dósa, Attila (2009), 'John Burnside: Poets and Other Animals', in *Beyond Identity: New Horizons in Modern Scottish Poetry*, Amsterdam: Rodopi, pp. 113–34.

Lacan, Jacques (1977), 'The Mirror Stage as Formative of the Function of the I as Revealed in Psychoanalytic Experience', in *Écrits: A Selection*, trans. Alan Sheridan, New York: W. W. Norton, pp. 502–9.

Lyotard, Jean-François (1979), *The Postmodern Condition: A Report on Knowledge*, trans. Geoff Bennington and Brian Massumi, Manchester: Manchester University Press.

Macfarlane, Robert (2015), *Landmarks*, London: Hamish Hamilton.

McLuhan, Marshall (1999), *Understanding Media: The Extension of Man*, Cambridge, MA: The MIT Press.

Merleau-Ponty, Maurice (2012), *The Phenomenology of Perception*, trans. Donald A. Landes, New York: Routledge.

Montaigne, Michel de (1993), *Essays*, trans. M. A. Screech, London: Penguin.

Morton, Timothy (2011), 'Mesh', in Stephanie LeMenager, Teresa Shewry and Ken Hiltner (eds), *Environmental Criticism for the Twenty-First Century*, London and New York: Routledge, pp. 19–30.

Morton, Timothy (2013), *Realist Magic, Objects, Ontology, Causality*, Ann Arbor: Open Humanities Press.

Ovid (2004), *Metamorphoses*, trans. David Raeburn, London: Penguin.

Poulet, Georges (1969), 'The Phenomenology of Reading', *New Literary History*, 1: 1, New and Old History (October), 53–68.

Weber, Max (1946), *From Max Weber: Essays in Sociology*, trans. H. H. Gerth and C. Wright Mills, New York: Oxford University Press.

Westling, Louise (2014), *The Logos of the Living World: Merleau-Ponty, Animals, and Language*, New York: Fordham University Press.

Zimmerman, Michael (1994), *Contesting Earth's Future: Radical Ecology and Postmodernity*, Berkeley: University of California Press.

CHAPTER 3

Modernity's Sylvan Subjectivity, from Gainsborough to Gallaccio

Catherine Bernard

Modernity has been a fiercely contested category for a long time now. And to consider this a truism has become something of a truism too, as if any discussion of modernity was of necessity trapped in a form of belatedness. That sense of critical infinite regress has often been seen as analogical to modernity's conflicted relation to its own present, as is evinced in Nietzsche's *Untimely Meditations*, Derrida's *Specters of Marx*, Bruno Latour's *We Have Never Been Modern*, or more recently Giorgio Agamben's 2008 essay 'What Is the Contemporary?' And Freud's concept of *Nachträglichkeit* is of course of strategic import here for the way it unhinges the subject's sense of self-presence in time.[1]

Similarly, the eurocentrism of modernity has been the object of systematic deconstructions, a task pithily summed up by the Argentinian-Mexican writer Enrique Dussel in his 1992 introductory Frankfurt Lectures:

> Modernity is, for many (for Jürgen Habermas or Charles Taylor, for example), an essentially or exclusively European phenomenon [. . .] I will argue that modernity is, in fact, a European phenomenon, but one constituted in a dialectical relation with a non-European alterity that is its ultimate content. Modernity appears when Europe affirms itself as the 'center' of a *World* History that it inaugurates: the 'periphery' that surrounds its center is consequently part of its self-definition.[2]

Postcolonial studies and connected history have of course contributed to our understanding of the way modern eurocentrism is locked in with its dark and repressed other. As Edward Said cogently argued, there would be no Mansfield Park – I will return to Austen later – without Sir Thomas Bertram's West Indies sugar plantations. As Terry Eagleton also contends, the forces of social and economic mutation at work in *Wuthering Heights* need an alien within – Heathcliff – to be fully unleashed.[3] As Sanjay Subrahmanyam also shows in his 2011

Three Ways to Be Alien: Travails and Encounters in the Early Modern World,[4] the budding of an inchoate European identity in the Renaissance needed the construction of *unheimlich* encounters on the borders of Europe.

European modernity is thus often constructed in agonistic terms, even when the alien nestles within that modernity in the making. Fallen women, foundlings, colonials must be dealt with and expelled for the system to adapt and survive. The Marquise de Merteuil must be disfigured by smallpox for Choderlos de Laclos's ambiguous *Liaisons dangereuses* to fulfil its allegorical agenda. Little Jo in *Bleak House* must die for the redemption narrative to fully work. The same sense of a conflicted modernity is to be found in philosophical accounts of modernity, from Adorno and Horkheimer to Bruno Latour and Jean-François Lyotard. The repression and foreclusion of otherness has thus been read as unavoidable to a system inherently binary rather than dialectical,[5] as if the dialectics of Enlightenment was bound to be negative; and we know how the modernist project reappropriated the power of negativity to radically subversive ends.[6]

Understanding the European mind in its relation to modernity may require a less aporetic approach to the dialectics of the modern, one less overshadowed by the power of Lyotard's *differend*[7] and his conviction that modernity has bred incompatible phrase regimes. Reintroducing the possibility of a sublation of the inner tensions of modernity would imply reading the modern in a more *poietic* vein, one which would perceive modernity as an ongoing practice, self-critically open to paradox and contradiction; an approach, in other words, less indebted to an absolutist definition of the modern and more atune to the productive potential of concepts once we agree that their reversibility may also have a hermeneutic effect. The emphasis on the hermeneutic productiveness of the approach – as opposed to a heuristic reading of the modern – cannot be too much emphasised as such attention to the *poietics* of tension entails a work, a task, rather than a revelation.

Such attentiveness to the power of paradox was one of Michel Foucault's most fruitful contributions to the genealogy of the modern. In his essay 'What Is Enlightenment?', first published in *The Foucault Reader* and which reworks an unpublished manuscript, Foucault redefines the Enlightenment as opening the possibility of a critical ethos working with or from within its inner contradictions. Rereading 'Was Ist Aufklärung?', a text published by Kant in the *Berlinische Monatsschrift* in 1784, Foucault rethinks the spirit of Enlightenment as an ongoing practice in self-definition, a discipline that would be no disciplining subjection but an exercise in dialectical criticity. For Foucault, modernity is not a historical moment but an 'attitude'[8] that is endlessly reactivated and which must contend with its inner splits, so that modernity should not be established as an absolute, requiring an other to assert itself, but as self-divided or, even more accurately, as a practice.

As one might expect from Foucault, such ethos is profoundly immersed in the material reality of historicity, and should be 'described as a permanent critique' of our historical being.[9] Here Catherine Porter's translation of Foucault's original text entails an intriguing misprision, choosing as it does to refer rather to 'our historical era'. Such misprision would no doubt warrant a full volume specifically devoted to what is culturally repressed in translation. Foucault's original text precisely refuses to narrow down the historical perspective to a specific context. In the original, that 'attitude' is not of a given place and age and cannot address 'our historical era'. It is precisely beyond place and age. It engages what Foucault defines in fact, as our '*être historique*':[10] our historical being, a form of historicity beyond the here and now of any specific 'historical era'. Such a transcension of history by historical criticity comes as no surprise if we remember Foucault's deep interest in Nietzsche's visionary dehistoricising of origins and his 'untimely meditations': I am referring here to Foucault's 1971 essay 'Nietzsche, la généalogie, l'histoire', also reprinted in the same reader. For Foucault, modernity's critical 'attitude' needs no other. The other, as defined by disciplinary order and as relayed by the symbolical imagination, lies within. Modernity's criticity 'consists of analyzing and reflecting upon limits'.[11] But those limits are not external to modernity and modernity's criticity lies in the possibility of their ongoing 'transgression'.[12]

OF TREES AND MEN

Modernity's internal dialogue with the other entails a dialectics which has been the subject of many a work of art. From the start, nature has embodied that otherness within; and we should not be surprised that a Romantic painter like Delacroix should have devoted such a large part of his fresco, *Jacob Wrestling with the Angel*, in St Sulpice church (Paris), to the vision of a mysterious, timeless nature, seemingly indifferent to the momentous fight taking place (see Figure 3.1).

The trees that dwarf the two protagonists of that dance-like struggle offer an enigmatic backdrop to the visual transcription of *Genesis*, chapter 32. An extension of the Angel's divine power, the trees also resist our temptation to read them only allegorically. Absent from the biblical source, they exist as and for themselves. In this late work of Delacroix's, they above all provide a wonderful terrain of experimentation with textures, colours and hues. They paradoxically look back and look forward. They rehearse the vision and manner of the Dutch landscape painters, of Nicolas Poussin and Claude, a vision that Constable and Gainsborough had already appropriated, in order to experiment with vision and texture. They also anticipate with later experiments with texture. They belong to the history of artistic modernity, as much as they belong to the history of visual allegory.

The critical modernity of Delacroix's trees lies in this paradoxical relation to the history of visual representation. Delacroix's reiteration of the sylvan motif captures something of a mute enigma; an enigma that is inexhaustible and incommensurate, that cannot be explained away by the art of quotationality

Figure 3.1 Eugène Delacroix, *Jacob Wrestling with the Angel (lutte de Jacob avec l'ange)*, 1861, Chapel of the Holy Angels, St Sulpice church, Paris, © Emmanuel Michot / COARC / Roger-Viollet

and that calls for renewed instanciation, again and again and again. Painted on the eve of nascent modernism, Delacroix's work captures modernity's 'attitude' at its most critical, when it pushes against the limits of representation, a tension that was, as we know, to be foundational to modernism's poetics of othering.

The context might be widely diverging but the end of *The Great Gatsby* also dramatises such a moment of criticity. Nick Carraway returns to Gatsby's house and walks down to the beach. He is, at that point, invaded with a vision of a sylvan world both elemental and mythical, a vision of 'the old island [. . .] that flowered once for Dutch sailors' eyes – a fresh green breast of the new world'.[13] The sylvan world he imagines is inscribed in the allegorical metatext of historical predestination: 'Its vanished trees, the trees that had made way for Gatsby's house, had once pandered in whispers to the last and greatest of all human dreams.'[14] Yet this world, from the start, resists all ideological subsumption. In front of it, consciousness is caught in a form of syncopation which the text necessarily aestheticises, yet immediately forecloses: 'man must have held his breath in the presence of this continent, compelled into an aesthetic contemplation he neither understood nor desired, face to face for the last time in history with something commensurate to his capacity for wonder'.[15] The sylvan universe conjured up by Fitzgerald is a liminal universe that produces a limit-experience. That experience is both intensely modern in its collusion with imperialism and already foregone, past, vanished, both intensely new and already archaic, both utopian and nostalgic, but nostalgic of a sense of belonging European man had not even intuited before.

Fitzgerald captures something here of the untimely criticity of modernity as a practice working against the limits of its own laws and desires. In the visionary eclipse of the trees, he also intuits the two dialectical modalities of Europe's modern mind. Pristine nature is soon to vanish, to be rationalised, yet it endures as the negative spectre of instrumentalised nature. The trees confronting the Dutch sailors thus embody the two modalities of man's relation to nature in the modern age. As a force soon to be subjugated, it already bears the mark of instrumental and experimental reason; as a repository for man's 'capacity for wonder', it also puts instrumental reason to the test of desire. Simon Schama's pithy definition of modern England's relation to nature: 'The greenwood was a useful fantasy; the English forest was serious business'[16] should in fact be reversed: 'The English/American forest was soon to be serious business; but the greenwood was a useful fantasy.' The vanished, visionary trees of America's 'fresh, green breast' push modernity's phenomenology to its limits. The new, imperial subject in the making can only experience himself as a historical/feeling subject, a subject whose reflexive expertise is grounded in an experience that is both rational and sentient, disciplined and *unheimlich*.

EXPERTISE AND SUBJUGATION

Eco-history has shown how European demographic expansion and European expansionism resulted in massive deforestation and the development of forestry,[17] timber being a material strategic to Europe's imperialist agenda, as early as the Renaissance period.[18] Taking up Kant's and then Foucault's question, 'What Is Enlightenment?', in his masterful study *Forests: The Shadow of Civilization*, Robert Pogue Harrison answers: 'A question for foresters.'[19] Of course, as Harrison also shows, such entanglement does not date back to the Enlightenment; it is inherent to civilisation itself, at all times, everywhere. As Alison Byerly also notes:

> The old question of whether a falling tree in the forest makes a sound
> if no one is there to hear it encapsulates the paradox: a tree standing
> in the forest is not part of the 'wilderness' unless a civilized observer is
> there to see it.[20]

From the start, forests have been inscribed in cultural economies that – as Byerly's empiricist reference suggests – are both structural and empirical. One may even argue that our relation to trees and forests is necessarily cultural insofar as it is always a felt, embodied relation. Modernity took that entanglement to its limits in the way it turned forests into a shared 'memory site'[21] in which modern men and women would experience themselves as cultural/ sentient beings even as they experimented with new forms of rationalisation.

The rationalisation of modern man's relation to the forest took the form of management and improvement. As Robert Pogue Harrison insists, the state or the landlord assumed then 'the role of Descartes' thinking subject'.[22] In Goethe's *Elective Affinities*, for instance, the book's motif of experimentation extends to the world of trees and Edward's management of his estate is utilitarian before it is Romantic. The 'improvement' of his estate's park tightly harnesses the picturesque aestheticisation of nature to another form of improvement depending on the rationalisation of agriculture. As Charlotte expresses her concern that the planned improvement may prove too costly, Edward retorts with economic arguments spelling the end of an outdated rural community and ensuring better returns:

> We have only to dispose of that farm in the forest which is so
> pleasantly situated, and which brings in so little in the way of rent: the
> sum which will be set free will more than cover what we shall require,
> and thus, having gained an invaluable walk, we shall receive the
> interest of well-expended capital in substantial enjoyment.[23]

The process of aesthetic autonomisation characteristic of modernity is well under way. Pastoral mimicry warrants agricultural rationalisation. Sense and sensibility collude in the same phrase regime that precisely subjugates the enjoyment of improved nature to an overarching utilitarian world view. Yet, as Goethe's advertisement also insists from the start, nature cannot be rationalised or aestheticised away:

> everywhere there is but one Nature, and even the realm of clear,
> rational freedom is run through with the traces of a disturbing and
> passionate Necessity, traces not to be erased unless by a higher hand,
> and perhaps not in this life.[24]

Nature resists, and any attempt at instrumentalising it cannot suppress its capacity to unhinge Enlightened reason and even undo the accepted binarism opposing reason and sensation.

Even more central to our argument is the way such sublation speaks of man's 'attitude' and his capacity to articulate and experience his sense of historical belonging. From Austen to Hardy and even Ford Madox Ford in *Parade's End*, from Gainsborough to Richard Long, the English imagination is structured around that complex and often unacknowledged negotiation between instrumental reason and historicised sensibility. Austen's England is indeed, as Jonathan Bate suggests, 'one in which social relations and the aesthetic sense [. . .] are a function of environmental belonging'.[25] As the running metaphor of improvement also shows, from *Sense and Sensibility* to *Mansfield Park*, Austen's England is one in which reason and emotion co-exist and even collude in the definition of the modern self as rational/ sentient, or as a fully phenomenological subject, self-reflexively thinking/ feeling *in* the world.[26]

Gainsborough's *Mr and Mrs Andrews* (1750) is also exemplary of such phenomenological negotiation. As the fierce art historical debates surrounding it have shown, its seemingly irenic natural setting is also an embattled ideological ground. Kenneth Clark's passing remark on Gainsborough's painting in his 1949 *Landscape into Art*[27] came under considerable flack from cultural theorists, geographers and eco-historians, from John Berger to Gillian Rose.[28] Clark's Rousseauistic reading of the work and the more recent culturalist and Marxist interpretations occupy two symmetrical positions representative of two antagonistic conceptions of modern subjecthood. In Clark's humanistic apprehension of Gainsborough's oil, modern subjectivity does not simply express itself through aesthetic contemplation. It invents itself *as* aesthetic contemplation.[29] Meanwhile, the phenomenological alchemy that turns landscape *into* art abstracts subjectivity. It lifts the subject above the economic and ideological apparatus of instrumental reason. The process of autonomisation at work here is well known and one could read Gainsborough's entire work as gradually intensifying that process of autonomisation, from the still relatively grounded vision of *Mrs and Mrs Andrews* or *The Gravenor Family* (1754) to the famed *Mr and Mrs William Hallett ('The Morning Walk')* (1785) or *Mrs Richard Brinsley Sheridan* (1785–7). Agonistic readings, such as Berger's or Rose's, denaturalise Gainsborough's aestheticised nature and its repressed economic realities. Aesthetic autonomisation is thus perceived as a strategy of containment that suppresses the underlying system of production.

I would like to argue for an even more dialectical approach to such layered images. Gainsborough's sylvan subjects are not so much conflicted as simply complex. The modern phenomenology in the making here is both rational and sentient,[30] both utilitarian and aesthetic, both modern and nostalgic. Recent studies in Gainsborough's rustic genre scenes, such as *Landscape with Wood-cutter and Milkmaid* (1755) (see Figure 3.2), or his other works in which pollards also feature, tend to show that such antagonistic interpretations fail to do justice to his layered imagination.

The scene in *Landscape with Woodcutter and Milkmaid* is intensely modern, in the full historical meaning of the term. As Elise Lawton Smith has recently shown,[31] it tells us of the current mutations of the rural world, the pollard trees standing for the waning economy of the commons. But the picture functions in other ways, as an allegory of course, warning the spectator against the dangers of idleness, Gainsborough harnessing the ancient idiom of allegory to the language of the modern work ethics. In the same landscape and the same sylvan vision, two cultures, two spatial economies, two models of selfhood come to cohabit.

Figure 3.2 Thomas Gainsborough, *Landscape with Woodcutter and Milkmaid*, 1755, oil on canvas, 106 cm x 128 cm, © His Grace the Duke of Bedford and the Trustees of the Bedford Estates. From the Woburn Abbey Collection

Pollards and timber are the symbols not so much of a changing world vision, but of the complexity of the modern. In *Pride and Prejudice*, the woods of Rosings in which Elizabeth Bennet learns to read Darcy and herself, as she rereads his letter, are a site of introspection in which the modern subject comes to experience herself as thinking and sentient, as fully phenomenological. But these woods are also the product of instrumental reason, that same reason that invented forestry and enclosed the commons. Similarly, Rousseau's cherished trees of Ermenonville are both fountains of emotion and potentially the liberty trees of the French Revolution (see Figure 3.3).[32]

The sylvan imagination of modern Europe is thus far more entangled than our obsession with ruptures and historical periodisation may imply. The anthropomorphic and pantheistic imagination of the likes of Charlotte Brontë in *Jane Eyre*, Wordsworth, Caspar David Friedrich, or Thomas Fearnley (see Figure 3.4) should not be read as merely antagonistic to changes in sensibility and economic conditions. *Jane Eyre*'s chestnut tree crystallises a sign system in which dominant, emergent and residual cultures – to resort to Raymond

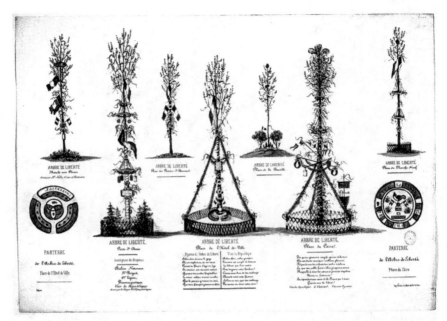

Figure 3.3 *Arbres de la Liberté*, print, Paris, Musée Carnavalet, © Musée Carnavalet/Roger-Viollet

Figure 3.4 Thomas Fearnley, *Slindebirken*, 1839, oil on canvas, The National Museum of Art, Architecture and Design, Oslo

Williams's taxonomy in 'Base and Superstructure in Marxist Cultural Theory'[33] – do not so much cohabit as function as one and fashion a subjectivity that sustains itself through a constant negotiation between seemingly contradictory aspirations and mind logics.

The phenomenological subject of modernity experiences herself as a sentient being through a contemplation whose empirical basis is also that of rational experimentation. This is the rational/sentient subjectivity that Joseph Wright of Derby captures in his 1768 *An Experiment on a Bird in the Air Pump*. Nature is subjugated in order for the subject of Enlightenment to come into his own. The same sublime nature that fuels Friedrich's or Fearnley's restless and wandering desire presses at the window of Wright of Derby's experimentation room and is kept at bay, as if foreclosed. A similar chiaroscuro technique is used by all three painters as an index of transcendance and also as a meta-pictorial instrument through which they experiment with vision and technique, thus anticipating later modernist experimentations.

The modern subject of epistemological reason is also the modern subject of phenomenology, grounded in empirical observation, looking both above and ahead, and yet also rooted in the here and now of her or his presence to the world of the senses and emotion. Acknowledging modern subjectivity as layered rather than conflicted implies we rethink modernity's relation to its own historicity, a historicity we have too often been taught to think of as agonistic and self-divided. To return to Foucault's argument, modernity might thus be approached as a self-reflexive practice enacting a sublation of binary tensions.

Jumping two centuries, I would like to try and see how contemporary art has reappropriated such critical historicity for a deconstruction of the suppressed narrative of modernity. Hamish Fulton's sylvan wanderings may provide ample material for such explorations, but I would like to turn to an installation by Anya Gallaccio – *Beat* (2002) – that forced the spectator to a violent experience of her or his own modernity by questioning the economy of aesthetic experience as engineered by the museum. *Beat* was commissioned by Tate Britain to coincide with Gainsborough's great exhibition also held at Tate Britain from October 2002 to January 2003. For *Beat*, Gallaccio took inspiration from the Tate Britain collections and 'began to consider the possibilities of working with that archetypal symbol of the British landscape: the oak tree'.[34] She 'fill[ed] the South Duveen galleries with whole tree trunks, with their bark intact but with their branches removed', thus ensuring 'their original and "natural" state is not forgotten'.[35]

As she has done previously, for instance in *Glaschu*, her 1999 in-situ work at Lanarkshire House, now the Corinthian, in Glasgow, Gallaccio uses site to reflect on the way it functions as a memory site. In the two installations, she more specifically produces embodied allegories of the English/British layered relation to nature. Nature's uncanny intrusion into the exhibition space does not merely transcend the nature/culture dichotomy; it discloses the overlooked, repressed memory of late modernity. Gallaccio's response to the two commissions is a political response that confronts modernity's ramified identity. In both cases, she engages with the artistic or visual language associated with the site's symbolical functions: a national museum in the case of Tate Britain, and not any museum, the museum solely devoted to the grand narrative of British art; a listed building, in the case of Lanarkshire House, formerly Glasgow's Sheriff Court and Justice of Peace Court, and which when extended by John Burnet in 1876–9, built on an earlier neo-classical building.

In *Glaschu* (Glasgow in Scottish Gaelic), Gallaccio chooses to reproduce a carpet design she had found in the archive of a local factory. Cracks created in the concrete floor of the neo-classical house allow foliage to grow through, producing the impression that nature may gradually invade that cultural site and reappropriate it.

In *Beat*, she enters in a dialogue with Gainsborough's conflicted vision of nature. Her agonistic installation taps into the hidden history of the building and also into the ideological subtext of much of Gainsborough's work and of the English cult of nature. Needless to say, the oak trees of the installation are powerful quotations of the landscape tradition of English painting. They are paradoxical, embodied abstractions of a grand narrative that itself is haunted by the memory of the lost forests of England. Not only is the oak tree, to use curator Mary Horlock's phrase, 'a powerful signifier of the British country-side';[36] here it is meant to function as a 'quasi-object', that is, one of those hybrids, neither fully natural nor exclusively cultural, which, Bruno Latour argues in *We Have Never Been Modern*, is the hallmark of our current sense of political and epistemological crisis.[37]

The objective reality of the installation is itself hard to circumscribe as it encompasses the site itself. The location is of course part of *Beat*'s meaning. Tate Britain's Duveen Galleries did not merely house Gallaccio's work. They were fully part of the work's quasi-object mechanism and were in their turn revealed as another sign system in which the museum, as imagined and funded by one of the icons of Victorian industrialism – the sugar magnate, Henry Tate – engineers a form of a-historical contemplation suppressing the museum's political rationale. That memory is present in the title of the installation, *Beat*, an ironical reference to the beetroots used in the production of white sugar. It is also embodied in another component of the installation: two slabs of molten sugar placed in the North Duveen.

As the third part of the installation makes clear – a hollowed root filled with water whose calm surface reflects the gallery space – *Beat* is intensely reflexive. Its ethical reflexiveness extends of course to the grand narrative developed by the museum and its complex dramatisation of the visitor's sense of cultural belonging; down to its most specific detail: the oak trees Gallaccio worked with originated from the Englefield Forestry Estate in Berkshire, a 'traditionally managed rural estate'[38] in its time painted by John Constable.

Beat's ethical reflexiveness is no intellectual play. It is embodied in the physical experience of the visitors who encounter the dead oaks as they enter the museum space. Gallaccio's installation functions as a phenomenological conceit. It develops a sustained allegory signifying the discursiveness of the museum experience through sensation. Confronted with the dead oaks, we can no longer ignore the fact that the museum is grave-like in more than one way.

Its celebration of the art of the past cannot be abstracted from a sense of 'our historical being' nestling in the dominant cultural apparatus, a sense that the museum conceals and represses.

Confronted with the dead oaks, the visitor is both necessarily shaken out of her or his complacency and forced to reflect. She or he may choose not to reflect and head straight to the galleries housing the permanent collections. But even that movement of denial is trumped by the overall reflexiveness of the work. *Beat*'s site-specificity turns space into a site of embodied intellection. Gallaccio's experimentation with space – a characteristic inherent to the very genre of installation art – offers a form of experiential criticity, in which aesthetic experience is newly endowed with a profound and disturbing historicity. Entering the museum we are forced to confront our own historicity, our own existence not only in the here and now of aesthetic contemplation but also as it survives through a long, conflicted history of denial.

Beat is thus both mausoleum and ghost chamber. As a quasi-object, it compels us to an embodied moment of reflexiveness. At the heart of the museum machinery, it harnesses sensation to a critical task that is both physical and intellectual. With it, modernity's sylvan imagination is meant to be understood for what it has always been: a contested and layered site, a site in which rationality and experience are interdependent. Its ethos remains intensely modern. Its criticity springs from the heart of modernity's embodied consciousness. The agonistic dialogue it initiates with our empirical memory is one in which our modernity does more than survive its own melancholy failure. That dialogue is one in which body and reason become fully productive of a historical reflexiveness that is both concept and practice.

NOTES

1. In the field of visual arts, such untimeliness might also be characteristic of the temporal turn of contemporary art; see Christine Ross, *The Past Is the Present; It's the Future Too*, London: Continuum, 2012.

2. Enrique Dussel, 'Eurocentrism and Modernity', *boundary* 2, The Postmodernism Debate in Latin America, 20: 3 (Autumn 1993), 65–76, 65. He is referring here to Jürgen Habermas's *The Philosophical Discourse of Modernity* (1985), Cambridge, MA: The MIT Press, 1987 and to Charles Taylor's *Sources of the Self: The Making of the Modern Identity*, Cambridge, MA: Harvard University Press, 1989.

3. See Terry Eagleton, *Heathcliff and the Great Hunger: Studies in Irish Culture*, London: Verso, 1995.

4. Sanjay Subrahmanyam, *Three Ways to Be Alien: Travails and Encounters in the Early Modern World*, Waltham, MA: Brandeis University Press, 2011.

5. On the subject, see a recent essay by French philosopher Jacob Rogozinski, *Ils m'ont haï sans raison. De la chasse aux sorcières à la Terreur*, Paris: Cerf, 2015.

6. Sanford Budick and Wolfgang Iser (eds), *Languages of the Unsayable: The Play of Negativity in Literature and Literary Theory*, Stanford: Stanford University Press, 1987.

7. Jean-François Lyotard, *Le Différend*, Paris: Éditions de Minuit, 1983.

8. Michel Foucault, 'What Is Enlightenment?', in *The Foucault Reader*, ed. Paul Rabinow, New York: Pantheon Books, 1984, pp. 32–50, p. 39.

9. Ibid. p. 42.

10. Michel Foucault, 'Qu'est-ce que les Lumières?', in Daniel Defert and François Ewald (eds), *Dits et écrits, 1976–1988*, Paris: Gallimard, coll. Quarto, 2001, pp. 1381–97, p. 1390.

11. Foucault, 'What Is Enlightenment?', p. 45.

12. Ibid. p. 45.

13. F. Scott Fitzgerald, *The Great Gatsby* (1926), Harmondsworth: Penguin Modern Classics, 1986, p. 171.

14. Ibid. p. 171.

15. Ibid. p. 171.

16. Simon Schama, *Landscape and Memory*, London: Vintage, 1995, p. 153.

17. See W. G. Hoskins, *The Making of the English Landscape* (1955), Toller Fratrum: Little Toller Books, 2013, pp. 84–90. For a synthesis of the research on the topic, see for instance Ian D. Rotherham (ed.), *Trees, Forested Landscapes and Grazing Animals: A European Perspective on Woodlands and Grazed Treescapes*, London: Routledge, 2013; John Sheail, 'The New National Forest, from Idea to Achievement', *The Town Planning Review*, 68: 3 (1997), 305–23. On eco-history, see Jean-Paul Deléage and Daniel Hémery's very early essay 'De l'éco-histoire à l'écologie-monde', *L'homme et la société*, 91: 2 (1989), 13–30.

18. See Jonathan Bate, *The Song of the Earth*, ebook, Cambridge, MA: Harvard University Press, 2002, ch. 1.

19. Robert Pogue Harrison, *Forests: The Shadow of Civilization*, ebook, Chicago: University of Chicago Press, 1992, ch. 3.

20. Alison Byerly, 'The Uses of Landscape: The Picturesque Aesthetic and the National Park System', in Cheryll Glotfelty and Harold Fromm (eds), *The Ecocriticism Reader: Landmarks in Literary Ecology*, Athens, GA: The University of Georgia Press, 1996, pp. 52–68, p. 58.

21. I am of course adapting Pierre Nora's meta-category: Pierre Nora (ed.), *Les lieux de mémoire*, Paris: Gallimard, 1984–92. In section 3 ('Les France') of volume 2 of this collective work, a chapter is devoted to the forest: Andrée Corvol, 'La forêt', in *Les lieux de mémoire*, Paris: Gallimard, coll. Quarto, 1997, pp. 2765–816.

22. Harrison, *Forests*, ch. 3.

23. J. W. Goethe, *Elective Affinities*, ebook, Boston: D. W. Niles, 1872, ch. 7.

24. Quoted in N. K. Leacock, 'Character, Silence, and the Novel: Walter Benjamin on Goethe's *Elective Affinities*', *Narrative*, 10: 3 (2002), 277–306,

p. 285. See also Walter Benjamin's essay 'Goethe's *Elective Affinities*', in Marcus Bullock and Michael W. Jennings (eds), *Walter Benjamin: Selected Writings. Volume 1, 1913–1926*, Cambridge, MA: The Belknap Press of Harvard University Press, 1996, pp. 297–359, p. 315.

25. Bate, *The Song of the Earth*, ch. 1.

26. On the complex relation between nature, naturalism and Enlightenment, see Taylor, *Sources of the Self*, pp. 328–30.

27. Kenneth Clark, *Landscape into Art*, London: John Murray, 1949, p. 34.

28. John Berger, *Ways of Seeing*, London: Open University, 1972, p. 107; Gillian Rose, *Feminism and Geography: The Limits of Geographical Knowledge*, London: Polity Press, 1993. See especially ch. 5, 'Looking at Landscape: The Uneasy Pleasures of Power', pp. 86–112.

29. On this process of aesthetic grounding, see once more Benjamin, 'Goethe's *Elective Affinities*', p. 315.

30. For a reading of the correlation to be established between Gainsborough's painterly vision and empiricism, see Amal Asfour and Paul Williamson, 'Splendid Impositions: Gainsborough, Berkeley, Hume', *Eighteenth-Century Studies*, 31: 4 (1998), 403–32.

31. Elise Lawton Smith, '"The Aged Pollard's Shade": Gainsborough's *Landscape with Woodcutter and Milkmaid*', *Eighteenth-Century Studies*, 41: 1 (2007), 17–39.

32. See Schama, *Landscape and Memory*, ch. 3.

33. Raymond Williams, 'Base and Superstructure in Marxist Cultural Theory', *New Left Review*, 1: 82 (November–December 1973); reprinted in Raymond Williams, *Culture and Materialism*, London: Verso, 1980, pp. 31–49.

34. 'Anya Gallaccio, 16 September 2002–16 January 2003', available at <http://www.tate.org.uk/whats-on/tate-britain/exhibition/anya-gallaccio> (last accessed 13 December 2016).

35. Ibid.

36. Mary Horlock, 'The Story so Far', in *Anya Gallaccio: Beat*, London: Tate Publishing, 2002, pp. 11–17, p. 12.

37. Bruno Latour, *Nous n'avons jamais été modernes*, Paris: La Découverte, 1991. The term is itself borrowed from Michel Serres's *Le parasite*, Paris: Grasset, 1980. A similar concept is used by David Matless in the introduction to his important book, *Landscape and Englishness*, ebook, London: Reaktion Books, 1998: 'The power of landscape resides in it being simultaneously a site of economic, social, political and aesthetic value, with each aspect being of equal importance'.

38. Horlock, 'The Story so Far', p. 12.

CHAPTER 4

Little Did They Know: Toward an Experiential Approach to the Theory of History

Sarah Pardon

It all starts with how we want to understand fiction. Ever since Hayden White has tried to make us aware of the employment of narrative strategies by the historian, we seem to be moving back and forth in an ongoing discussion on the relation between fiction and history writing. To be brief, we can argue along with literary theorist Roland Barthes[1] and narrativist Hayden White[2] himself that the scientific institutionalisation of history has caused us to turn a blind eye to the many similarities that can be found between historical and fictional representations.[3] Or we can in line with Lubomír Doležel make a clear-cut distinction between the two autonomous worlds of representation based on their contrasts in reference (obligation vs choice) and their main object (truthfulness vs credibility).[4] Doležel furthermore asserts that H. White, in the wake of Barthes, makes the unfortunate mistake of equating the constructivist side of history writing with the process of fictionalisation (Doležel 2010: 21). According to Doležel, this equation is fatal. As he explains, 'the fatal double equation "emplotment = literary operation = fiction-making" is instituted in the postmodernist paradigm not by analysis but by a substitution of synonyms, or more precisely, by a substitution of terms that White considers to be synonymous' (Doležel 2010: 15). In her attempt to explain and defend White's view on fiction, Ann Rigney emphasises a couple of the positive connotations that we have with fiction: it is a term that indicates the act of construction and the use of our imagination (Rigney 2001: 5). With this positive view on fiction in mind she explains that:

> When White referred to historical narratives as 'verbal fictions', he was clearly out to provoke people into thinking more deeply about the permeability of the border between historical writing and other forms of expression and about the role of imagination in producing history. (Rigney 2001: 5–6)

Dorrit Cohn, in contrast to Ann Rigney, sums up the negative traits we may associate with fiction. She points at the referential injustice that fiction may imply: deception, untruth, lie (Cohn 1999: 2–8). In line with this negative view on fiction, she explains that White 'expressly blocks out the referential level of historical narrative' (Cohn 1999: 114). My own starting point is that all historical representations, regardless of their referential claims, share the ability to provide the reader with a sense of comfort due to the existence of dramatic irony. When all has passed and every possible turn of event has taken place, we can find solace in our knowledge that from our retrospective positions we can, at least, gradually start to reconstruct what has happened.

My intention is to move away from any opinion about history writing and fiction based on a plea for either a diffusion or a strict division between the two. My research does not start with a closer look at what fiction means and how it can help us to change our views on some of the more solid ideas on objectivity and neutrality in the construction of history writing. Nor do I want to make a plea for either fiction or history writing as the type of writing where we may best become aware of an authentic experience of the past. Rather, I want to put focus on the common ground between fiction and history writing by putting all attention to the concept of a historical experience. What I want to bring forward is how both history writing and fiction are equally concerned with evoking an image of the past in our mind. As such, I treat them as equals if it comes to the question of how they come to terms with a historical experience of the past. This is not just a mere act of diplomacy. The purpose is to formulate an answer to the question presented by postmodernist historian Keith Jenkins: 'Why history?' (Jenkins 1999). Why should we still write, study and theorise about history if we are burdened with the realisation that it is a linguistic reconstruction with recognisable preconceptual forms[5] and shapes much like any other type of text or narrative? Or in Jenkins's words:

> If every reading of the 'real' world is ultimately an effect of that constitutive/performative reading, then why should we bother with postmodern 'reading's rather than the modernist ones we've got used to . . . in the end, why bother with anything? (Jenkins 1999: 5)

His advice, fitting for a postmodernist, is to remain calm in the face of such relativistic circumstances. He argues that it is a simple fact of life that human beings will be bothered with such questions. So why shouldn't we?, is his answer (Jenkins 1999: 5). I want to answer the question from the position of the reader. In addition, I have asked myself what we try to accomplish by reading historical representations and what happens to readers when they read representations of the past. This focus on the reader allows me to explain why there is a continuous appeal to re-examine historical events in all their forms and shapes.

In order to study this process I bring together two views on aesthetic experience that, when put together, take into account both the beginning and the end of the mediation process of reading historical representations. At the beginning of this process, as Anton Froeyman remarks in this volume, Chapter 6,[6] we can situate the idea of historical experience by Frank Ankersmit. Ankersmit, in the words of Ewa Domańska, 'pushes historical theory beyond the linguistic turn' (Domańska 2009: 176) by exchanging his interest in narratives for one that deals with our experience of the past. In order to understand this shift, we first need to be aware of a firm distinction Ankersmit makes between historical research and historical writing. The former is about making true statements about the past whereas the latter deals with the way narratives shape our understanding of the past (Ankersmit 1983: 8; 2005: 52–3; 2012: x). By making such a distinction, Ankersmit recognises historical research as an invaluable field of research in its own right, yet he also makes it positively clear that his own research does not involve any pursuit of facts, but instead, centralises on our relationship with the past (Ankersmit 2002: 53). Like Ankersmit, I want to turn the focus to how the past evokes an image in the mind. I think it essential for our understanding of the past to incorporate his view on how historical representations mediate a historical experience that precedes and exceeds our linguistic attempts to deal with the past. It is on the level of historical representation that we wish to come to terms with an absent past. As Ankersmit elucidates, 'representation aims at making an absent reality present again and thus at being "as good as" reality itself' (Ankersmit 2012: 57).

What I want to add is the question of how language is positively involved in this process. Ankersmit moves language out of the picture in order to bring us in contact with what lies underneath it: an authentic experience. As Ankersmit explains, '[l]anguage is where experience is not, and experience is where language is not' (Ankersmit 2005: 79). It is not my intention to skip experience and move over to language without looking back at the experiential level of history writing. Rather, I want to see how language and experience are complementary forces that are at work whenever we try to make sense of the past. The place *par excellence* to study the reconciliation between experience and language is the reading process. Here I address a number of insights borrowed from Wolfgang Iser who is known to foreground the actualisation of images during the reading process of the literary text (Iser 1995: 140–3). As he explains, 'the meaning of the literary work remains related to what the printed text says, but it requires the creative imagination of the reader to put it all together' (Iser 1995: 142). According to Iser, the literary text refers to a reality that has no existence of its own (Iser 1971: 8; 1997: 38). As such, Iser only focuses on the aesthetic experience of literary texts. I want to use his insights in matters of the reader's actualisation process and aesthetic response in the light of historical representations. The turn to Iser makes it possible for me to include the final stages of the reading process where the mediation of the historical experience through means of the text's guidance is activated by the reader's imaginative capabilities.

So far, the reason to talk about dramatic irony in the light of the reader has helped me to move away from a number of problems. First of all, it allows me to move away from a discussion of fiction and referentiality and move over to experience as a common denominator of fiction and history writing. Second of all, this angle makes it possible to reconcile language with experience in the process of reading. The outcome is a consideration of history writing and fiction on the level of their imaginative appeal. The next step is to consider how different depictions of the past, ranging from the more truthful to more inventive, employ different or similar linguistic means in order to capture that same sense of historical experience. In order to put theory into practice, I put my attention to a particular historical event: the assassination of JFK during his motorcade campaign through the streets of Dallas on 22 November 1963. Little did he or his companions know that they were on the road to tragedy. To this day, the JFK murder presents itself as an epistemological riddle. After more than fifty years we do not seem to be any closer to a definite answer as to why and how John F. Kennedy found his death. Or to put it in Patrick O'Donnell's words, the JFK murder exposes us to 'the gap between knowledge and truth that the assassination symptomizes' (O'Donnell 2000: 53). It is a historical event that seems to resist closure and instead continues to question itself. Timothy Melley rightly observes that despite the 'endless hermeneutic conundrums of the case' (Melley 2000: 134) the interpretation of the JFK assassination comes down to a rivalry between two interpretations: it is either a one-man show or a product of grand conspiracies (Melley 2000: 134–5). Due to this avalanche of new theories and interpretations, the event continuously confronts us with the limits of our knowledge about the past. Next to that it also challenges us to come to terms with a growing awareness of the multiple ways in which language can be used in order to cope with a tremendous experience of loss over the past.

In the following I want to look more closely at how experience and language are reconciled during the reading process of the two pivotal historical figures of this historical drama.[7] A referential approach, one that we may associate with Doležel and Cohn, will most likely put emphasis on how the novelist, due to his or her referential freedom, has a bigger repertoire of formal representations at hand such as internal focalisation and I-narration. A narrativist approach may reveal that similar plot techniques and narrative strategies are used among the novelist and the historian. With my angle directed towards the imaginative, I want to show that flexibility and solidity are not just matters that can be related to the ontological status of the text. The representation of historical characters is not just a matter of looking at the level of flexibility that is allowed in accordance to the level of fictionality of the historical representation that is involved.

THE REPRESENTATION OF HISTORICAL FIGURES

The head shot that killed the President has been repeatedly viewed and reviewed via the offices of the Zapruder 'home movie' – its individual frames blown up, enhanced, and magnified – as if it were possible to derive the truth of the event from the sheer iterability of its mediations. In the same vein, taken as a headless project that bears an amazing

consistency in terms of its implicit desires and goals, the seemingly
unlimited flood of information about and historical reinterpretations
of the assassination and the events leading up to it seek to pin down
the logic of presidential murder. (O'Donnell 2000: 45)

With this passage O'Donnell adequately uses the image of losing one's head
as a way to describe both JFK's murder and the everlasting emergence of
new theories on what actually happened on that fateful day. JFK's head
has, certainly since the murder, attracted a lot of attention. The position of
the President's head and neck have been re-examined from a series of ever-
changing viewpoints that tried to determine once and forever how many shots
were aimed from which corner by how many people. In turn, Lee Harvey
Oswald's head has also naturally provoked enormous attention. Needless to
say, both the heads of these historical figures provoke a desire for continuous re-examination. My own interest in their heads does not extend to any
physical or mental examination. Rather, I want to analyse how these two historical figures are represented differently as they each have been historically
condemned to take up the role of antagonists in the continuous portrayal of
the mystery murder of JFK. The questions I pose are the following: can we
consider the representation of historical figures as headless projects in terms
of invention? Are novelists by definition allowed greater freedom in order to
develop any kind of representation to suit the head, body and limbs of their
historical figures? Or can we find similarity in the techniques of representation of one historical figure in a variety of historical texts ranging from the
more imaginary to the more faithful?

I want to bring attention to the fact that we cannot represent JFK in the
same way that we can represent Lee Harvey Oswald. They both call upon a
different image and a different set of questions in our mind. This variety of
images and questions to a great extent influences the selections of formal representations that fall in line with the reader's sense of an authentic experience
of the past. What is more, the demand for a series of particular forms of representation can be traced in both fictional and factual accounts. So even if fiction
may allow for a more imaginative representation – such as an I-narration or
internal focalisation – we can still trace similar techniques of solid and more
fluid formal representation in both fictional and factual accounts for the same
historical figure. In order to analyse how the flexibility of the representations
of these figures can be stretched, I introduce the term 'avertability'. I want to
analyse to what extent (because it is a matter of degree) a historical character
will allow for more strict or fluid forms of representations. The question I want
to pose is: how many formal strategies of invention can a historical character
tolerate before our barrier of our so-called suspension of disbelief is crossed?
Of course, the notion of our barrier in this definition needs some explication.
Genre conventions and the actual historical context of the reader, it should be
noted, play an important role in determining when such an abstract barrier is

crossed. A remark made in conversation by Julian Wolfreys on the importance of an authentic experience may be most helpful to further clarify what I mean by this term. It is a term that refers to those moments when the reader accepts the experience of a historical character as an authentic one. As a general guideline, I would say that the crossing of this boundary may best be explained by the occurrence of an authentic experience of the past by any reader. Readers, in such a case, go through an authentic experience whenever their expectation of the past coincides with the aesthetic response that is affected through the text. It is not a matter of finding the perfect match, however, as readers may also feel positively curious at finding out new ways of imagining a historical character. Rather, it is a matter of degree where a representation of a historical figure can move on a scale from most credible to absolutely incredible and, therefore, inauthentic. By focusing on two historical characters in a selection of truthful and imaginary depictions, I want to detect how the flexibility of a character's representation depends not only on the text in which it appears but also on the experience that the character evokes. The starting point is that not every character calls upon a similar experience of the past.

JFK: THE MYTHICAL AND SOLID SIGN

Let us start with an analysis of JFK. This name covers an entire range of images that come close to that of a mythical god, but also to that of an imaginative and detached persona. More than anything else, he is often considered in terms of the images that have been projected onto his identity. Thomas Brown, for instance, has devoted an entire study to how the death of JFK has provided the Americans with a blank page on which they have projected their own idolisations and disillusionments with the course of US policy after the 1960s (Brown 1988). John Hellman, who wants to revise Brown's approach, goes so far as to say that there is not only a Kennedy text on which images are being written. Rather, Kennedy and his advisors wilfully assumed the role of author/actor during his lifetime, so as to further elaborate on a mythical yet distant image of Kennedy's own self (Hellmann 1990: 744–6). These images, Hellman points out, are drawn from a discourse rooted deeply in 1950s Hollywood culture, with associations of glamour actors such as Cary Grant or Jimmy Stewart (Hellmann 1990: 748). His image, Hellman argues, is also constructed on the role of a hero that Kennedy designed for himself during political moments of crisis. As an example Hellman points to the U.S. Steel crisis of 1962 in which JFK played the hero who did not want to play along with the capitalist games of big companies (Hellmann 1990: 751–2).[8] Finally, the name JFK is also collectively remembered in connection to the myth of improvement or the 'promise of a better world', as Patricia K. Felkins and Irvin Goldman call it (Felkins and Goldman 1993: 447). As they explain, 'Kennedy's assassination is the tragic context in which archetypal images of life and death, the Promise and the loss of Promise, dramatically collide'

(Felkins and Goldman 1993: 449). Owen Dudley Edwards, in his review of a nostalgically written portrait of JFK, writes that '[s]uddenly the dead Kennedy became what he had been for relatively few in life – the hope of the future, the hero, the Prince of youth' (Edwards 1984: 413). This is, again, where the image of Camelot comes into play. For many, JFK could have been America's knight in shining armour. We can notice a certain eagerness to believe that JFK would have made better decisions in foreign policies. As Diane Kunz points out, '[n]ot surprisingly, no aspect of the Kennedy legend has proved more durable than the notion that, had he lived, the United States would never have become mired in the Vietnam conflict' (Kunz 1999: 368). The association of Camelot with JFK remains a powerful to this day.[9] This becomes clear from biographies such as Seymour Hersh's *The Dark Side of Camelot* (Hersh 1998) or Kunz's virtual history 'Camelot Continued: What If John F. Kennedy Had Lived?' (Kunz 1999) which use the image of Camelot in order to paint a more negative picture of the Kennedys and their legacy.

By reading about JFK in fictional and factual representations, we hope to unravel his slippery private self we think is hidden more or less behind his Hollywoodesque public display. The image of JFK seems to resist any form of proximity: he remains an elusive character of mythical proportions. This becomes obvious when we look at the moment of exposition, or the introductory pages, of the character of JFK in a variety of texts. Norman Mailer, for instance, who has published a set of journalistic articles and letters about JFK, talks about his encounter with this presidential presence in terms of alienated familiarity. Mailer recognises in JFK, for instance, an air of 'detachment of a man who was not quite real to himself' (Mailer 1964: 46). It leads Mailer to ponder on the relation between JFK's image and the use of distant media:

> He would seem at one moment older than his age, forty-eight or
> fifty, a tall, slim, sunburned professor with a pleasant weathered
> face, not even particularly handsome: five minutes later, talking to
> a press conference on his lawn, three microphones before him, a
> television camera turning, his appearance would have gone through
> a metamorphosis, he would look again like a movie star, his coloring
> vivid, his manner rich, his gestures strong and quick, alive with that
> concentration of vitality a successful actor always seem to radiate.
> (Mailer 1964: 48)

Mailer finds JFK most suitable for the contradictory medium of television, which gives us at once an impression of immediacy while at the same time covering great geographical distances. So distance works with JFK. He can be as up-close as you want, but he will always remain a detached figure who, above all, embraces contradictory forms of charisma: sometimes a distracted professor, at other times a confident and cheeky actor. The easiness by which he switches from one image to the next can be aligned with JFK's famous pragmatic viewpoint as a politician. As Henry Pachter observes, '[h]e was above all a political operator, and he tried to persuade others that he was neither a capitalist nor a socialist, neither a reactionary nor a progressive, but a pragmatist' (Pachter 1966: 6). What is even more important to consider is how a figure of such mythical allure simply always remains at a certain distance from us. JFK is an ungraspable figure who always emanates power, strategy and therefore also solidity. His image is not random, it is well chosen. There always seems to be a controlling and strategic hand behind all his public display, much like the novelistic presence of a narrator. This quality plays an important role in general when it comes to the selection of credible narrative strategies that usually surround the depiction of the figure of JFK. My analysis of a number of diverse representations will show that he is usually portrayed by firmly contoured narrators. The selection of the following fictional fragments are ordered according to their increasing tolerance for invention for the representation of JFK: we will gradually get closer to his mind and thoughts. The first example confirms a rather safe and formally distant representation of JFK's outward appearance. I compare this with various attempts to represent JFK's inner consciousness, ranging from distant and safe third-person narration to more adventurous attempts in the shape of first-person narration. We could argue that the latter examples are more 'fictional' in the sense that the author has taken more imaginative 'risks', so to speak, in order to fill in the persona of a restricted historical character. Usually such characterisations are considered to be more inventive when compared with a more distant (and therefore safer) depiction of JFK. What I intend to show, however, is that even though the measures to depict JFK become more and more adventurous with each new example that I present below, the basic foundation remains somewhat similar: each time, the choices of formal narrative strategies confirm and strengthen our idea that JFK is a solid figure that cannot tolerate a lot of confusion between the narrator and the character.

The question that naturally occurs during the fictionalisation of JFK's mind is: to what extent can we fictionalise his personality? Jeff Smith reminds us, here, that:

> It was a long time before presidents could readily be made 'real' even in the very conventional terms of fictive realism, and a still longer time before they were fully embodied in fiction, with all the messy intimacy that the term body implies. (Smith 2009: 282)

If anything, Smith argues, the 1960s and 1970s made it possible to imagine a president in the light of his weaknesses. He remarks that at the time 'analysts fretted that the presidency's demands were simply more than mere mortals could bear' (Smith 2009: 165). The assassination, Smith suggests, did nothing but affirm the fragility and weakness of a person in such a high office (Smith 2009: 166). So any attempt to further fictionalise his voice is also an attempt to return to a memory of JFK as someone made of flesh and blood. Someone who can be approached just like any other fictional character nowadays, by means of his inner voice. This is exactly where the appeal of JFK lies: we want to make him touchable. However, many fiction writers have ventured into a deeper psychological inspection of JFK's consciousness in an attempt to get nearer to this otherwise mythical character. In order to capture the nuances of the ways in which JFK's mind is internally made accessible, I rely on Cohn's notion of psycho-narration. Psycho-narration is a form of third-person narration where the character's consciousness is still obviously embedded within the discourse of a narrator (Cohn 1978: 21–6). The narrator, in such a case, takes the liberty of talking indirectly about a character's thoughts and feelings. Cohn distinguishes between two types of psycho-narration: the dissonant and the consonant form. The former deals with a type of narration where the narrator has a firm and distant grip on the character's mind (Cohn 1978: 28–9), whereas the latter present a narration where the narrator wilfully adapts to the figural voice – that is, the character's voice – and is therefore described by Cohn as 'ungraspably chameleonic' (Cohn 1978: 30). In the following analysis, I will present a number of fragments that introduce JFK. I want to argue that in such cases it is no surprise that we will find a dissonant form of psycho-narration. This particular form supports the idea that JFK is above all a solid figure who, habitually, will only tolerate a clear and firm mediation of the voice of his consciousness.

We can find such an example in Jeff Greenfield's *If Kennedy Lived: The First and Second Terms of President John F. Kennedy: An Alternate History*, an alternate history that follows the contours of a novel (Greenfield 2013). Jeff Greenfield opts for an account of JFK based on a combination of a historian's distant voice of what happens after the shooting combined with a number of quoted comments from JFK's known entourage such as Ted Sorensen, Arthur Schlesinger and Norman Mailer. The combination of comments by recognisable historical characters and a counterfactual description of the historical facts easily fuels the reader's sense of dramatic irony. We can, for instance, read an observation made by Sorensen about JFK's response to the shooting: 'It was, as Ted Sorensen said later, "vital that the President reject the notion that the shooting was somehow evidence of a national sickness, that there was any kind of collective guilt for what had happened"' (Greenfield 2013: 42). Observations by Schlesinger appear too, as we can read in the following comment, '"[a]s long as you're being morbid," said Schlesinger, "if it had stopped raining in Dallas, and the bubble top wasn't on your car, it *has* occurred to me to wonder where we'd be in Vietnam . . ."' (Greenfield 2013: 158). The alternate voice of Norman Mailer, echoing his actual voice from the Presidential Papers, furthermore, notices the Superman qualities of this vivid example of JFK after his near-death experience (Greenfield 2013: 158–9). The narrator furthermore clarifies that the emergence of a hippie generation in the 1960s could be explained from the general optimism that was already there thanks to JFK's peace-making policy (Greenfield 2013: 151). Finally, The Beatles also join in to meet with a very approving JFK (Greenfield 2013: 157). All of this makes Jeff Greenfield's alternate history a very enjoyable read that often feeds into our sense of dramatic irony. His work continuously relies on and tests the reader's possible knowledge of the JFK policy right before he got shot.

Overall, the novel gives us a picture of JFK based on a presentation of direct quotes from JFK and many of his followers next to a historian's distant voice that helps to situate the context. However, at the very beginning of the novel, we come across a scene that offers a more inventive excursion into JFK's mind as he is just about to head out for the Dallas motor route. It is no surprise that here we can find a lot of room for reflection from both the narrator and character. After all, we are dealing with a moment in history that very much appeals to our imagination. The introductory scene starts off cautiously enough with a typical heterodiegetic narrator who knows more than his character and has firm control over his character's gaze and subsequent thoughts. We can find an example of the narrator's direction of the president's gaze in the following statement:

> His hosts had borrowed priceless paintings from local museums –
> a Monet, a Picasso, a Van Gogh – but his eyes were drawn to the
> gloomy weather, and to a large crowd gathered on the sidewalk eight
> stories below: a fitting blend of bad and good news for this trip.
> (Greenfield 2013: 1)

In the following quote, however, we can witness different attempts at getting a glimpse of JFK's consciousness:

> At every stage of the visit so far – from the dedication of the United
> States Air Force School of Aerospace Medicine in San Antonio, to a
> Houston dinner for Congressman Albert Thomas, to the motorcade
> route to and from the airports – the crowds had been large and
> enthusiastic. *If we get a break in the weather*, he thought, *we can let
> the crowds get a good look at us here and in Dallas and Austin; maybe
> that'll shake some cash loose from the big-money boys.*
> Only . . . there were clouds hanging over this Texas visit that had
> nothing to do with the weather.
> For one thing, the Democratic Party was in the middle of a full-
> fledged civil war between conservative Democrats, led by Governor
> John Connally, and liberals led by Senator Ralph Yarborough [. . .]
> That had produced exactly the kind of headline John Kennedy did
> *not* want to see, splashed across the front pages of the Dallas papers.
> (Greenfield 2013: 2)

A lot of things are happening here in this particular fragment. What is perhaps most obvious to notice is the use of what Cohn calls quoted monologue. This is a category that falls under a second type of third-person narration that she develops, next to psycho-narration. Quoted monologue is a technique that refers to a construction in the narrative where it seems that the narrator makes use of direct quotation in order to make the thoughts of a character visible to the reader (Cohn 1978: 58–63). Indeed, in the fragment we notice a number of clearly defined referential indicators. We know that it is JFK who is thinking those words because they are italicised and, of course, because we can read 'he thought'.[10]

At first sight we may be doubtful whether the following line 'Only . . . there were clouds hanging over this Texas visit that had nothing to do with the weather' presents us with the thoughts of the narrator or of JFK. After all, it is plausible that we continue to read JFK's thoughts on the political debates of the time. In that case, we would not be dealing with quoted monologue, but narrated monologue, a form where we cannot draw a clear line between the narrator's voice and the character's (Cohn 1978: 99–102). This is Cohn's third and final type of third-person narration. However, there are clear signals in the text that suggest otherwise. My own reading would be to consider this fragment as a moment where the narrative zooms out and jumps from a momentary gaze inside JFK's thoughts to a larger reported reflection by the narrator on the particularities of the time. I find it much more likely that JFK's thoughts are only made accessible in the italicised text and the rest of the information is conveyed by a distant and controlling narrator. The most obvious sign is the alternation of a present tense that is used in the quotation and the past tense in the informative comments. Indeed, a change in basic tense is the most common grammatical indicator for the use of quoted monologue embedded in the reporting style of the narrator (Cohn 1978: 62–3). Cohn furthermore clarifies that:

> A monologist in a third-person context is not the uniquely dominant voice in the text we read. He is always more or less subordinated to the narrator, and our evaluation of what he says to himself remains tied to the perspective (neutral or opiniated [sic], friendly or hostile, empathic or ironic) into which the narrator places him for us. (Cohn 1978: 66)

In this case, the narrator's comments serve as a means to introduce the reader into the political moment of the time, not as a means to get familiar with JFK's thought process. Finally, we get access to JFK's opinion by means of a form of dissonant psycho-narration where the narrator talks about JFK in the third person ('the kind of headline John Kennedy did *not* want to see'). Here, again, we arrive at a reporting remark made by a knowledgeable narrator. All in all, we can say that the narrative information is distributed in a stable and consequential way. The narrator wilfully and accurately indicates when JFK is thinking. So even if we venture into JFK's head, the means to do so remain solid and clear. There is no merging of the narrator's voice with the character's voice.

Even though a first step towards a more personalised invention of JFK's human consciousness has already occurred in the previous example, it can still be considered as a safe one in the sense that it is embedded in the third-person narration. We take a riskier leap into the imagination when JFK is represented by means of a first-person narration. We can find an example that comes very close to such a narration in Jeff Golden's *Unafraid: A Novel of the Possible* (Golden 2008). It is a story that consists of a number of layers. In the alternate history of this novel the Kennedy family has ordered a biography of JFK. Caroline Kennedy, JFK's daughter, is reading the manuscript for the first time. The text of the manuscript is formally distinct from the representation of Caroline's reading experience and further comments by means of a different typeface. The reader and Caroline read the manuscript at the same pace. This is obvious in moments when Caroline's thoughts suddenly appear in a different typeface in order to comment on the previous text from the manuscript or whenever the typeface of the manuscript comes to an abrupt end and we continue to read a conversation between Caroline and the author of the biography, who happens to be around, about what was just made available in the manuscript. In the manuscript, JFK is represented by means of the already familiar techniques. Mostly this part of the book consists of dialogues and JFK is characterised as a persistent president with outspoken ideas on human rights and anti-war statements by means of direct quotations. It is only in the parts where Caroline appears that we may come across a personal account delivered by JFK in seeming I-narration delivered by the president as Caroline tries to remember her conversations with her father. In this case, we are still dealing with an example of quoted monologue, yet it is remarkable that any signs of a referential marker of the quotation are left behind. This adds to the dreamlike state of Caroline's memories of her father. We can find such an example of a more risky representation of JFK in the following passage:

> He said it was, but not in the way most people think. I'm supposed to have had this near-death experience, the tunnel of light and the divine embrace and so on and so forth, and woken up some kind of holy man. It's a lovely story but it's not what happened. I didn't visit the sweet by-and-by. I never lost consciousness except when they put the mask over me in surgery. Not that getting shot doesn't have a way of focusing your attention on what matters. It has a way of lifting your head up out of whichever ridiculous thing you happen to be obsessing over at the moment. (Golden 2008: 105)

This is an example of Cohn's so-called unsignalled quoted monologue (Cohn 1978: 62–3). It still serves as an example of a direct use of quotations as it is preceded by an obvious 'He said'. Here, JFK recounts the event of the missed shooting to Caroline. Notice that we are working with an intermediate figure, the daughter. She functions as a substitute for the reader, yet at the same time, this particular role is narrowed down to that of the listener. In terms of creating counterfactual information, Jeff Golden is taking a huge leap. Even though he uses Caroline's vague memory of a quoted monologue in order to grasp her father's voice, we still get the impression that we are reading a more direct form of I-narration by JFK. After all, JFK becomes a screen onto which a set of ideological high hopes are being written. It becomes doubtful whether this depiction of JFK can carry such a load of great expectations to the point where it could conflict with our sense of an authentic experience of this historical figure.

In sum, we can say that JFK gives rise to a number of questions that mostly deal with the juxtaposition of public and private persona. In general, we can say that the image of a distant mythical being is most helpfully supported by distant representational strategies. Moments of closer introspection, as can be gathered from the previous examples, have been explored as well. However, some caution seems to be necessary when the author wants to personalise a historical figure of such mythical measures. Also, it should be observed that when such a 'trespassing' occurs from outer observation to inner speculation, it is usually signposted by well-defined forms: we can tell where the voice of the narrator stops and where the mind of JFK starts wandering. There is no obvious confusion of the lines that indicate who is talking and who is thinking. The narrator is presented as an instance that can give the reader access to inner thoughts as well as someone who governs knowledge from all quarters. If we relate this to the event of JFK being murdered, we could say that his mythical charge has come to a final stop at the day of his murder. As the bullet shoots right through his body and his life ends, all the layers of mythical allure and unaccomplished promises get locked up within the frame of the proper name. John F. Kennedy, the sign that says: could have been, would have been, should have been, if only he was given the chance. This definite ending makes the mythical status even more entrancing: it circulates within his fixed entity. He is a concealed sign in the sense that his representations favour firm contours for the voice of the narrator and the character. The *degree of avertability* is guided by a question of proximity: we want to get closer to JFK, yet, at the same time, we also expect a certain solidity in the representation of his mind. By reading into his character we hope to get a closer picture of who he really was and what he could have accomplished.

LEE HARVEY OSWALD: THE MYSTERIOUS AND INQUISITIVE SIGN

The mind of Lee Harvey Oswald provokes a number of questions that are very different from the ones that we were driven to ask as we were contemplating the character of JFK. We turn to Oswald if we want to get answers on questions about what happened on that fateful day. As Mailer observes in his biography of Oswald, '[i]f a figure as large as Kennedy is cheated abruptly of his life, we feel better, inexplicably better, if his killer is also not without size' (Mailer 1995: 607). He can either gain this size by being backed up in his action by the involvement of a number of threatening and all-controlling organisations, or, his psyche can become the central focal point in order to explain the causal relations between Oswald and the murder of JFK. Throughout all this, Oswald remains a sign that shows resistance to readability. Dewey talks about Oswald as a 'familiar, if troubling text' (Dewey 2006: 94). For all we know, he *is* the assumed murderer, yet there are many theories out there that contradict this very assessment. Therefore, his proper name signals a sense of uncertainty and shiftiness. In his attempt to capture Oswald's psyche, Mailer states, '[t]he difficulty with closing the case on Oswald is that every time one shuts the door, a crack opens in the wall' (Mailer 1995: 622). This difficulty, I would argue, can easily be traced back to the cloudy facts that surround Oswald's personal life. (Why did he travel to Russia? Why did he come back to America? How could he pay off his debt to the American state for his travelling expenses after he returned from Russia?) This, finally, results in possible portrayals of his character that are a lot more flexible and fluid than the ones we have seen of JFK. These questions, furthermore, are most commonly projected on representations that give an account of what happened before the shooting. In line with this observation, I am going to look at two texts that delve into Oswald's consciousness before the shooting took place: Don DeLillo's *Libra* (DeLillo 1989) and Norman Mailer's *Oswald's Tale: An American Mystery* (Mailer 1995). Here we get examples of one counterfactual biographical novel that is clearly imaginatively free and a nonfictional biography that is guided by the author's hope of staying as close to the factual reality as possible. The otherwise limited attempts to venture into Oswald's conscious mind allow me to venture even more into these two very specific texts in which his mind is so central to the story.

In DeLillo's *Libra*, the proper name Lee Harvey Oswald is subjected to a lot of instability. First of all, its contours become blurred when aliases and pseudonyms start to emerge such as Lee, Leon, Alek James Hidell. As Kavadlo states, Oswald 'uses and plays upon language to hide and protect himself, as though names or words can provide sanctuary and comfort for the body' (Kavadlo 2004: 53). The further blurring of lines between narrator and character also returns in the representation of Lee Harvey Oswald's voice. The following fragment is an example of a recurring poem in *Libra* on the name Hidell:

A man in a white tuxedo introduced the bathing beauties by name. Sincere applause. The two men went into the chill night. It was late and quiet and Lee pulled his windbreaker tight around him. Konno stood smoking, hunched away from the wind, knees bent, looking down an empty neon street.

Take the double-*e* from Lee.
Hide the double-*l* in Hidell.
Hidell means hide the *L*.
Don't tell.   (DeLillo 1989: 90)

What is important to notice in this fragment is the lack of clarity about who provides us with this information. Is it the narrator who gives the reader an ironic wink from the present time as he delivers the poem or does the poem originate from the confused mind of Lee Harvey Oswald himself? Or to phrase it in the narratological language of Cohn: the fragment starts off cautiously enough by giving the impression that we may be dealing with a distant and heterodiegetic narrator. It soon becomes clear that the narration is an example of consonant psycho-narration as the third-person narrator includes sensory experiences of the character in his discourse ('Sincere applause'). The narrator, therefore, already hints at the fact that he is able to remain close to Oswald's mind. However, due to the lack of clear quotation marks surrounding the poem, it becomes unclear what the source is that presents us with these lines: the narrator in retrospect or the experiencing Oswald? This is a question that remains unanswered. In line with the previous analysis of JFK, which started with classic examples of his depiction, we may well consider this fragment as a typical example of how we may expect Lee Harvey Oswald's consciousness to be represented: one moment he is cautiously portrayed by a clearly contoured narrator, the next moment we do not know where the narrative information is coming from. It is an example of what I have earlier called an absent form of narration. As the narrator disappears behind the wings of the stage, Oswald's voice appears, but it appears with no clear definitions. As Lentricchia furthermore explains,

> The omniscient third-person narrator 'DeLillo' becomes first-person consciousness trapped in the system, without the warning of 'he thought' or 'he felt,' or the safety of quotation marks, in the midst of a paragraph, often in the midst of a sentence: 'DeLillo's' voice fades into his major characters, he becomes Ruby or Oswald, or the crowd gaping at Kennedy, or Mrs. John Connolly in the limousine speeding to Parkland Hospital. (Lentricchia 2007: 210)

Lentricchia deliberately surrounds the author's name with quotation marks to signal the absent state of the narrator and, therefore, the necessity to include the author's name to fill up the absence of the narrator (Lentricchia 2007: 210). With Kennedy we have seen that the referential indicators are usually stable and well defined. This should come as no surprise. We only need to think of the proper name JFK. The abbreviation of the president's name alone has a certain ring of solidity and steadfastness to it. Apart from the fluid use of mixed names, we also learn in *Libra* that Oswald's proper name, in contrast to JFK's, is also changed through time. When Oswald finally gets arrested, he notices that everyone starts to use his name differently. Suddenly, people talk about his full name. This is where his name, according to Oswald, gains its fullest meaning in history. As we read in *Libra*: '[o]nce you did something notorious, they tagged you with an extra name, a middle name that was ordinarily never used. You were officially marked, a chapter in the imagination of the state' (DeLillo 1989: 198). From that moment on, his name apparently needs to be pronounced in its full shape so that it can carry the wide range of questions and unresolved mystery that emanates from it. As José Noya explains, '[t]he name becomes an imposition masking the secret that cannot be named in the official denominations' (Noya 2004: 272). History has put a stamp of meaning on his name, one of never-answered mystery, and by doing so, it has changed his name forever.

Not only his name in *Libra*, but language as a whole is subjected to an extreme extent of flexibility for Oswald. As Glen Thomas asserts, 'Oswald is marked as one who is the victim of a form of linguistic alienation' (Thomas 1997: 111). According to Thomas, Oswald 'is continually frustrated in his attempts to place himself within discourse and to find the conventional form or meaning for his words' (Thomas 1997: 111). DeLillo captures this nicely by referring to Oswald's dyslectic problems. He depicts an Oswald who determinedly jots down ideas and descriptions in his diary while bearing in mind that someday someone will study his writings. As for the struggle he has with writing, we read the following:

> Let them see the struggle and humiliation, the effort he had to exert to write a simple sentence. The pages were crowded, smudged, urgent, a true picture of his state of mind, of his rage and frustration, knowing a thing but not able to record it properly. (DeLillo 1989: 211)

In his writing, after all, Oswald can gain a sense of determination over the fluidity of the signs that dance in front of his eyes. When it comes to his sense of reality, however, his surroundings become as fluid as his grip on language, as the following passage may show:

> He walked invisibly through layers of chaos, twilight Tokyo. He walked for an hour, watching neon lights pinch through the traffic haze, with English words jumping out at him, TERRIFIC TERRIFIC, under the streetcar cables, past the noodle shops and bars. He saw Japanese girls walking hand in hand with U.S. servicemen, six doggie bakers and cooks by the look of them, all wearing jackets embroidered with dragons. It was 1957 but to Lee these men had the style of swaggering warriors, combat vets taking whatever drifted into meathook reach. (DeLillo 1989: 83)

As with the previous passage, we may at first get the impression that we are dealing with an innocent portrayal of Oswald's outward behaviour by means of a reporting heterodiegetic narrator. Again, the narrator is quick enough to include an exaggerated form of Oswald's visual experience within his discourse. With phrases such as 'by the look of them' the representation of Oswald's gaze remains close to the character's experience. Finally, the narrator seems to take a step back and gives us a retrospective comment about the time and about the confusion that Oswald experiences with the city. In general we can say that the city of Tokyo resists any stable reading for Oswald: lights dazzle his eyes and he has to walk through the mazes of traffic. He allows his imagination to run as free as much as his grip on language is fluid as well. Words and signs seem to jump into his vision as rapidly as new and fantastic explanations of the people that surround him in the streets. They can become a warrior in a heartbeat. Nothing remains steady. As Kavadlo explains, when the struggle to obtain a grip over language and the world becomes too much, Oswald turns to violence in order to maintain a clear position within history (Kavadlo 2004: 67). In the case of the motorcade route as presented in the Warren Commission Report, everything that was planned was natural and convenient. Here, the surroundings of Oswald are anything but natural or convenient. The same can be said about the choice of representation: the consonant form of psycho-narration supports the general idea of fluidity and unsteadiness that we can trace back in the formerly discussed representations of Oswald.

The image of Lee Harvey Oswald can be shifty and elusive, but it is a different kind of shiftiness than that of the set of images that cling to the figure of JFK. Whereas JFK's images seem to be controlled and decisive (the hero during crises, the actor on a television screen, the learned professor in an interview), the images of Lee Harvey Oswald defy solidity. Lentricchia detects in the language of *Libra*'s JFK something Arthurian and Shakespearean whereas Oswald has to make do with pronunciations associated with John Wayne (Lentricchia 2007: 199). This marks JFK as 'a seeker of traditional cultural sanction and empowerment' and Oswald as 'the plaything [. . .] of Hollywood's image factories' (Lentricchia 2007: 199). JFK, then, has a sense of purpose whereas Oswald is at a loss. Kavadlo, with regard to Oswald, states that 'just as Oswald never gets to know himself and others cannot see through to him, the reader feels a constant distance between him- or herself and the protagonist' (Kavadlo 2004: 52). As we can read in the following passage, Oswald is neither here nor there. He is not distant like JFK, because distant still implies that there is a possibility of being connected. Oswald, by all means, is completely unattached, as we can read in the following lines:

> He paused, measuring how he felt. Inside the bouncy music and applause, he occupied a pocket of calm. He was not connected to anything here and not quite connected to himself and he spoke less to Konno than to the person Konno would report to, someone out there, in the floating world, a collector of loose talk, a specialist who lived in the dark like the men with bright lips and spun-silk wigs. (DeLillo 1989: 89)

Here, and in many other places in *Libra*, Oswald is represented as a man who wants to be part of a bigger chain of historical theories. He lacks a sense of belonging, a central core, to which he can relate. This is also reflected in the narrative strategies for depicting his character. Take, for instance, the next passage from *Libra*:

The autumn damp took hold. Lamplight shimmered in networks of alleys crowded with wooden houses and shops. They'd taken away his American space. Not that it mattered. His space had been nothing but wandering, a lie that concealed small rooms, TV, his mother's voice never-ending. Louisiana, Texas were lies. They were aimless places that swirled around the cramped rooms where he always ended up. Here the smallness had meaning. The paper windows and box rooms, these were clear-minded states, forms of well-being. (DeLillo 1989: 86)

The first two sentences may well be spoken by an omniscient sort of narrator, yet we soon come across expressions that are derived from Oswald's mind. There is a tendency to remain so close to Oswald's mind that we may even be hesitant to call this passage an example of psycho-narration. Rather, the discourse in this passage can be read as narrated monologue. This is Cohn's third type of third-person narration, where there occurs, as she explains, '[a] transformation of figural thought-language into the narrative language of third-person fiction' (Cohn 1978: 100). As such, the figural (i.e. the character's) voice is mixed with the narrator's. Though the narrator is of course always present as a mediating instance, here, we get the illusion of a disappearance act: there seems to be no mediating force present between the narrator's rendering of Oswald's experience and Oswald's own thoughts. Even though we can only talk about an act of disappearance and not a real absence, we can see how this illusion is at work here. Indeed, such complete diffusion of the two discourses (the narrator's and the character's) seems a suitable form to capture the fluid sign that is Lee Harvey Oswald. He seems to have lost his space as well as his own boundaries. He has become someone who floats around with no clear definitions or anchor points

We can find a similar mechanism of floating references and fluidity in the nonfictional account of Mailer's Oswald. Mailer takes his time to explain that his book, despite a number of fictionalising strategies, is above all a nonfictional account of Oswald. He categorises his book as a 'peculiar form of nonfiction' (Mailer 1995: 353), a status that is dependent on the 'mystery of the immense dimensions of Oswald's case' (Mailer 1995: 353). O'Donnell even describes Mailer's book as 'a nonfictional bildungsroman' (O'Donnell 2000: 66). Mailer furthermore states that, 'it is most certainly not fiction. The author did his best to make up no dialogue himself and attribute no private motives to his real characters unless he was careful to label all such as speculation' (Mailer 1995: 353). Curiously, Mailer thinks it is fiction because of the inclusion of his own speculations, yet here he remains most faithful to some of the typical shifters of historical discourse that Roland Barthes identified.[11] He simply extends their degree of suggestiveness. Even though he claims to steer away from any interior motives of the characters, the main task that he sets himself is to get closer to the mind of Oswald. So even though we are dealing with a so-called nonfictional account, the sign of Oswald remains subjected to a high level of fluidity. Even when the author wants to shy away from any fictional exploration of Oswald's consciousness, a mixture of different narrative voices continues to emerge within his biography and these narrative voices usually follow one another in rapid succession. Rather than discussing a myriad of quotes from one text, as in the previous analysis of *Libra*, it is therefore much more appropriate to pick one extensive passage that serves as an example of how one fragment may contain a myriad of narrative attempts to capture Oswald's mind.

I will start off, however, with a particular passage that meets with more traditional expectations of the nonfictional biography. After all, Mailer's biggest concern, as with most biographers, lies with an adequate and complete representation of Oswald. He regularly admits that it is not an easy task to pin down Oswald within the realm of the nonfictional. However, he remains hopeful to achieve an all-round understanding. As he states,

> If to some degree he will always remain mysterious, that contributes
> nonetheless to our developing sense of him. He is a man we can never
> understand with comfort, yet the small mysteries surrounding him
> give resonance to our comprehension. An echo is less defined than the
> note that created it, but our ear can be enriched by its reverberation.
> (Mailer 1995: 539)

In order to meet with the demand of a full and comprehensive depiction of Oswald's character, Mailer relies on a massive amount of documents. The purpose is to let the accumulation of facts finally speak for the character of Oswald. The many interviews, transcripts and conversations do indeed give some insight into Oswald's character at a certain moment of time. However, Mailer needs to rely on his voice as a narrator when he has to deal with the development of Oswald's character between one given moment in time and another. He illuminates Oswald's development by means of such remarks as 'It is *almost certain* that Lee Oswald at fourteen and fifteen shared this point of view' (Mailer 1995: 370, my emphasis). The overall effect is, as O'Donnell explains, one where the studied object has to become an active agent. As he explains:

> Arguably, the general project of *Oswald's Tale* involves a collapsing
> of the subject into the object, for while he capitalizes on the surplus
> of information that accrues as the tale gets told, Mailer is interested in
> constructing a historical figure who has multiple, subjectival choices
> at every turn, and therefore, is indeterminate, obscured. (O'Donnell
> 2000: 66)

How does this manifest itself on the level of narration?

Let us take an example from one of the many personalised accounts of the interviewees when they talk about Oswald. Rimma, an Intourist guide, appears to be a most interesting example as she shows a certain degree of extravagance in her language and expressions. This makes it easier to analyse the narrative manipulations within this particular text. Let us take a look at the following passage that deals with Oswald:

> But he was still upset he had to go to Minsk. He had no idea where it was. Had never heard of it. Rimma told him it was a good city, which was true. She often took foreigners to Minsk in a railroad coach on trips. She liked its newest hotel, their Hotel Minsk. People in Minsk, she told him, are much better than in many other places. But he was depressed. He wanted her to accompany him on his all-night allroad trip from Moscow to Minsk, but by now he understood that everything was not so simple as he had thought before – everything was more serious than he had thought. In America, when he took his decision to go to Russia, he must have been like a child, but then in these days he grew up, you see. So now, he understood that even if Rimma wanted, she couldn't leave her job and go with him. He understood it was impossible. He knew it was a very serious place here.
> [. . .]
> December 31
> New Year's Eve, I spend in the company of Rosa Agafonova at the Hotel Berlin. She has the duty. I sit with her until past midnight. She gave me a small Boratin clown. (Mailer 1995: 63–4)

What may come as an initial surprise if we look at the first paragraph is that the interview is not laid out in a conventional manner where interviewer's questions and interviewee's answers are framed in separate blocks of text and where the answers given by the interviewee are represented by means of a first-person version. Rather, several interviews with the same person are reworked to fit into one coherent personal account. The voice of the interviewer is left out in order to maintain the coherent structure of the interviewee's account. Rimma and Oswald are both treated from an equal distance in the narration: they both appear to be characters who are framed in a third-person narration. As a consequence, it may appear at the outset that we are dealing with a dissonant form of psycho-narration. It seems as if a neutral and distant narrator is giving us indirect information on what Oswald and even Rimma feel. We may know that the information is provided to us through an interview, yet the formal exposition of the information is reminiscent of novelistic attempts to capture a consciousness. This impression is finally interrupted with the line 'he must have been like a child', which is a clear indication that whoever is narrating does not pretend to have access to the minds of the characters and is only making an estimation. Here the narrator breaks the illusion of having access to the aspirations of Oswald and Rimma. An additional 'you see' may well remind the reader that this is a second-hand story delivered by an interviewee, Rimma, who wants to explain the situation. Once her personal account is finished, we abruptly find a diary input by Oswald, one of the documents that Mailer has consulted and occasionally puts in-between personalised accounts of the interviewees. According to Cohn, the diary is closely related to autonomous monologue where the reader is confronted with an immediate unrolling of a mental process in a present moment (Cohn 1978: 208–9). The sequence of different immediacies of time gives a fragmented view of the depiction of the character's agency: once an object of an after-the-fact narration, at other times a subject who gives an account of an immediate experience. As we can see, a multitude of narrative situations is used in order to frame Oswald's mind.

Overall, we get the impression that there is no firm narrative grip over Oswald. He remains ungraspable. He is a ghost who needs to be detected from the many different viewpoints that are available. In this respect, O'Donnell notices that:

> Oswald's opacity predominates until the very end of the story, when he is transformed into the singular, tragic lone gunman of the theory the narrator proffers as the one that most likely follows when the facts are combined with knowledge of Oswald's character. (O'Donnell 2000: 66)

On the whole, we can say that Oswald's character calls upon a fluid representation. O'Donnell summarises it cleverly:

> Mailer's Oswald, like DeLillo's, is a figure of multiplicity, but with agency added; he is a figure of identification and difference, but his differentiation in *Oswald's Tale* is a matter of the author's keeping in play as many alternative Oswalds as possible rather than portraying him as a nomadic cipher ever available to the semiotic regime of the moment. (O'Donnell 2000: 73)

So whether Oswald appears in fiction or nonfiction, he remains a sign that resists any ultimate interpretation. He calls upon an experience of confusion over who he is and what he has done. This puts a set of demands and expectations on the formal representations of his character that are very different from the ones we have seen on JFK. As this fluid form of representation is a lot more challenging than the classical and safe ones that we have seen with JFK, it may be no surprise that, in general, we can find less inventive representations of Lee Harvey Oswald than of JFK.

CONCLUSION

It is my conclusion that the representations of historical figures cannot be understood as headless projects. The experience that arises from each individual historical figure determines to a great extent which formal representations are considered to be more credible. These representational conventions affect both fictional and factual accounts. I do not mean to object to the idea that we can expect more interpretatively free portrayals of a historical figure in a fictional text than in a factual one. I agree that we can easily detect more careful approaches to the representation of the human consciousness of a historical figure when it is done by a traditional historian or biographer. What I want to foreground, however, is that each historical figure individually calls upon typical questions that arise from the experiences that we have when imagining said historical character. This is where fiction and history writing share a common ground. They are both dependent on the experience of a historical character. Finally, these experiences determine the way in which a historical figure is given shape. The flexibility in representing a historical character cannot only be explained by looking at the fictional status of a text. It is also a matter of a response to the many images and questions that we imaginatively connect with historical characters when constructing their identity in written form.

NOTES

1. Most notably in 'The Discourse of History' (Barthes 1989b: 127–41).
2. Most notably in *Metahistory: The Historical Imagination in Nineteenth-Century Europe* (White 1993).
3. For the sake of my argument I have grouped Barthes and H. White together as two likeminded theorists whose goal it is to make us aware of the construction of history writing as a discourse with narrative strategies. It should be noted here that the relationship between their views on history writing is a bit more complicated than that. Put generally, one could say that Barthes's take on history writing is marked by a desire to reveal the illusionist construction of objectivity and neutrality in the discourse of the narrating historian whereas H. White argues for an awareness of the construction of objectivity and neutrality among historians by pointing at their use of narrative frameworks and preconceptions in order to reconstruct the past. For a comprehensive study of the relation between their viewpoints, see Kansteiner 1993.
4. Doležel argues that, '[t]he contrast in truth-conditions between historical and fictional texts is pragmatic. It is a condition of a successful (felicitous) functioning of these texts as communicative acts, a prerequisite for achieving their respective aims. Fictional texts, liberated from truth-valuation, construct sovereign fictional worlds which satisfy the human need for imaginative expanse, emotional excitement, and aesthetic pleasure. Historical texts, constrained by the requirement of truth-valuation, construct historical worlds which are models of the actual world's past. One and the same historical event or sequence of events (historical period, life, and so on) can be modeled by various historical worlds. In a critical testing, these

worlds are assessed as more or less adequate to the actual past' (Doležel 1998: 793). See also Doležel 2010.

5. In order to explain what I mean by preconceptual forms, I want to refer to what White calls 'the poetic act' of the historian, or, what happens before the writing stage. According to White, the historian relies first of all on 'general notions of the forms' which he or she shares with an audience. This will help the historian to perceive of a possible story or outline of the events he or she is studying. It will finally bring the historian to an understanding of the past by means of formulating a story (White 1985: 86).

6. He also mentions it more elaborately in Froeyman 2012: 397.

7. This reflection forms part of my PhD research *Little Did They Know: Place, Time and Character in Historical Representations*, which is a project funded by FWO at the university of Ghent. In this research I have addressed a specific entity per chapter in relation to historical experience: in the first chapter I address issues of space and facts (chapter 'Little') and in the second I discuss narration in the light of our background awareness of time (chapter 'Did'). In the third chapter I explain my findings on character representation in historical fiction a bit more elaborately (chapter 'They'). Each chapter should be considered as a theoretical exercise that begins from one distinctive starting point: I foreground the effects of dramatic irony and historical experience in the process of reading as two key notions to help us understand our relation with the past. This I explain in the final chapter 'Know'.

8. For a more detailed survey of the construction of the JFK image by John Hellman, see his *The Kennedy Obsession: The American Myth of JFK* (Hellmann 2000).

9. See also Rosenberg's observation of the likeness between the Arthurian hero survival and the many rumours about JFK's secret survival (Rosenberg 1976).

10. For the sake of clarity I here apply Cohn's standardised term 'quoted monologue'. In order to further specify the type of quoted monologue, we may also talk about 'quoted interior monologue' to indicate the italicised words by JFK in the above-mentioned passage. Cohn clarifies her own sporadic use of this term as follows: 'I [. . .] use the combined term "quoted interior monologue," reserving the option to drop the second adjective at will, and the first whenever the context permits' (Cohn 1999: 13).

11. Following Jakobson's take on linguistics, Roland Barthes distinguishes between a number of shifters in the discourse of history that confirm the presence of a constructed narrator's voice in history writing. He talks about listening and organisational shifters. Shifters of organisation are utterances by which the historian/narrator announces a certain movement in the discourse (e.g. *here were are* or *as we have seen before*). The shifters of listening give an indication of the historian's relationship with his or her

source material. This happens when historians explicitly verbalise what they can possibly know by using such phrases as 'To my knowledge' or 'As I have heard' (Barthes 1989a: 128–9).

WORKS CITED

Ankersmit, F. R. (1983), *Narrative Logic: A Semantic Analysis of the Historian's Language*, The Hague: Nijhoff.

Ankersmit, F. R. (2002), *Historical Representation*, Stanford: Stanford University Press.

Ankersmit, F. R. (2005), *Sublime Historical Experience*, Stanford: Stanford University Press.

Ankersmit, F. R. (2012), *Meaning, Truth, and Reference in Historical Representation*, Leuven: Leuven University Press.

Barthes, R. (1989a), 'The Discourse of History', in *The Rustle of Language*, trans. R. Howard, Berkeley: University of California Press, pp. 127–40.

Barthes, R. (1989b), *The Rustle of Language*, trans. R. Howard, Berkeley: University of California Press.

Brown, T. (1988), *JFK: History of an Image*, Bloomington: Indiana University Press.

Cohn, D. (1978), *Transparent Minds: Narrative Modes for Presenting Consciousness in Fiction*, Princeton: Princeton University Press.

Cohn, D. (1999), *The Distinction of Fiction*, Baltimore: Johns Hopkins University Press.

DeLillo, D. (1989), *Libra*, London: Penguin.

Dewey, J. (2006), *Beyond Grief and Nothing: A Reading of Don DeLillo*, Columbia: University of South Carolina Press.

Doležel, L. (1998), 'Possible Worlds of Fiction and History', *New Literary History*, 29: 4, 785–809.

Doležel, L. (2010), *Possible Worlds of Fiction and History: The Postmodern Stage*, Baltimore: Johns Hopkins University Press.

Domańska, E. (2009), 'Frank Ankersmit: From Narrative to Experience', *Rethinking History*, 13: 2, 175–95.

Edwards, O. D. (1984), 'Review: Remembering the Kennedys', *Journal of American Studies*, 18: 3, 405–23.

Felkins, P. K. and Goldman, I. (1993), 'Political Myth as Subjective Narrative: Some Interpretations and Understandings of John F. Kennedy', *Political Psychology*, 14: 3, 447–67.

Froeyman, A. (2012), 'Frank Ankersmit and Eelco Runia: The Presence and the Otherness of the Past', *Rethinking History*, 16: 3, 393–415.

Golden, J. (2008), *Unafraid: A Novel of the Possible*, Ashland, OR: Hellgate Press.

Greenfield, J. (2013), *If Kennedy Lived: The First and Second Terms of President John F. Kennedy: An Alternate History*, New York: New American Library.

Hellmann, J. (1990), 'The Author and the Text', *American Literary History*, 2: 4, 7473–755.

Hellmann, J. (2000), *The Kennedy Obsession: The American Myth of JFK*, New York: Columbia University Press.

Hersh, S. (1998), *The Dark Side of Camelot*, London: HarperCollins.

Iser, W. (1971), 'Indeterminacy and the Reader's Response in Prose Fiction', in J. H. Miller (ed.), *Aspects of Narrative: Selected Papers from the English Institute*, New York: Columbia University Press, pp. 1–45.

Iser, W. (1995), *The Implied Reader: Patterns of Communication in Prose Fiction from Bunyan to Beckett*, Baltimore: Johns Hopkins University Press.

Iser, W. (1997), *The Act of Reading: A Theory of Aesthetic Response*, Baltimore: Johns Hopkins University Press.

Kansteiner, W. (1993), 'Hayden White's Critique of the Writing of History', *History and Theory*, 32: 3, 273–95.

Kavadlo, J. (2004), *Don DeLillo: Balance at the Edge of Belief*, New York: Lang.

Keith, J. (1999), *Why History? Ethics and Postmodernity*, London: Routledge.

Kunz, D. (1999), 'Camelot Continued: What If John F. Kennedy Had Lived?', in N. Ferguson (ed.), *Virtual History: Alternatives and Counterfactuals*, New York: Basic Books, pp. 368–92.

Lentricchia, F. (ed.) (2007), *Introducing Don DeLillo*, Durham, NC: Duke University Press.

Mailer, N. (1964), 'The Third Presidential Paper – The Existential Hero', in *The Presidential Papers*, London: Andre Deutsch, pp. 25–63.

Mailer, N. (1995), *Oswald's Tale: An American Mystery*, New York: Random House.

Melley, T. (2000), *Empire of Conspiracy: The Culture of Paranoia in Postwar America*, Ithaca: Cornell University Press.

Noya, J. L. (2004), 'Naming the Secret: Don DeLillo's "Libra"', *Contemporary Literature*, 45: 2, 239–75.

O'Donnell, P. (2000), *Latent Destinies: Cultural Paranoia and Contemporary US Narrative*, Durham, NC: Duke University Press.

Pachter, H. (1966), 'JFK as an Equestrian Statue: On Myth and Mythmakers', *Salmagundi*, 1: 3, 3–26.

Rigney, A. (2001), *Imperfect Histories: The Elusive Past and the Legacy of Romantic Historicism*, Ithaca: Cornell University Press.

Rosenberg, B. A. (1976), 'Kennedy in Camelot: The Arthurian Legend in America', *Western Folklore*, 35: 1, 52–9.

Smith, J. (2009), *The Presidents We Imagine*, Wisconsin: The University of Winsconsin Press.

Thomas, G. (1997), 'History, Biography, and Narrative in Don DeLillo's *Libra*', *Twentieth-Century Literature*, 43: 1, 107–24.

White, H. V. (1985), 'The Historical Text as Literary Artifacts', in *Tropics of Discourse: Essays in Cultural Criticism*, Baltimore: John Hopkins University Press, pp. 81–101.

White, H. V. (1993), *Metahistory: The Historical Imagination in Nineteenth-Century Europe*, Baltimore: Johns Hopkins University Press.

CHAPTER 5

'The Heart cannot forget / Unless it contemplate / What it declines': Emily Dickinson, Frank Ankersmit and the Art of Forgetting

Páraic Finnerty

> To move away from the pedestrian world of daily reality to that of art and poetry is extremely difficult, but once this step has successfully been made, one has entered a world in which everything is permitted.
>
> F. R. Ankersmit, *Sublime Historical Experience* (2005: 429)

> Imagine the extremest possible example of a man who did not possess the power of forgetting at all and who was thus condemned to see everywhere a state of becoming.
>
> F. Nietzsche, 'On the Uses and Disadvantages of History for Life' (1997: 62)

Most critics of nineteenth-century literature would be surprised to discover that Frank Ankersmit, a renowned scholar of historiography, the philosophy of history and historical theory, uses lines by the reclusive American poet Emily Dickinson to encapsulate his ideas about how humanity relates to the past. The lines 'The Heart cannot forget / Unless it contemplate / What it declines' from her 1883 poem 'To Be Forgot by thee' (Dickinson 1998: 1405; Fr1601) are an epigraph for and discussed briefly within Ankersmit's 2001 essay 'The Sublime Dissociation of the Past: Or How to Be(come) What One Is No Longer', a revised version of which forms the central and titular chapter of his book *Sublime Historical Experience* (2005). While many Dickinson scholars would concur with Harold Bloom's assessment of Dickinson's 'startling intellectual complexity' and 'cognitive originality', as well as his belief that in her 'lyrical mediations' she 'rethought everything for herself' (Bloom 1995: 291), few would expect to find in her writings ideas relevant to humanity's relationship to and representation of the past. Ankersmit's incorporation of Dickinson into his discussion of historical experience is, however, in line with recent scholarship of the poet that has challenged an earlier view that she 'did not live in history and held no view of it' (Johnson 1958: xx) and 'epitomize[d] almost to the point of parody the gender expectations of her society: that women remain domestic, modest, and hidden' (Wolosky 2013b: 79). Resisting 'the tendency to privatize Dickinson' and position the poet and her writings outside history, recent critics have shown that Dickinson was 'vitally engaged with multiple aspects of her culture – literary, social, cultural, religious, and political' (Mitchell 2000: 2; Miller 2012: 2).

Representative of this approach is the important essay collection *Emily Dickinson and Philosophy* (2013), which situates the poet 'within the intellectual culture of her time', such as Common Sense philosophy, Higher Criticism, German Idealism and New England Transcendentalism, and demonstrates her anticipation of concepts and perspectives associated with later philosophical movements such as existentialism and phenomenology by drawing parallels between her ideas and those of Friedrich Nietzsche, Emmanuel Levinas, Jean Paul Sartre and Martin Heidegger (Deppman et al. 2013: 5). Yet the closest this collection, or Dickinson scholarship more generally, comes to a discussion of Dickinson's ideas of history is Daniel Fineman's essay 'Against Mastery: Dickinson Contra Hegel and Schlegel'. 'Dickinson's poetic practice', Fineman argues, draws on 'Hegel's method of progressive negation, of sublation, coupled with a Schlegel-like sense of the necessary systematic ironies resident in acts of comprehension'; however, she counters their shared 'presumption of totalization and mastery that comes from a masculine orientation' by foregrounding 'the interplay between the immediate sensory demands of language as object and the always-frustrated desire for final meaning' (Fineman 2013: 88, 89, 90). As Fineman puts it,

> [her] lyrics appear to realize in miniature the Hegelian trajectory
> of history: they gain a new object and enlarged vision out of the
> progressive cancellation of their own initial foci . . . [; however,
> she] does not share Hegel's faith that history advances because
> the revolutionary understanding of the last paradigm's incomplete
> knowledge, its negativity, is the very means to the next period's fuller
> sight. (Fineman 2013: 85–6)

Rejecting the possibility of progressive forms of comprehension, Dickinson's writing, in form and in content, foregrounds the uncertain, fragmentary and incomplete; in her work, the 'insufficiency of language to experience means that no depiction is ever final: ultimately finality is not attainable or even desirable' (Wolosky 2013a: 138). Viewed within this context, Ankersmit's orientation to Dickinson's work is less surprising as both he, particularly in *Historical*

Sublime Experience, and the Amherst poet are interested in experiences – complex, mysterious or sublime – which, once acknowledged, challenge orthodox conceptions of language, truth and knowledge. As Ankersmit puts it, 'Where you have language experience is not, and vice versa. We have language in order not to have experience and to avoid the fears and terrors that are typically provoked by experience' (Ankersmit 2005: 11). Dickinson, like Ankersmit, is fascinated and imaginatively exhilarated by the fearful and terrifying 'void of being', the formlessness and nothingness hidden from us by fictive ideas and reality effects, without which we would be 'exposed to the nature of actuality plain before human beings got at it and (contingently) real-ized it' (Jenkins 2008: 547).

This chapter examines Dickinson's representations of past experiences and her exploration of forgetfulness in the context of Ankersmit's ideas about humanity's experience of the past. For Ankersmit, historical writing stems from and attempts to remedy humanity's experience of its separation from the past and its desire for access to this foreclosed realm. The division between the past and present becomes most pronounced and undeniable at moments of social and political upheaval, which generate sublime experiences as a former worldview disturbs the mental categories and frameworks through which a current world order is understood and perceived. He offers the French Revolution, Industrial Revolution and Death of God as examples of events which cataclysmically changed 'the life of [individuals] in every conceivable aspect' and represent 'the most decisive and profound changes' that people in the West have 'undergone in the course of their history' (Ankersmit 2005: 323). Such 'historical change' makes itself 'felt with traumatic intensity' in the case of individuals and resounds 'in the collective consciousness of a whole generation', creating 'an insurmountable barrier between past and present that could impossibly be denied or undone' (Ankersmit 2005: 143). At such moments of dramatic transformation, there is a collective 'forgetting [of] a previous world and . . . shedding [of] a former identity' as a condition of 'entering a wholly new world' (Ankersmit 2005: 323). Such forgetfulness is a collective response to the 'fact of [such] a rupture with the past and [is] how this rupture is experienced by the human individual'; what is abandoned or forgotten is experienced in its absence, associated with a mythic world that is 'forever and irrevocably outside [one's] reach', and sublimely encountered as an epistemological and conceptual challenge to a current worldview (Ankersmit 2005: 188, 189). Ankersmit's ideas offer a new way of understanding much-discussed features of Dickinson's work, especially her preoccupation with past events and experiences, loss and memory, and, most strikingly, her couching of these in imagery and language associated with the sublime and in relation to psychological self-division and incomprehensible states. These elements of her writing along with her figurations of death, violence and revolution are indicators of what Ankersmit terms sublime historical experience, reflecting her position as writing after the American Revolution and during a shift within her Anglo-American culture which, put in Ankersmit's terms, involved the loss of a 'former identity' centred on religious belief, and the designation of a new secular and sceptical identity 'precisely in terms of what has been discarded and surrendered' (Ankersmit 2005: 13). Similarly telling of Dickinson's sensitivity and response to her culture's mood and collective consciousness is her specific attention to the theme of forgetfulness, which first appears in her letters to Abiah Root from the late 1840s and early 1850s. In these communications, she expresses her refusal to profess publicly her Christianity at a time of religious revival in Amherst, when all of her family and most of her friends and neighbours were experiencing the joys of a declaration of faith. Ideas about forgetting, conceptualised in these early letters, recur in later poems that explore the pain of being forgotten and the difficulty of forgetting. Her repeated concern with the concept and practice of forgetting signifies her participation in what Ankersmit calls the 'avalanche of literature' that poeticises change-overs from one order of things to another (Ankersmit 2005: 366)

A WORLD WE HAVE LOST

Ankersmit's citation of Dickinson draws her into his argument about the limitations placed on our understanding of how we experience the past by the ways in which it is rhetorically, textually and narratively constructed by historical writing (see Domańska 2009: 181–2). What is left out of historical writing is historical experience, of which he predominantly discusses two main types: subjective and sublime. Subjective historical experience occurs as a reaction to the distance and difference between the past and present, for example, in 'a direct encounter not only with the past in its quasi-noumenal attire but *also* with the aura of a world we have lost' (Ankersmit 2005: 265). Sublime historical experience, in contrast, happens at a devastating and exhilarating 'divergence of present and past' or an 'experience of the past breaking away from the present':

> The past is then born from the historian's traumatic experience of having entered a new world and from the awareness of irreparably having lost a previous world forever. In such cases the historian's mind is, so to say, the scene on which the drama of world history is enacted. (Ankersmit 2005: 265)

Sublime historical experience shapes historical consciousness and writing, but is also, for him, available to any individual (although he focuses on the historian) who witnesses or records the dramatic separation of present and past: 'subjective historical experience may well give rise to a feeling of loss and disorientation – and then some of the sublimity of the [other] type of historical experience will be imparted to subjective historical experience' (Ankersmit 2005: 266). In this context and while acknowledging that from the nineteenth century onwards historians have connected the identity of a nation, people or institution with establishing information and forms of knowledge about past events, Ankersmit argues that forgetting or losing a collective identity is just as fundamental to the way in which we relate to and construct historical discourse. Such forgetting, for him, is connected with the category of the sublime, which to a large extent is the 'philosophical equivalent of the psychological notion of trauma' (Ankersmit 2005: 318). Whereas traumatic experience can challenge our sense of identity, sublime experience requires the abandonment of a past identity and its accompanying conceptual patterns of thought, feeling and belief. Historical transformation rests on a process of forgetting: 'one has become what one is no longer': 'one's former identity, is now transformed into the identity of the person who *knows* (and no longer *is*) his former identity' (Ankersmit 2005: 333). Our collective identity then is defined by 'what we are no longer, by what we have forgotten and repudiated' (Ankersmit 2005: 340). Having described the process of forgetting as 'the lost object, is *first*, pulled within the subject in order to be, *next*, repelled again as a criticised object – where it will, *lastly*, forever remain part of the subject in this guise', Ankersmit adds: 'this is, summarized in one sentence, the entire mechanism I am describing in this chapter (and, even more succinctly, encapsulated in Emily Dickinson's poem that I used as its epigraph)' (Ankersmit 2005: 341). He goes on:

> forgetting is possible only on the condition of a perfect memory (think again of the Dickinson poem). The past first has to be fully admitted to our identity, to be recognized as a world that we have left behind us, and only then can it be discarded and give way to a new identity. (Ankersmit 2005: 343)

Before offering a fuller interpretation of this Dickinson poem within the context of her frequent inquiry into the topic of forgetting, it is important to consider her writing's fixation on the past and its replaying and dissection of prior experiences and events in relation to Ankersmit's theory. Alfred Habegger, for example, notes her regular scrutiny of 'acts of memory' and personal history in relation to singularity, and gains and losses, a practice intensified at various points in her writing career. Typically, in these poetic 'backward glances', her speakers attempt but often fail to draw 'a firm line between past and present' (Habegger 2001: 499, 531). In one poem, 'Remembrance has a rear and front' (Dickinson 1998: 485, Fr1063), remembrance is presented as a gothic house full of dangerous 'Fathoms' and refuse, while in another, 'To flee from memory' (Dickinson 1998: 1161–2, Fr1343), the vault of memory is something that must be kept closed or a place from which a speaker tries but inevitably fails to flee (see Habegger 2001: 525–37). David Porter argues that in fact her poetry is dominated by this 'back-looking view' and speakers who record their experience of 'living after things happen', 'living in the aftermath' (Porter 1981: 9). Many of these aftermath poems centre on a retrospective explication and re-experiencing of a past crisis or profound loss that has shattered thought and language. In one such poem, the speaker struggles to delineate a past occurrence that transcended conventional categories and expectations, and caused an unravelling of identity and meaning:

> I felt a Cleaving in my Mind –
> As if my Brain had split –
> I tried to match it – Seam by Seam –
> But could not make them fit –
>
> The thought behind, I strove to join
> Unto the thought before –
> But Sequence ravelled out of Sound –
> Like Balls – upon a Floor –
> (Dickinson 1998: 812; Fr867B)

Dickinson's frequent descriptions of such scenes of former awe and terror in which epistemological and ontological connections and associations are compromised have been identified as her specific take on the Romantic sublime. In such poems, Dickinson, according to Gary Lee Stonum, is attracted to the liminal state or threshold position between the 'actual intensity of the past moment', either traumatic or ecstatic, and a future or imagined resolution; as such she prolongs the sublime encounter that discomposes experience and identity, skirting the closure, coherence and mastery associated with the reactive stage of the orthodox sublime (Stonum 1990: 160).

The provocative parallels between features in Dickinson's sublime constructions of looking back on former states of being and Ankersmit's delineation of the sublime experience of a sundering of the past and present suggest her poetry as the unexpected 'scene on which the drama of world history is enacted' (Ankersmit 2005: 265). 'I felt a Cleaving in my Mind' along with other similar retrospective poems map the idea of language as no longer offering what Ankersmit calls 'the shield protecting us against the terrors of a direct contact with the world as conveyed by experience' (Ankersmit 2005: 11). Moreover, in line with Ankersmit's ideas, Dickinson represents the experience of the past as a grappling with the sublime; it is 'as close to death as one may come'; as 'nothing less than an act of suicide'; as an occurrence so world shattering that '"normal" patterns of experience are disrupted' and an 'abyss [emerges] between two different historical or cultural identities' (Ankersmit 2005: 325, 343, 346, 327). Poems such as 'It Was Not Death, for I Stood Up' (Dickinson 1998: 379–80, Fr355), 'I felt a Funeral in my Brain' (Dickinson 1998: 365–6, Fr340) and 'I heard a Fly buzz – when I died –' (Dickinson 1998: 587, Fr591) cover existential territory that correlates with what Ankersmit terms authentic experiences: '[w]e die a partial death at such moments since all that we are is then reduced to just this feeling or experience' (Ankersmit 2005: 228). In these poems a former event causes 'cognitive rupture' and 'the decomposition of sequential thought', and marks a death-like 'rupture between normal understanding and the sublimely traumatized consciousness' (Stonum 1990: 173, 74). Connoting sublime historical experience, these speakers recall but seemingly fail to transcend the dread and thrill of prior sublime encounters, that take them beyond language and familiarity to the realm of alterity; each speaker seems 'to objectify a former self, as if [she] had suddenly become an outsider to [her] own (former) self' (Ankersmit 2005: 347). That these past events are over, yet they inspire a desire to explicate and re-experience them, anticipates Ankersmit's sense of the 'sublime discrepancy between the desire of being and that of our knowledge of the past'; such poems are in microcosm 'account[s] of the experiences of rupture with all "the worlds we have lost"' (Ankersmit 2005: 359).

As Ankersmit theorises it, sublime historical experience generates not only the type of epistemological and ontological dissociation in such poems, but more specifically creates a range of interrelated paradoxes connected to subjectivity:

> [it] is the kind of experience of forcing us to abandon the position
> in which we still coincide with ourselves and to exchange this for a
> position where we relate to ourselves in the most literal sense of the
> word, hence, as if we were two persons instead of just one. (Ankersmit
> 2005: 347)

Dickinson's poems on memory and aftermath conjure up what Ankersmit describes as 'feelings of a profound and irreparable loss, of cultural despair, and of hopeless disorientation', but also often explicitly infer that 'a former identity is irrevocably lost forever and superseded by a new historical or cultural identity' (Ankersmit 2005: 324). For him, however, what has been seemingly lost in this process has, on some level, also been retained:

> One now is what one is, because one no longer is what one was – and
> this not being any longer what one was, is what one has essentially
> now become. It is as if something has been turned inside out. One
> has discarded (part of the) past from one's identity, and in this sense
> one has forgotten it. But one has not forgotten *that* one has forgotten
> it, for that one has forgotten precisely *this* is constitutive of the new
> identity. (Ankersmit 2005: 333)

He goes on: '[c]onstitutive of the identity of contemporary Western [humanity] is [its] realization of being no longer part of a prerevolutionary, preindustrial, and still predominantly Christian [world]' (Ankersmit 2005: 333). Complicating the notion of psychical integrity and foregrounding the idea of selves (and texts) divided against themselves, Ankersmit's ideas evoke one the most ubiquitous attributes of Dickinson's poetry. As Virginia Jackson puts it, self-division is 'the signature characteristic of the subjectivity Dickinson bequeaths to literary history' and has 'often been understood as the sign of Dickinson's modernity':

a reader of Dickinson can generate a long list of chasms, fissures, maelstroms, cleavings, self-burials, and horrors that irrevocably divide one part of the 'I' from another. Nearly all of the commentary devoted to Dickinson has centred on the question of these self-splittings, and especially on the referent of this schizophrenic subjective representation: sheer grief, lost love, physical and psychic pain, gendered, artistic, and sexual misinterpretation and oppression have all vied as explanations for the missing referent of the crisis. (Jackson 2005: 223)

Of course, such psychological dissonance may not have a personal cause but rather represent the workings of larger cultural and social forces. Paul Crumbley argues that such thematic and imagistic self-division is reinforced formally by semantic and syntactic doubling in Dickinson's writing, creating 'the simultaneous presence of diverse points of view'. For him, these features reflect the tension between a cultural reticence advocated for women and American ideals of individualism and independent self-expression (Crumbley 2010: 14). Alternatively, placed within Ankersmit's framework, Dickinson's self-divided speakers and correlate imagery can be viewed as her mirroring the effects of sublime historical experience: when one looks at oneself 'from the perspective of [an] outsider' or 'as if [one] were looking at somebody else' (Ankersmit 2005: 349). Ankersmit writes:

sublime experience confronts us with contradictions, oppositions, or paradoxes that are utterly unthinkable within [the] 'normal' patterns of experience. And this is precisely what becomes a possibility if we erect the shield of representation in ourselves, or, rather between the person we are now and the one we were before. We have then made room in ourselves for the epistemological paradoxes that are the defining characteristic of the sublime. (Ankersmit 2005: 346–7)

Provocatively, in some of her representations of self-division in poems such as 'He was my host – he was my guest' (Dickinson 1998: 1508, Fr1754) and 'I make His Crescent fill or lack –' (Dickinson 1998: 788–9, Fr837), Dickinson presents the idea of a current identity being confronted by a former one: she considers the idea of a past self or event haunting or possessing the mind and bifurcating the identity (see Finnerty 1998). Such poems describe something similar to the moment when, as Ankersmit puts it, 'we suddenly become aware of a *previous* identity of ourselves, of the kind of person that we had been up to now and had never realized that we were' (Ankersmit 2005: 349).

For Ankersmit, periods of transition not only cause an individual to see a former self as if it were 'the self of some other person', they also create a sense in which the 'moving to a new and different world really is and also *requires* an act of violence' and 'hostility' to 'the lost object after our having internalized it and made it into a part of our own identity' (Ankersmit 2005: 343–5).

Reflecting the violence that Ankersmit associates with this process, Dickinson's retrospective poetry often draws on forceful imagery to connote, for example, a 'cleaving' in the mind, signifying the destruction of thought, feeling and identity. Cataloguing some of Dickinson's most violent imagery, Camille Paglia describes her poetry as 'a war of personae, a clash of opposites; it is sexually, psychically, morally, and aesthetically bivalent' (Paglia 1991: 657). Additionally, recent scholarship has pointed out Dickinson's appropriation of imagery of social upheaval and political revolt to underline her sense of her position in the midst of competing versions of truth generated by political, industrial, intellectual and scientific revolutions that were dramatically transforming her life and the life of her community (see Crumbley 2015). Her poems feature 'not only political revolt but also an implicit reference to the external teleological force conventionally regarded as compelling such upheaval' and draw on a contemporary discursive 'juxtaposition of stark, incompatible opposites, many of them defined in politically and religiously charged language' (Kohler 2010: 29). Corroborating Ankersmit's complication of any straightforward transition from past to present, such forceful imagery in Dickinson's work encodes an existential wavering before entry into 'a wholly new world' and a level of hostility towards a former identity, but also points to the difficulty of forgetting. Just as Ankersmit makes forgetfulness a key component in periods of historical transitions when one identity is lost or abandoned for another, it is also a recurring theme in Dickinson's writings.

I TRIED HARD TO FORGET YOU

Ankersmit's discussion of forgetting begins with the story of Kant's dismissal of Lampe, his once faithful and dutiful servant, for stealing:

> Nevertheless, Kant was not at ease with his Roman *severitas*, and
> he kept worrying about poor Lampe. In order to get rid of this most
> unwelcome manifestation of *Neigung*, he pinned above his desk a
> little note with the stunning text 'Lampe vergessen' – forget Lampe.
> (Ankersmit 2005: 317)

In Dickinson's extant letters to friends and family, she frequently uses the words forget, forgot, forgetting and forgotten (MacKenzie 2000: 260–2), usually to express either her fear of being forgotten by those she loves (Dickinson 1958: 109, 119, 189, 222, 223, 224, 302, 319, 322, 396, 430) or to reassure correspondents that she will not forget them (Dickinson 1958: 113, 136, 223, 226, 243, 367, 389, 390, 721, 843). While clearly drawing on nineteenth-century letter-writing conventions tied to promises, tokens and assertions of remembrance (Messmer 2001: 219–21), Dickinson does not merely suggest that she won't forget her correspondents, but rather that she *can't* forget them. Like Kant, she needs to be 'helped [to] forget'; must 'try' to forget; or will 'slowly forget' (Dickinson 1958: 96, L35; 186, L79; 907,

L1047). She tells one friend, 'sometimes I shut my eyes, and shut my heart towards you, and try hard to forget you because you grieve me so, but you'll never go away'; to another she confesses, 'And I know I'll *remember* [the time we shared], for it's so precious to me that I doubt if I could forget it, even if I should try' (Dickinson 1958: 176–7, L73; 197, L86). She constructs herself as someone who never forgets (see Dickinson 1958: 103, 197, 211, 215, 224, 266, 304, 713, 834): 'I dont forget you a moment of the hour'; 'To never forget you – is all we can'; and 'to forget you would be impossible' (Dickinson 1958: 223, L103; 612, L555; 620, L567). Elsewhere in her letters, her unflinching remembrance is connected with (or used as a substitute for) divinity's omniscient memory: she writes, 'To be remembered is next to being loved and to be loved is Heaven' (Dickinson 1958: 487, L361) and advises against the 'timid mistake about being "forgotten," shall I caress or reprove? Mr. Samuel's "sparrow" does not "fall" without the fervent "notice"' (Dickinson 1958: 708, L724). Similarly, in other letters, Dickinson uses the word forget to assert her love or devotion to friends and implies that they have usurped God's (or religion's) place within her devotional hierarchy. She tells her friend Susan Gilbert in 1852:

> Friends are too dear to sunder, Oh they are far too few, and how soon they will go away where you and I cannot find them, dont let us forget these things, for their remembrance now will save us many an anguish when it is *too late* to love them! (Dickinson 1958: 211, L94)

In another letter to Emily Fowler Ford, in 1854, she writes: 'it makes me so happy to think of writing you that I forget the sermon and minister and all, and think of none but you' (Dickinson 1958: 293, L161). She spells out the implications for God of her lifelong idolatry of her dearest friends in a letter from the late 1850s: 'My friends are my "estate." Forgive me then the avarice to hoard them! . . . God is not so wary as we, else he would give us no friends, lest we forget him!' (Dickinson 1958: 339, L193).

She first employs the word forget and its correlates in letters to Abiah Root from the mid-1840s to early 1850s which refer to their membership of a group, known as the 'five', that also included Harriet Merrill, Abby Wood and Sarah S. Tracy. The letters react to the dissolution of the group owing primarily to Abiah, Harriet and Sarah moving away from Amherst. Although only her letters to Abiah are extant, Dickinson appears to have written persistently to all three in an attempt to preserve these bonds of friendships, forged while they were students at Amherst Academy (see Habegger 2001: 179–87). Wanting, as she puts it in one early 1845 letter, 'Harriet, Sarah & your own dear self to complete the ancient picture' (Franklin 1995: 14, L8), she sets out to remind these women of their 'old & I fear forgotten friends' (Dickinson 1958: 46, L15) and of 'forgotten' joyful times they once shared (Dickinson 1958: 67, L23). Although providing early examples of Dickinson's often hyperbolic and witty epistolary style, these letters dwell on loss or impending loss, of times, people and seasons 'gone': she 'sentimentalise[s] opon the past' and the 'golden links' that bound all five together (Franklin 1995: 17, L9; 28, L39). Having promised to send Abiah a forget-me-not from her garden in one 1846 letter (Dickinson 1958: 18, L7), in the next, she refers to Harriet, from whom she hasn't received a reply to two letters: 'I really cant help thinking she has forgotten the many happy hours we spent together, and though I try to banish the idea from my mind, for it is painful to me, I am afraid she has forgotten us, but I hope not'; she ends the letter 'Don't forget your aff friend Emily E D' (Franklin 1995: 14, 16, L8). When Abiah replies, a not-forgotten Dickinson mentions 'a China mug with forget me not' before inquiring: 'Have you heard a word from H. Merrill or S. Tracy. I consider them lost sheep . . . I cant think that they have forgotten us, [but wonder] why they should delay so long to show any signs of remembrance' (Franklin 2005: 18, L9; see also 21, L12). Dickinson's concern about not hearing from her friends is heightened by the death, in 1844, of her close friend, Sophia Holland, which had a devastating effect; Dickinson makes clear that she will 'never forget' her dearly departed companion (Dickinson 1958: 32, L11).

Her above reference to her friends as 'lost sheep' and a later reference to 'that prodigal – Hatty Merrill' who has 'entirely forgotten us' (Franklin 1995: 21, L12) are noteworthy as she had recently told Abiah of her penchant for quoting from the Bible ('Excuse my quoting from Scripture, Dear A for it was so handy in this case I couldnt get along very well without it'), as well as of her identification with Eve ('I have lately come to the conclusion that I am Eve, alias Mrs Adam') (Franklin 1995: 14, L8; 18, L9). These allusions are provocative considering that Dickinson composes these letters at a time of a religious revival in Amherst when she resisted the pressure on her to convert. The attenuation of these early female friendships, conceptualised through the topic of forgetfulness, is inextricably connected with their affirmations of faith and her refusal. Her letters interconnect her frustrated desire for and resistance to such a profession with her, at times, desperate attempt to preserve a world of female companionship that is being destroyed by spiritual as well as physical distance. Dickinson confides that although she recognises that she will never be happy or find peace 'without I love Christ', she soon 'forgets' the practices that faith requires:

> I was almost persuaded to be a Christian. I thought I never again
> could be thoughtless and worldly – and I can say that I never enjoyed
> such perfect peace and happiness as the short time in which I felt I had
> found my savior. But I soon forgot my morning prayer or else it was
> irksome to me. One by one my old habits returned and I cared less for
> religion than ever. (Dickinson 1958: 27, L10)

Sceptical and then devotional, she records her hopes that 'the golden opportunity is not far hence when my heart will willingly yield itself to Christ, and that my sins will be all blotted out of the book of remembrance' (Dickinson

1958: 28, L10). Here, combining faith and doubt, hope and despair, we have a fledgling example of a representative feature of Dickinson's writing: its yoking together and offsetting of 'stunningly opposed options' and 'unruly set[s] of contesting impulses' (Crumbley 2010: 45, 5). Moreover, the letter foreshadows a growing connection between her forgetting Christ and sense of being forgotten by Him (in the sense that her sins will be remembered) and her friends.

After Abiah converts in 1846, not long after their mutual friend Sarah Tracy also declares her faith, Dickinson presents herself as the isolated figure who 'did not give up & become a Christian'; she confides: 'I had quite a long talk with Abby while at home, & I doubt not she will soon cast her burden on Christ. She is sober, & keenly sensitive on the subject & she says she only desires to be good' (Franklin 1995: 25, L23). After Abby converts, in 1850, the painful personal and spiritual consequences of Dickinson's resistance are apparent: 'I am feeling lonely; some of my friends are gone, and some of my friends are sleeping – sleeping the churchyard sleep'; when she walks among the graves, she wonders who will 'come and give me the same memorial', adding:

> but I never have laid my friends there, and forgot that they too must
> die; this is my first affliction, and indeed 'tis hard to bear it – to those
> bereaved so often that home is no more here, and whose communion
> with friends is had only in prayers, there must be much to hope for,
> but when the unreconciled spirit has nothing left but God, that spirit is
> lone indeed. (Franklin 1995: 26, L39)

Ironically, she draws on the language of religion – communion, prayers, spirit – to express her 'unreconciled' spiritual revolt; she is not only forgotten by her friends, but is even more alone because her only alternative is to turn to a God she cannot embrace. Without heavenly salvation and its human equivalent, memory, she feels truly forgotten. Her rebellion is figured as immaturity and immorality, suggesting, on the one hand, levels of uncertainty about the personal stand she is taking, yet, on the other, showing her wittily pitching her defiance in the terms of the religious discourse she is rejecting. She tells Abiah:

> You are growing wiser than I am, and nipping in the bud fancies
> which I let blossom – perchance to bear no fruit, or if plucked, I may
> find it bitter. The shore is safer, Abiah, but I love to buffet the sea – I
> can count the bitter wrecks here in these pleasant waters, and hear the
> murmuring winds, but Oh I love the danger! You are learning control
> and firmness – Christ Jesus will love you more – I'm afraid he dont
> love me any! (Franklin 2005: 29, L39)

She goes on also to contrast her danger-loving seafaring scepticism with the newly devotional Abby, who is 'more of a woman than I am, for I love so to be a child – Abby is holier than me. . . . she will be had in memorial when

I am gone and forgotten'. Drawing on sermon language of unity, spirit and bonds, she pledges herself to her holy friends as a means of counteracting religion's eclipsing of their friendship: 'we are growing away from each other, and talk *even now* like strangers. To forget the "meum and teum" *dearest* friends must meet *sometimes*, and then comes the "bond of the spirit" which if I am correct is "unity"' (Franklin 1995: 28, L39). Like other nineteenth-century writers, she creates writing that presents a double vision of religion, giving a traditional or conventional language a radical and sceptical twist (Morgan 2010: 19–22). Yet Dickinson is not simply appropriating and reformulating religious discourse, sermons or dogma for her own artistic, even parodic purposes (Morgan 2010: 93–8, 178–218); her letters equate lost female friendships with a loss of certainty and a sense of community that went along with a religious outlook, which she cannot accept and yet is constitutive of her identity.

Commenting on these letters, Habegger suggest that 'Abiah and Abby's retreat to the safety of standard beliefs and feelings posed a challenge to the poet's expressive drive, helping explain both her sentimental returns to the past and her teasing recklessness' (Habegger 2001: 181). Considering the role Ankersmit assigns to myth in the developing of historical consciousness and the historical sublime, it is provocative that Dickinson's discourse of forgetting coincides with her creation of the myth of a 'collective', idyllic female-centred past 'outside the course of history', an identity-defining realm prior to a world of socialisation (Ankersmit 2005: 368). The preoccupation of her poetry, as already noted, with re-visiting and re-experiencing sites and moments from the past is, at times, accompanied by the idea of a utopian world of girlhood that, as she told Susan Gilbert, for the bride and 'plighted maiden' 'seem[s] dearer than all others in the world' (Dickinson 1958: 210, L93) (see Eberwein 1985: 103–6; Messmer 2001: 180–90). In a similar manner, her love poems tend to re-play a past loss and to idealise and desire reunion with the lost object, person or time period. The sublimity of such poems 'originates from this paradoxical union of the feelings of loss and love, that is, of the combination of pain and pleasure in how we relate to the past' (Ankersmit 2005: 9). This trajectory confirms Ankersmit's association of the past with lost love – absent and 'precisely because of this, always so very much and so very painfully present' – and with 'lost worlds' that take on the characteristics of 'myth' by being that to which we cannot return, 'however strong the nostalgic yearning for these lost paradises may be' (Ankersmit 2005: 325). Interestingly, as in these early letters, in some of these poems, Dickinson draws on religious discourse – imagery of churches, sacrament, conversion, vows, crucifixes, martyrdom and heavenly reunion – to represent human love, blurring the line between love and faith, a loved figure and Christ. In so doing, Dickinson is not merely connecting moments of loss with sublimity (via an inextricable divinity), but also using religious discourse to reflect on some level the dissociation, difficulty and pain Ankersmit associates with abandoning a former self, associated in this case with orthodox religion, and the way in which such 'discarded identities' remain present not only in their absence, but through acts of imaginative appropriation (Ankersmit 2005: 367).

Ankersmit's ideas illuminate the ways in which in these letters Dickinson's new identity as non-conformist and religious sceptic emerges out of the orthodox identity that she presents herself as forgetting and abandoning. Drawing on and undercutting religious discourse, her sentimentalisation of the past and determination never to forget her friends transform her into a *faithful* friend. She asks Abiah Root: 'Have you forgotten your visit at Amherst last summer, & what delightful times we had? I have not' (Dickinson 1958: 57, L23). Again, after Abiah attended Mount Holyoke's Commencement in August 1848 and ignored her, Dickinson makes her position clear: 'Slowly, very slowly, I came to the conclusion that you had forgotten me, & I tried hard to forget you, but your image still haunts me, and tantalizes me with fond recollections' (Franklin 1995: 27, L39). Having made the difficulty of forgetting clear, in one of her last letters to Abiah, dated 1852, she hyperbolically reprimands her friend, underlining her faithfulness to their past friendship and 'school day memories':

> Hard hearted girl! I dont believe you care, if you did you would come
> quickly and help me out of this sea, but if I drown, Abiah, and go
> down to dwell in the seaweed forever and forever, I will not forget
> your name, nor all the wrong you did me! (Franklin 1995: 29, L69)

These letters reveal Dickinson's participation in her culture's incorporation of identities tied to religious faith and authority into new secular subjectivities and the translation of religious notions such as heaven and an afterlife into new less dogmatic and even non-religious concepts (see St Armand 1984). More precisely, following Ankersmit's work, we see Dickinson position herself rebelliously and nostalgically within 'an idyllic, pre-historical, and quasi-eternal and quasi-natural past' as a means of escaping a future marked by female conformity and the end of personal freedom and characterised by religious compliance (Ankersmit 2005: 366).

In Dickinson's epistolary discourse on forgetfulness, there are traces of the mechanics of a powerfully emergent discourse of modernity tied to materialism, empiricism and science which is already challenging religion for cultural dominance. Her writings, in Ankersmit's terms, are an 'externalization of a drama that was, in fact, enacted in the mind' as 'a previous world' tied to Christian faith was being 'forgotten and repudiated' to the point that individuals were experiencing what Freud would later call a 'melancholic reaction to traumatic loss' (Ankersmit 2005: 340–1). The lost friendships Dickinson mourns and can't forget are, on one level, what is traumatically being lost, yet, on another level, what is also vanishing is a once dominant religious world picture. The letters show that neither loss can be easily forgotten: one is mourned explicitly, the other implicitly. Interrelating these losses, she substitutes preservation through human memory (and writing) for immortalisation through religious faith and presents herself as usurping God and/or Christ's place as the eternally faithful friend who will never forget.

THE ART OF FORGETTING

The theme of forgetfulness in Dickinson's poetry, which exemplifies her career-long attention to neglected, unnoticed and inconsequential events, objects, creatures and people, has not been fully explored. Perceptively, Jane Eberwein notes that although '[d]eprivation is, after all, a universal human experience though one easily forgotten', '[s]uch forgetfulness would be unlikely for Emily Dickinson', who presents herself as 'a lifelong quester searching for a treasure already experienced but lost long ago' (Eberwein 1985: 65). The image of the quester of a past treasure is a fitting one, suggesting that her poetry's exploration of deprivation is, like historical writing, 'situated in the space enclosed by [the] complimentary movements of the discovery (loss) and the recovery of the past (love) that constitute together the realm of historical experience' (Ankersmit 2005: 9). The speakers of her aftermath poems cannot forget: from a present instance, they articulate a previous 'moment of loss', when the past having 'broken off' became something to know or describe rather than experience (Ankersmit 2005: 9). Expanding on the topic of forgetting in the Abiah Root letters, Dickinson's poetic exploration of this subject focuses on the pain of being forgotten, as well as attempts to complicate power dynamics between the person who forgets and the person forgotten. As in her earlier letters, forgetting is interconnected with larger questions about death, the afterlife and God, but also presented as a difficult but advantageous activity, which is defined as an art or discipline, something that could be learnt or taught as if it were a lesson at school.

Two early poems, both dated 1858, tackle the topic of forgetting in a sustained way. The first of these, 'Oh if remembering were forgetting –' (Dickinson 1998: 65, Fr9), is a riddle-like poem in which the speaker reverses the meaning of forgetting: 'Oh if remembering were forgetting – / Then I remember not! / And if forgetting – recollecting – / How near I had forgot!' (Dickinson 1998: 22, Fr9). Despite the inversion, the speaker is someone who can only reach the enviable position of having 'forgot' or 'remembered not' if these now mean having remembered. The poem underlines the connection between the conscious process of forgetting and the activity of remembering, which first drew Ankersmit to Dickinson's poetry. Revisiting these oppositional terms in a later poem, from 1874, Dickinson's first stanza distinguishes between the slightly less offensive idea of never having been remembered and the more obnoxious one of having been forgotten, which stems from a deliberate and conscious practice:

Whether they have forgotten
Or are forgetting now
Or never remembered –
Safer not to know –
(Dickinson 1998: 1154–5, Fr1334)

The poem ends with the suggestion that if one has been forgotten, it is better
not to know: the 'miseries of conjecture' are softer than 'a Fact of Iron Hard-
ened with I know'.

The other 1858 poem on forgetfulness, 'There is a word' (Dickinson 1998:
93–4, Fr42), also uses hard, forceful imagery, in this case martial imagery, to
emphasise the power of the word 'forgot', whose 'barbed syllables' can wound
even those who are 'armed'; this word divides the world into the fallen (the
forgotten) and 'the Saved' (the remembered). The word 'saved' provocatively
summons up a religious context for the poem's second stanza:

Wherever runs the breathless sun –
Wherever roams the day,
There is it's noiseless onset –
There is it's victory!
Behold the keenest marksman –
The most accomplished shot!
Time's sublimest target
Is a soul 'forgot'!
(Dickinson 1998: 92, Fr42A)

'Forgot' is a forceful and injurious word because it conceptualises the idea
that one has been forgotten by a victorious and powerful other. Provocatively,
considering the religious connotations of 'saved' and 'soul', the poem, like the
letters to Abiah, connects human forgetfulness with God's. The idea is that the
forgotten soul abandoned by God or a god-like figure is the 'sublimest target',
inspiring awe and terror. These ideas are repeated in other poems: one poem
speculates that 'There dwells one other Creature / Of Heavenly Love – forgot –'
(Dickinson 1998: 567–8, Fr570), while another imagines 'a meek apparreled
thing' 'forgot by Victory' (Dickinson 1998: 111, Fr67). Additionally, the afterlife circumstances of the dead, a recurring subject in Dickinson's poetry, are
considered in relation to forgetfulness. One speaker reassures that the dead
have not forgotten the living: 'Though in another tree' they look 'just as often /
And just as tenderly', noticing all from 'above' (Dickinson 2005: 171, Fr130).
In 'My Wars are laid away in Books –', the speaker declares that although
she has battled throughout her life, she expects an encounter with a final foe
who has already taken the 'best' and neglected her. Although it is unclear if
the foe is death or God, what most concerns her is that she is 'not forgot /
by Chums that passed away' (Dickinson 1998: 1385, Fr1579). Challenging these
suggestions, other poems depict heaven as a realm of forgetfulness. In 'I shall

know why – when Time is over –', the speaker imagines lessons being taught by Christ in the 'fair schoolroom of the sky' that will explain and justify 'each separate anguish' and help the speaker 'forget the drop of anguish / That scalds me now – that scalds me now!' (Dickinson 1998: 243, Fr215). Without the last line's mocking repetition, other poems suggest that if among the 'Redeemed', one's 'Barefoot time [will be] forgotten', or that through 'faith' 'The Mold-life' will be 'all forgotten – now – / In Extasy – and Dell –' (Dickinson 1998: 507, Fr496; 559, Fr559). But, in other poems that gloss forgetting, not remembering one's earthly life once in heaven may represent a loss of one's personal identity, individuality and 'boundaries' (Dickinson 1998: 275, Fr255; 523, Fr513). Certainly, forgetting is connected with Death's 'diviner Classifying' and 'Democratic fingers' that remove 'Color – Caste – Denomination –' and brand; 'all [are] forgotten –' (Dickinson 1998: 788, Fr836).

If God and death are associated with forgetfulness, then the forgetful beloved wields a god-like power over the one who fears being or has been forgotten. In 'Poor little Heart!', the speaker reaches out to a figure who has been forgotten, addressing a heart, either her own or another's, that has been forsaken by others (Dickinson 1998: 242–3, Fr214). As in her letters to Abiah, such poems express the pain of being forgotten by those who are precious and valued: 'Precious to Me – She still shall be – / Though She forget the name I bear' (Dickinson 1998: 710–11, F751). While other poems foreground forgetfulness within unequal relationships between speakers and addressees (Dickinson 1998: 624, Fr635; 781, Fr827), one poem shifts the balance by having its speaker identify with a forgiving Christ in the aftermath of his betrayal by Peter, a friend and disciple who had so vociferously expressed the expanse of his fidelity:

> He forgot – and I – remembered –
> 'Twas an everyday affair –
> Long ago as Christ and Peter –
> 'Warmed them' at the 'Temple fire'.
>
> 'Thou wert with him' – quoth 'the Damsel'?
> 'No' – said Peter – 'twasn't me –
> Jesus merely 'looked' at Peter –
> Could I do aught else – to Thee?
> (Dickinson 1998: 256, Fr232)

In one final example, 'That she forgot me was the least', Dickinson adds the experience of humiliation to her discussion of this topic; her speaker states that what injured her most was the idea that she was 'worthy to forget' and that her continued assurance to her beloved of 'Faithful[ness]' and 'Constancy' was transformed into 'something like a shame' (Dickinson 1998: 1490–1, Fr1716). The poem 'To be forgot by thee', from which Ankersmit quotes, reverses the disregard associated with forgetfulness in so many of her other forgetting poems, with the speaker redefining it not as evidence of neglect, but rather as an indication of remembrance and attention. In line with Ankersmit's ideas, forgetting is constituted by remembering; to be forgotten is to be raised from oblivion into renown, to leave ordinary time and enter the realm of myth:

> To be forgot by thee
> Surpasses Memory
> Of other minds
> The Heart cannot forget
> Unless it contemplate
> What it declines
> I was regarded then
> Raised from oblivion
> A single time
> To be remembered what –
> Worthy to be forgot
> My low renown
> (Dickinson 1998: 1405, Fr1601)

As part of her analysis of the nature of forgetting, in a series of poems Dickinson considers what 'helps us to forget –' (Dickinson 1998: 334, Fr315). As Ankersmit puts it, 'Not forgetting but being able to forget is the real issue here, for we should realize that it is truly part of our identity, of the kind of person that we are, that we are capable of forgetting a certain part of our past (or not)' (Ankersmit 2005: 333). He goes on: 'we are not only the past that we (can) remember . . . but we are also the past that we can forget' (Ankersmit 2005: 333). These Dickinson poems examine forgetting as an intricate practice that if learned could offer an alternative to the obsessive remembrance and memorialisation that stifle change in so many of her aftermath poems. In the first of these poems, a self-divided speaker makes a deal with her heart:

> Heart! We will forget him!
> You and I – tonight!
> You may forget the warmth he gave –
> I will forget the light!
>
> When you have done, pray tell me
> That I may straight begin!
> Haste! lest while you're lagging
> I remember him!
> (Dickinson 1998: 109, Fr64)

Forgetting means a conscious endeavour that involves the prospect of self-betrayal and further self-division; it underlines the foolhardiness of any conscious practice of forgetting which is, as other poems have implied, merely a form of remembering. The same idea is presented in another poem where the speaker considers how happy she would be if she could only forget her sadness, a prospect made more fraught because of her recollecting of summer ('Bloom') in November. The poem ends with the speaker imagining a 'bold', deadly act, in defiance of learning and with a child-like forgetting of implications, of searching in coldness for a summer's blossom:

> How happy I was if I could forget
> To remember how sad I am
> Would be an easy adversity
> But the recollecting of Bloom
>
> Keeps making November difficult
> Till I who was almost bold
> Lose my way like a little Child
> And perish of the cold.
> (Dickinson 1998: 942, Fr1080)

Drawing on similar nature imagery, another poem suggests a preference for a setting as opposed to a rising sun, for a dramatic exit rather than staying on stage, for dying rather than waning. Yet essentially the speaker wants the perspective of a natural world associated with 'beautiful forgetting', sweetness and sorrow and loss (Dickinson 1998: 1187; Fr1366A). In another poem, nature offers the 'promise [of] return'; however,

> One thing of it we covet –
> The power to forget –
> The Anguish of the Avarice
> Defrays the Dross of it –
> (Dickinson 1998: 1325; Fr1516B)

The speaker covets nature's unconsciousness of its own patterns and processes: its power to forget.

In two other forgetting poems, Dickinson uses schoolroom imagery to underline the difficulty of forgetting. Such imagery is alluring considering the happiness and friendship Dickinson associated with her time at Amherst Academy, and the pressure placed on her to convert while she was studying at Mount Holyoke (see Habegger 2001: 139–66, 191–212). While the idea of having forgetting as a subject on the school curriculum is suggestively counterintuitive, it may tap into aspects of her formative education that she wanted to forget. Moreover, although both institutions were religious in ethos, Dickinson was given a broad education in which science featured strongly and the poet enjoyed and clearly benefitted from studying botany, geology and astronomy. In other words, her schooling was a site of historical transformation that pitted Christianity against science, while officially attempting to reconcile the two. Do these poems anticipate Nietzsche's sense of the liberation, possibility and opportunity that forgetting brings and the horror of not being able to forget? Or Ankersmit's belief in the importance of forgetting for historical progress and cultural and personal advancement? In the first of these poems, the speaker is unable to obey a powerful male instructor's charge to forget and becomes the 'Dunce' of the class. But, the poem claims, it is the 'dull lad' who should be loved best; his failure to learn to forget is a sign of his devotion:

> Did we disobey Him?
> Just one time!
> Charged us to forget Him –
> But we couldn't learn!
>
> Were Himself – such a Dunce –
> What would we – do?
> Love the dull lad – best –
> Oh, wouldn't you?
> (Dickinson 1998: 320, Fr299)

Even more explicitly, in 'Know how to forget', which has two versions, one written in 1862 and the other in 1865, Dickinson reverses the idea of school as a place of education and learning, making it a place where students unlearn and where the art of forgetting should be taught. The earlier version asks an instructor:

> Knows how to forget!
> But – could she teach – it?
> 'Tis the Art, most of all,
> I should like to know –
>
> Long, at its Greek –
> I – who pored – patient –
> Rise – still the Dunce –
> Gods used to know –
>
> Mould my slow mind to this Comprehension –
> Oddest of sciences – Book ever bore –
>
> How to forget!
> Ah, to attain it –
> I would give you –
> All other Lore –
> (Dickinson 1998: 415, Fr391)

The speaker suggests that despite her patient efforts at studying forgetting, she remains a 'Dunce', failing at its 'Comprehension'; it is more challenging than Greek and the 'Oddest of sciences'. The speaker would *literally* give up all other knowledge to master forgetfulness. Here, forgetting is positioned within the context of oppositional forms of knowledge evident in her own schooling: Greek, a language associated with an ancient world of 'Gods', superstition and myth, is opposed to science, centring on empiricism, experiment and categorisation. Implicit here is the idea that while forgetting may lead the child into error, it also offers emancipation from past mistakes and particularly from those who have forgotten her. In the longer 1865 version of the same poem (Dickinson 1998: 416), Dickinson makes the same overall point in a more effusive and detailed way. The speaker implies that forgetting is the 'Easiest of Arts, they say / When one learn how', yet one that, as with 'Science', requires 'Sacrifice': 'Dull Hearts have died / In the Acquisition'. These lines indicate that science has appropriated a concept so central to Christianity: 'Sacrifice for Science / Is common, though, now'. Having gone to 'School', the speaker is no wiser about how to forget: 'Globe did not teach it / Nor Logarithm Show', and she turns to a Philosopher and Rabbi for advice and 'to be[come] erudite / Enough to know!'. Full of questions, the speaker asks if there is a particular book that would teach it, if forgetting, like astronomy, requires 'Telescopes', or if it is an invention and therefore has 'a Patent' (Dickinson 1998: 416, Fr391B). The poem stresses that despite its importance, forgetting is unteachable because of its inextricable relationship with remembering; it is much more complex than the process of acquiring a body of knowledge, it is about discarding, abandoning and shedding an identity.

CONCLUSION

The Ankersmit sentence used as an epigraph for this chapter offers one way of thinking about Dickinson as the Romantic artist who removes herself from the 'pedestrian world' to a world of art and poetry and the possibility they offer (Ankersmit 2005: 429). In contrast, reading Dickinson in the light of Ankersmit's theories suggests that her representations of loss, past experience, self-division, the incomprehensible, violence and death, along with her discourse on forgetfulness, tap into and reflect her culture in the midst of radical transformation as religious authority is being cumulatively undermined by the influence of science, as well as by new political, social and cultural ideas. The parallels between Ankersmit's theories about sublime historical experience and the Dickinson sublime stem from the common influence of the Romantic sublime on their work. In other words, Ankersmit's ambition to rehabilitate 'the romanticism moods and feelings as constitutive of how we relate to the past' (Ankersmit 2005: 10) means he conceptualises historical experience as a nineteenth-century poet might. As Dickinson puts it, 'Did we not find (gain) as we lost we should make but a threadbare exhibition after a few years' (Dickinson 1958: 923, PF71). Such a movement of loss and gain calls to mind Ankersmit's overarching claim about historical experience: that each time 'humanity or a civilization enters a truly new phase in its history, a new mythical sublime comes into being as this civilization's cold and fossilized heart that will forever be handed on to those living in all its later phases' (Ankersmit 2005: 366). Dickinson's writings are marked by these trajectories and point to her ambivalence about such transition: while she certainly embraces the freedom that cultural forgetting can bring, there are also hints in her work of her concerns about the moral, social and political repercussions for her culture of losing its anchorage to the metaphysical order and authoritative structure that religion provided.

WORKS CITED

Ankersmit, F. R. (2005), *Sublime Historical Experience*, Stanford: Stanford University Press.

Bloom, Harold (1995), *The Western Canon: The Books and School of the Ages*, London: Papermac, pp. 291–309.

Crumbley, Paul (2010), *Winds of Will: Emily Dickinson and the Sovereignty of Democratic Thought*, Tuscaloosa: University of Alabama Press.

Crumbley, Paul (2015), 'Back Talk in New England: Dickinson and Revolution', *Emily Dickinson Journal*, 24: 1, 1–21.

Deppman, Jed, Marianne Noble and Gary Lee Stonum (eds) (2013), *Emily Dickinson and Philosophy*, Cambridge: Cambridge University Press.

Dickinson, Emily (1958), *The Letters of Emily Dickinson*, 3 vols, ed. Thomas H. Johnson and Theodora Ward, Cambridge, MA: The Belknap Press of Harvard University Press.

Dickinson, Emily (1998), *The Poems of Emily Dickinson*, 3 vols, ed. R. W. Franklin, Cambridge, MA: The Belknap Press of Harvard University Press.

Domańska, Ewa (2009), 'Frank Ankersmit: From Narrative to Experience', *Rethinking History*, 13: 2, 175–95.

Eberwein, Jane Donahue (1985), *Dickinson: Strategies of Limitation*, Amherst: University of Massachusetts Press.

Fineman, Daniel (2013), 'Against Mastery: Dickinson Contra Hegel and Schlegel', in Jed Deppman, Marianne Noble and Gary Lee Stonum (eds), *Emily Dickinson and Philosophy*, Cambridge: Cambridge University Press, pp. 85–104.

Finnerty, Páraic (1998), '"No Matter – now – Sweet – But when I'm Earl": Dickinson's Shakespearean Cross-Dressing', *The Emily Dickinson Journal*, 7: 2, 65–94.

Franklin, R. W. (1995), 'Emily Dickinson to Abiah Root: Ten Reconstructed Letters', *Emily Dickinson Journal*, 4: 1, 1–43.

Habegger, Alfred (2001), *My Wars Are Laid Away in Books: The Life of Emily Dickinson*, New York: Random House.

Jackson, Virginia (2005), *Dickinson's Misery: A Theory of Lyric Reading*, Princeton: Princeton University Press.

Jenkins, Keith (2008), 'Cohen Contra Ankersmit', *Rethinking History*, 12: 4, 537–55.

Johnson, Thomas (1958), 'Introduction', in *The Letters of Emily Dickinson*, 3 vols, ed. Thomas H. Johnson and Theodora Ward, Cambridge, MA: The Belknap Press of Harvard University Press, pp. xv–xxii.

Kohler, Michelle (2010), 'Dickinson and the Poetics of Revolution', *Emily Dickinson Journal*, 19: 2, 20–46.

MacKenzie, Cynthia Jane (ed.) (2000), *A Concordance to the Letters of Emily Dickinson*, Niwot: University of Colorado Press.

Messmer, Marietta (2001), *A Vice for Voices: Reading Emily Dickinson's Correspondence*, Amherst: University of Massachusetts Press.

Miller, Cristanne (2012), *Reading in Time: Emily Dickinson in the Nineteenth Century*, Amherst: University of Massachusetts Press.

Mitchell, Domhnall (2000), *Emily Dickinson: Monarch of Perception*, Amherst: University of Massachusetts Press.

Morgan, Victoria N. (2010), *Emily Dickinson and Hymn Culture: Tradition and Experience*, Aldershot: Ashgate.

Nietzsche, Friedrich (1997), 'On the Uses and Disadvantages of History for Life', in *Untimely Meditations*, ed. Daniel Breazeale, trans. R. J. Hollingdale, Cambridge: Cambridge University Press, pp. 59–123.

Paglia, Camille (1991), *Sexual Personae: Art and Decadence from Nefertiti to Emily Dickinson*, Harmondsworth: Penguin.

Porter, David (1981), *Dickinson: The Modern Idiom*, Cambridge, MA: Harvard University Press.

St Armand, Barton Levi (1984), *Emily Dickinson and Her Culture: The Soul's Society*, Cambridge: Cambridge University Press.

Stonum, Gary Lee (1990), *The Dickinson Sublime*, Madison: University of Wisconsin Press.

Wolosky, Shira (2013a), 'Truth and Lie in Emily Dickinson and Friedrich Nietzsche', in Jed Deppman, Marianne Noble and Gary Lee Stonum (eds), *Emily Dickinson and Philosophy*, Cambridge: Cambridge University Press, pp. 131–50.

Wolosky, Shira (2013b), *Feminist Theory Across Disciplines: Feminist Community and American Women's Poetry*, New York: Routledge.

CHAPTER 6

Reading Microhistory: Three Layers of Meaning

Anton Froeyman

INTRODUCTION

Few developments in the writing of history have had such effect on both the public and the professional sphere as microhistory. Historians such as Emmanuel Le Roy Ladurie and Carlo Ginzburg not only revolutionised the way many professional historians thought about how stories of the past should be written, they also reached a surprisingly large lay audience while doing so. Emmanuel Le Roy Ladurie's classic *Montaillou*, for example, over six hundred pages long and loaded with footnotes, went straight up to the top of the non-fiction billboard charts and has sold over two million copies.[1] Le Roy Ladurie's second major microhistorical work, *Carnival in Romans*, was adapted to a successful television series.[2] Nevertheless, microhistory, although often criticised by professionals, was never regarded as mere populist fancy. Many professional historians were inspired by it, and many more agreed that it brought a new and valuable perspective into the discipline.

However, although much has been written about microhistory, there has been no consensus and arguably not even a plausible theory on what this new perspective exactly consists of. Microhistory is of course essentially defined by the scale of its subject, but scale alone is not enough to be innovative. People have been doing historical research on the micro level all along, largely non-academic, under the banner of local history. One need only think of biographies, family histories, village histories . . . The difference with microhistory, most people believe, is that microhistory is supposed to have some bearing on the general level while local history is not. The micro level would then be a means to make a certain point on a more general level, and not an end in itself. To quote Giovanni Levi paraphrasing Clifford Geertz, 'Historians do not study villages, they study *in* villages.'[3]

The problem is that it is not really clear what this general level is and how the 'microscopic' observations in microhistorical works relate to it. In this chapter, I will state that we can distinguish three layers within this general level. They will serve as 'layers of meaning' from which a microhistorical study derives its surplus value when compared with local history. These layers are the cognitive, the experiential and the ethical. I claim that the contribution of most if not all microhistories does not lie in the first layer, but rather in the second and third. The method I will use in making this claim is based on a Kuhnian understanding of the workings of science. I believe that scientific disciplines, such as microhistory, are not based on abstract principles, credos or commandments, but rather on concrete canonical examples. Therefore, the core of my argument is formed not (only) by abstract logic and argumentation, but by references to the classics of the genre. The works I will refer to are Emmanuel Le Roy Ladurie's *Montaillou* and *Carnival in Romans*, Carlo Ginzburg's *The Cheese and the Worms*, Giovanni Levi's *Inheriting Power*, Natalie Zemon-Davis's *The Return of Martin Guerre*, Robert Darnton's *The Great Cat Massacre*, Gene Brucker's *Giovanni and Lusanna* and Patricia Cohen's *The Murder of Helen Jewett*. I do not pretend that this is a complete list of all the relevant classics in microhistory. Rather, this list is a compromise between representativeness and manageability.

THE COGNITIVE LAYER

The cognitive is the first and most obvious layer a microhistorical work could add to. Just as the use of a microscope can make a biologist change his or her hypothesis about the workings of an organism, a closer look at a certain historical situation can reveal previously unknown information about its workings, and eventually lead to the formulation of new hypotheses. Giovanni Levi gives us an example from his own work.[4] Historians have long thought that land transactions in early modern Italian peasant societies were regulated by something like a free market based on individual commercial interests. When we look more closely, however, at the social and family ties between agents of a specific region, it seems to be the case that these land transactions were actually a way of charity and forging social cohesion, much more than an exchange out of commercial interests. This is an example of how microhistory, the study of social relations in a specific region, can indeed be used to make a general point, in this case the economic system in early modern Italy. The explanatory structure is that of a case study: a general hypothesis asserts something, a single case proves to be different from what the hypothesis predicts. Hence the general hypothesis is rejected or said to hold only for a more limited number of cases. If all microhistories had such an explanatory structure, our story would end here, and we would have found the difference between local history and microhistory.

However, this is not the case. Let us think of *Montaillou* or *The Cheese and the Worms*.[5] Both works do not make a general point. Their aim is purely descriptive. They do not state that their objects of study, the village of Montaillou and the miller Menocchio, can be used to prove or falsify some general hypothesis about villages or the beliefs of people in general. Both Montaillou and Menocchio are unique: Montaillou because of its status as a heretical village and the fact that it was rather isolated from the familiar structures of feudal society, and Menocchio because of his intermediate position between high and low culture. If these subjects are supposed to be examples or instances of a general kind of some sort, they are very badly chosen indeed. Even in Levi's own *Inheriting Power*, from which our example of the possible cognitive merits of microhistory stems, the general point is not how land transactions occurred. Rather, what his book basically is about is the story of how one man, Giulio Cesare Chiesa, was able to acquire and transmit (hence the title) such an amazing amount of power, despite the regulations imposed by the ruling class.[6]

More generally, the idea that microhistorical research can lead to a more or less general claim about a certain society does not work well with the fact that many, if not all, microhistories are written about outsiders or extraordinary events that are, if anything, more *atypical* of a certain society than typical. One need only think of events such as the eighteenth-century cat massacre described by Robert Darnton,[7] or Le Roy Ladurie's *Carnival in Romans*,[8] Natalie Zemon-Davis's return of Martin Guerre[9] or Patricia Cohen's murder of a nineteenth-century prostitute.[10] Darnton even explicitly denies that *The Great Cat Massacre* represents a typical case of anything at all.[11]

Could it not be then that the relation of a microhistorical event to a macrohistorical structure is different from the relation of an example or an instance to a general category or law? Maybe there is some other way in which the study of microhistorical events has bearing on a more general level. A small-scale event might be regarded as a Freudian slip of the tongue in which some general but normally subaltern aspects of a certain society suddenly come into the spotlight.

Microhistory is indeed often seen in this light, as studying the global through the local. The central concept here is Clifford Geertz's 'thick description', and the paradigm example is Geertz's own 'Deep Play: Notes on the Balinese Cockfight'.[12]

So-called thin description is a description of what obviously happened, from a sort of 'I-am-a-camera' point of view.[13] Thick description on the other hand, the hallmark of interpretative anthropology, is a description in terms of meaning. It aims to unearth what a certain event means (or meant) for the native. In doing so, it penetrates into the symbolic 'architecture' of an individual or a society. Geertz himself, for example, first describes the Balinese cockfight and the wagers surrounding it as any of us would do at first sight, by just saying what physically happened.[14] Starting from a sense of wonder at the fact that the cockfight seems to be so important for the Balinese, as well as from a typological distinction between different kind of fight, ('deep' and 'shallow' ones, based on the amount of money involved), Geertz goes on[15] to a more general analysis of the symbolic and social importance of the cockfight. The cockfight seems to be a performative ritual in which the Balinese men at the same time construct and represent their masculinity and social bonds. Hence the importance of this event for an understanding of Balinese society as a whole.

As has been amply noted, Geertz's work in general and the Balinese cockfight in particular have been of great influence to microhistorians.[16] The historian most profoundly influenced by Geertz is probably his Princeton colleague, Robert Darnton, particularly in the essay 'The Great Cat Massacre' in his book bearing the same name.[17] In order to see how Geertz's views translate to the writing of history, it is a good idea to take a closer look at Darnton's essay.

In the essay 'Workers Revolt: The Great Cat Massacre of the Rue Saint-Séverin', Darnton describes a riotous massacre of cats which contemporaries believed to be hilariously funny. The intriguing thing here is that we as people from the twenty-first century do not get the joke. We generally just think it's cruel towards all those poor cats. At first sight, the Great Cat Massacre is a lot like the Balinese cockfight. What first looks like a somewhat strange and insignificant event on closer inspection appears to be laden with all kinds of symbolic meaning and social stratifications. Like Geertz, Darnton first lays out a 'thin' description of the event and then descends into its deeper layers in order to reveal a multitude of meaning. The cat massacre he describes appears to be an expression of a socio-economic imbalance between employers and employees,[18] a symbolic identification of pets with their bosses,[19] a carnival tradition of reversal of the social order, a cultural *je-ne-sais-quoi* about cats[20] and the practice of charivari.[21]

Despite the fact that *The Great Cat Massacre* is obviously inspired by Geertz's essay on the Balinese cockfight, there is one difference that cannot be ignored. While the cockfight is a common practice in Balinese society, the great cat massacre was an exceptional event. Although we should keep in mind that Geertz explicitly states that the cockfight is not the master key to the understanding of the Balinese,[22] it is still an essential part of it. And it is only because the cockfight is so omnipresent in the life of the average Balinese man that Geertz is able to derive general characteristics of Balinese society from it. The cat massacre described by Darnton, on the other hand, is a singular and unique event, and it cannot be said to be essential to a certain society or a historical period. Because of this, Darnton does not really *derive* anything new from the event he describes. The economic imbalance, the carnival and charivari traditions, the symbolic identification of pets and bosses and the sexual connotations of cats were already known facts. The fact that they played a part in a cat massacre does not really add anything to our knowledge of the society they belong to. The social and symbolic structure of Balinese society, on the other hand, was not known in advance, and Geertz really needed the key of the cockfight in order to find out about it.

Following this, I believe that it is wrong to say that microhistory is just a straightforward application of Geertzian anthropology to the writing of history. It most definitely is not. Geertz (and Geertzian anthropologists) tries to describe a society, while Darnton (and other microhistorians) describes one singular event. Once again, the problem here is that microhistory tends to focus on the exceptional rather than the common. It is still not clear how such a focus on one exceptional event can give us any knowledge about a society or a historical period. Dominick LaCapra, among others, has criticised Carlo Ginzburg's *The Cheese and the Worms* precisely because of the fact that an individual such as Menocchio, always an outsider, cannot be used as evidence for a general (cognitive) claim about the relation between high and low culture.[23] The things we learn from Menocchio are only really true of Menocchio himself. Conversely, Richard Brown argues in favour of Patricia Cohen, stating that she does not simply tell the story of Helen Jewett, the murdered prostitute, but that she shows us a great deal about gender relations in nineteenth-century New York as well. Nevertheless, the general points Cohen makes (for example ,on the nature of nineteenth-century newspapers in her second chapter, on the place of prostitution in society,[24] on literacy and gender roles[25] and on the gender roles of prostitutes[26]) could have been made equally well without reference to what happened to Helen Jewett. Jewett's fate does not serve as evidence of any kind for such general claims, only as an illustration. So although a work such as *The Murder of Helen Jewett* does make general claims, it does not do so *because* it is a microhistory, but rather *despite* its being one. The general historical information (about economic situations, gender roles, class conflicts, etc.) given in microhistory is usually derived from other historical studies or, if it stems from original research (such as Cohen's research on the nineteenth-century press), could in itself just as well have been conducted in a non-microhistorical format. The portrayal of outsider characters such as Menocchio or Helen Jewett and exceptional events such as the Great Cat Massacre or the Romans Carnival simply do not make a cognitive contribution to the general claims that no doubt appear in microhistories.

Why is it then, if not on cognitive grounds, that microhistorians have such a fascination with the outsiders of history?

THE EXPERIENTIAL LEVEL

Adrian Jones has made the point that there is an essential difference between those texts that present a thesis or a claim about something and those texts that aim to transfer meaning or a feeling.[27] Clifford Geertz, on the other hand, once made the bold statement that the success and the quality of an anthropological study do not primarily depend on the quality of its cognitive claims, but rather on its ability to transfer a feeling of 'having been there'.[28] So Geertz argues that anthropological texts are not of Jones's first kind, but of the second.

Now, in the West, we have gradually grown accustomed to the idea that works of non-fiction should present some kind of thesis. But if Geertz is right, an anthropological work should not really do so. If the value of an anthropological book is measured by its ability to transfer a feeling rather than warrant a claim, our criteria of valuation of anthropological writing change. We should not look at what claims anthropologists make, what kind of evidence they use and how they use it. Rather, we should look for the textual techniques they use to paint the image of the world they describe and to generate sympathy (or antipathy) for the people they study and interact with. This of course does not mean that evidence or facts do not play a part. What it does mean is that the aim of the representation of anthropological data in an anthropological work of non-fiction is not to convince the reader of a certain thesis, but to transfer a feeling of 'what it is like to be there'. Factual accuracy is as important in the second as it is in the first aim, so again, it is not an issue at stake here. Nevertheless, I agree with Hayden White that the feeling of 'being there', the authenticity of a piece of historical writing, depends less on the facts than on the way these facts are presented.[29]

One could say that a piece of historical writing always presents a thesis, since it states that certain things happened in the past. This is, however, not the way in which the word is used here. The term 'thesis' refers to an explanation of a certain historical event or feature, an equation of two (kinds of) historical events or features (a claim such as 'A is actually B') or an application of a more or less general law.[30]

I argue now that microhistory is, generally speaking, similar to what Geertz believes anthropology to be. The aim of most microhistories is to transfer a feeling rather than to prove a thesis, and many distinctive features of the genre can only be seen in this light, as literary means to create an effect of 'having been there'. Le Roy Ladurie formulates this quite explicitly in his *Carnival in Romans* and in *Montaillou*, affirming that feelings, not concepts, are what his books are about:

> In a city the size of Romans, all the participants in a revolution
> knew each other. They hated each other passionately, cordially, and
> personally. It was the kind of hatred which only the small can feel
> towards the mighty, and was far more concrete than a simple, abstract
> 'class consciousness'. Hatred was aimed at those too-comfortable
> citizens who had for so long handled the community finances.[31]

> But Montaillou itself is much more than a courageous but fleeting
> deviation. It is the factual history of ordinary people. It is Pierre and
> Béatrice and their love; it is Pierre Maury and his flock; it is the breath
> of life restored through a repressive Latin register that is a monument
> of Occitan literature. Montaillou is the physical warmth of the *oxtal*,
> together with the ever-recurring promise of a peasant heaven.[32]

Or take, as a very fine example of being-there, Natalie Zemon-Davis's description of the judges in the court room on Martin Guerre's trial at Toulouse:

> The Criminal Chamber, or La Tournelle as it was called, was one
> of the five chambers of the Parlement and made up of a rotating
> group of ten to eleven judges and two or three presidents. Those
> who happened to be sitting on it for the appeal of 'Martin Guerre'
> included some of the luminaries of the court. There was the learned

Jean de Coras, with all his legal publications. There was Michel Du
Faur, former judge in the Sénéchaussée and now a president of the
Parlement; from a family of distinguished men of the law, he was
married to a Bernuy, whose dowry came from profits in the Toulouse
pastel-dye trade. Jean de Mansencal himself, the first president of the
Parlement, came down from the high chamber for the last days of
the trial. Owner of a splendid Renaissance house in the city, he also
had property in the diocese of Lombez, not far from the village where
Arnaud du Tilh was born.[33]

Zemon-Davis could have just summed up the judges, but her choice of describing them one by one, using the repetitive formula 'there was . . ., there was . . .'
gives us the impression that someone is pointing at the important people and
explaining to us who they are. The little word 'himself' adds to this impression, and gives us something of the same awe towards de Mansencal that the
common people present at the moment itself must have felt. The fact that
Zemon-Davis goes through the trouble of describing the court room in this
way shows that she has something else in mind than a simply objective description of Martin Guerre's trial. She wants us to relive it, to see it through the eyes
of a contemporary.

TECHNIQUES OF 'BEING THERE'

One of the most important techniques used in creating an effect of 'being
there' is rather obvious actually, a story of 'how I got there'. This is quite common in anthropology. For example:

In the cool of the early morning, just before sunrise, the bow of
the *Southern Crow* headed towards the eastern horizon, on which
a tiny dark blue outline was faintly visible. Slowly it grew into a
rugged mountain mass, standing up sheer from the ocean; then as we
approached within a few miles it revealed around its base a narrow
ring of low, flat land, thick with vegetation. [. . .] In an hour or so
we were close inshore and could see canoes coming round from the
south, outside the reef, on which the tide was low. [. . .] The ship
anchored on a short cable in the open bay off the coral reef. [. . .] For
the first time, perhaps, he began to doubt of having left what was to
him the civilization of Tulagi [. . .] Feeling none too certain myself
of the reception that awaited us – though I knew it would stop short
of cannibalism – I reassured him, and we began to get out the stores.
Later we went ashore in one of the canoes. [. . .] We were surrounded
by crowds of naked chattering youngsters, with their pleasant light-
brown velvet skins and straight hair, so different from the Melanesians
we left behind. They darted about splashing like a shoal of fish, some
of them falling bodily into pools in their enthusiasm. At last the long
wade ended, we climbed up the steeply shelving beach, crossed the

soft, dry sand strewn with the brown needles of the Casuarina trees – a home-like touch; it was like a pine avenue – and were led to an old chief, clad with great dignity in a white coat and loin-cloth, who awaited us on his stool under a large shady tree.[34]

'Arrival stories', as they are called,[35] are somewhat of a typical feature of interpretative anthropology. They allow the reader to identify with the author and empathise with his or her feelings in order to get a taste of 'how it really was to be there'. Of course, writers of microhistories do not have time machines, so a literal (and truthful) adoption of this technique is not an option. But there are ways to adapt. A first one is using a historical character to introduce us to the lost world of the past. The historian will introduce a character, will try to get us to sympathise with him or her, and then lets the character take us on an introduction to the historical world in which the events the microhistorian will describe take place. Once we are sufficiently at our ease in the historical world the author wants us to be in, we can be left on our own and we can turn our attention to other matters, be it characters, events or situations. Patricia Cohen's *The Murder of Helen Jewett* is a clear example. In the first pages of the book, the book (and reader) focuses on Rosina, Helen Jewett's prostitute friend who discovers her corpse.[36] As we identify with Rosina, we are introduced to the world of the Victorian brothel, and we discover the central character of the book, Helen Jewett, as Rosina discovers her burnt body. As Rosina and her contemporaries embark on a fascinated search for the murderer, we as readers embark on a quest for the inner world of thoughts of this mysterious prostitute. The shepherd Pierre Maury in *Montaillou* is another fine example. The book starts off with a description of the ecology, economy and social structure of the village of Montaillou and its surroundings. In two of the first chapters (the fourth and fifth), we meet the first person we as readers can identify with, Pierre Maury.[37] Le Roy Ladurie then gives us a narrative of the life of Pierre Maury, which conveniently, due to the fact that Maury is a wandering shepherd, takes us on an introductory tour of Montaillou and its surroundings. Through Maury's diachronic narrative, we are introduced to the historical world the author wants to portray.

However, historical characters themselves are not always needed to produce the effect of an arrival story. Some authors only use a few sentences. Robert Darnton, for example, invites his readers to embark on a journey with him,[38] and Natalie Zemon-Davis tells the readers of *The Return of Martin Guerre* that Jean De Coras, her most important source, will 'initiate' us into the 'hidden world of peasant sentiment and aspiration'.[39] Both of these statements are meant to get the reader's curiosity going and to convince him or her that what follows will not be an abstract description, but an exciting journey of new experiences. A somewhat different technique, with a similar effect though, is used by Gene Brucker in *Giovanni and Lusanna*. Brucker starts his book by telling us how he accidently stumbled on the extraordinary document which is now about to reveal its secrets.[40] This is a way of letting the reader identify with the author and become contaminated by his curiosity.

A second important way of letting the reader *feel* history, maybe the most important one of all, is identification with the characters. Microhistorians describe their characters in a way that makes it easy to identify and empathise with them. Pierre Maury again, the main character from *Montaillou* (published in the 1970s) looks suspiciously like a hippie. He is a free spirit, a little bit naïve (not too much though), a wanderer, unbound by social conventions, he has a lot of friends and girlfriends, is susceptible to non-catholic spirituality and always tries to do good to everyone. How could we, especially if we were living in the second half of the 1970s, not identify which such a character? Le Roy Ladurie even helps us a little bit more. When he is introduced, Le Roy Ladurie inserts a little title: 'Pierre Maury, the good shepherd'.[41] He talks about 'our hero'[42] and contrasts him with the treacherous, power-hungry and perverted priest, Pierre Clergue. In this kind of situation it is almost inevitable for the reader to identify with Pierre Maury, the good shepherd. Similarly, Le Roy Ladurie refers to Paumier from *Carnival in Romans* as 'our man'[43] and Robert Darnton refers to some of his characters as 'our bourgeois',[44] 'our author',[45] 'our Montpelliérain'[46] or 'our policeman'.[47] Carlo Ginzburg for his part uses an opposition similar to the one in *Montaillou*, between the naïve, stubborn and creative Menocchio and his bloodsucking inquisitors. We as readers are clearly expected to root for the poor miller, who tries to resist but who is in the end submitted to the thorough and unforgiving questioning and torture by the inquisitors. For example, Ginzburg calls the inquisitor 'unrelenting',[48] and states that he 'put Menocchio on the spot'.[49] Ginzburg also says the following things about poor old Menocchio, obviously meant to create pity:

> The aura of martyrdom in which Menocchio envisioned his own death makes one think that all his talk was nothing more than the pathetic fancies of an old man. After all, he had nothing left. He was alone now: his wife and his closest son were dead. He must not have been on good terms with his other children: 'And if *my* children want to go their own way, good luck to them', he declared disdainfully to Simon. But that mythical Geneva, the home (or so he thought) of religious freedom, was too far away; this, and his tenacious loyalty to a friend who had stood by him in a moment of difficulty, had kept him from flight. Evidently, on the other hand, he couldn't repress the passionate curiosity about things pertaining to the faith. So he lingered there awaiting his persecutors.[50]

Rejected by his children who considered him a burden, a disgrace in the eyes of the village, a ruin for his family, he passionately longed to be restored to that Church that had once separated him from herself, and even marked him visibly as reprobate. Because of this he was making a pathetic gesture of homage to his 'superiors': 'inquisitors' (understandably in first place) and then in succession 'bishops, vicars, priests, chaplains, and curates'. It was a useless act of submission, in a sense, because when he wrote this, the investigation of Menocchio by the Holy Office had not yet resumed. But the uncontrollable yearning 'to seek exalted things' tormented him, filled him with 'anxiety', made him feel guilty 'and in disgrace with the world'. And then he desperately cried out for death. But death had bypassed him: 'It has done just the opposite, it has taken away a son of mine . . .; and then it has wanted to take my wife . . .' At that moment he cursed himself: 'if only I had died when I was fifteen' – before growing up and becoming the man he was, to his disgrace and that of his children.[51]

Dramatic words indeed. Patricia Cohen equally arouses pity with her heroine (because in her eyes she really is something of a heroine) Helen Jewett, when after many pages of rather distanced discourse analysis and descriptions of the economic and social situation of the brothel business she suddenly tells us the following:

> In her mind, their love transcended her other sexual liaisons,
> occupying a different realm. Setting Robinson apart might be
> expected in a prostitute who kept her heart from other customers,
> but Jewett typically drew her many clients into a circle of friendship
> and romance. In this letter Helen discloses a deeper set of feelings,
> bordering on dependency, for an idealized Robinson. He had truly
> hurt her.[52]

Coming after more than two hundred pages of mystery, speculation about Jewett's origins and discourse analysis, these sentences are really a dramatic and moving turn to the sentimental. The effect is so strong exactly because of its contrast with the somewhat more scholarly analyses preceding it. The contrast is even greater because of the conciseness of the little sentence 'He had truly hurt her.' We as readers feel something of a shock, and by doing so we again identify with Jewett herself, as Richard Robinson's betrayal was such a sudden shock to her.

At other places as well, it is clear that Cohen wants us to root for the independent women in the brothel business, for example by calling the attacks by people who were offended by the brothel business 'bully attacks' by 'ruffians',[53] and by describing her alleged murderer, Richard Robinson, clearly the bad guy of the story, in the following way:

> This slight young man of nineteen demonstrated an uncanny ability to
> play the con artist. Lying came easily to him; in conversations about
> the Jewett case with utter strangers he boldly plumped for his own
> probity while completely misrepresenting himself.[54]

In Cohen's portrayal, Robinson looks remarkably like a sociopath: he has no trouble lying, was able to charm and lie at will, had no remorse of any kind and could not cope with rejection.

Natalie Zemon-Davis for her part wants us to identify with Martin Guerre's wife, Bertrande de Rols, who, she complains, has all too often been portrayed as an obedient nobody.[55] Take this typical description: 'But the obstinate and honorable Bertrande does not seem a woman so easily fooled, not even by a charmer like Pansette.'[56]

A third important way of creating the feeling of 'being there', of letting the past speak for itself, as it were, is the use of direct discourse and free indirect discourse. Carlo Ginzburg's *The Cheese and the Worms*, for example, has direct discourse on almost every page, and the spine of the text is indeed formed by a conversation, the one between Menocchio and his inquisitors. Le Roy Ladurie's *Montaillou* and *Carnival in Romans* as well are absolutely loaded with direct discourse. Gene Brucker and Natalie Zemon-Davis are somewhat more modest in their use, but still employ it quite often.[57] Patricia Cohen and Richard Darnton employ it in a more sporadic way.[58] This may be a conscious strategy, but much more likely it is just the consequence of the nature of their sources. Direct discourse is a hazardous enterprise for a historian, and is usually not made up,[59] but taken directly from the sources, typically from trial reports and inquisitorial hearings, one of the only historical sources to contain transcriptions of actual spoken discourse, or at least something close enough. In any case, microhistorians are inclined to use as much direct discourse as the sources allow them.

Besides direct discourse, they also make ample use of free indirect discourse. Free indirect discourse can be seen as a mixture between direct and indirect discourse, and can be used instead of 'normal' third-person narration to generate sympathy with a character and a more direct contact with the narrated situation. Take this example from *The Return of Martin Guerre*:

> For the Chamber had to decide what to do about the woman prisoner in the Conciergerie. What could one say about the beautiful wife so easily deceived and so obstinate in her error? After much discussion, the judges agreed to accept her good faith; the female sex was, after all, fragile.[60]

Of course Zemon-Davis herself does not belief that the female sex is or was fragile; the judges do. But by leaving this fact implicit rather than stating it explicitly, Zemon-Davis allows us to take a point of view which is closer to that of the judges themselves. Used in this way, free indirect discourse blurs the distinction between the point of view of the author and that of her characters. As a result, this leaves us with a more direct experience of historical reality then we would have had if Zemon-Davis had written something like 'They accepted her good faith because they believed the female sex to be fragile.' Free indirect discourse allows for an identification of the reader with a character without being limited to actual recorded direct discourse. Here, it allows Zemon-Davis to make an educated guess about the judges' motivations and let the reader experience them for him- or herself. If she had simply told us the motivations in indirect discourse, we would not been able to really 'experience' or 'feel' them. If, on the other hand, she had used direct discourse ('"The female sex is fragile," the judges said'), she would have been open to the justified criticism of historical inaccuracy, since there is no indication whatsoever that the judges did literally say that. Free indirect discourse is therefore an important instrument for the microhistorian. It allows him or her to let the reader have a look into the heads of the characters without making a strong historical claim that cannot be warranted. Not surprisingly, free indirect discourse can be found in most microhistories.[61]

At this point, we have given an explanation for some distinguishing textual features of microhistory such as the use of direct and free indirect discourse and the use of arrival stories. We have not, however, touched on one of the most distinguishing features of microhistory, namely, the fascination of microhistorians with the outsiders of history. In order to do so, we have to introduce some theoretical concepts. We have seen that microhistory aims primarily at the creation of a feeling of 'being there', and not at some sort of cognitive explanatory argument. The Dutch historians Johan Huizinga and Frank Ankersmit have argued that an experience of the past, such as the feeling of 'being there', is fundamentally at odds with our cognitive discourse about the past.[62] The more we write about history, the more context we create, the more we will have the feeling that the reality of the past itself is buried under a layer of discourse and contextualisation. The more we know about the past, the less likely we are to be surprised, intrigued or amazed by it. In other words, the more we know the past, the less we can experience or feel it. This entails that historical experience has to find a way around the mainstream historiography. And this is why, in my opinion, microhistorians are fascinated by the outsiders of history. Emmanuel Le Roy Ladurie and Gene Brucker formulate this point quite literally:

> Our documents have permitted us to break through the superficial crust of feudal relations; this fresh and nutritious crust with which historians of the oldest farm life have contented themselves for so long, limited by their sources and their desire not to make a fool of themselves.[63]

> Lusanna was an extraordinary woman, who does not fit neatly into any of the standard roles of chaste wives and widows or cloistered nuns that were defined for women of her time and social rank. She was obviously a woman of strong passions, who found little satisfaction in her marriage and was prepared to risk dishonor to follow the dictates of the heart.[64]

Let us take Menocchio as another example. If Ginzburg had given a biography of a typical nobleman/intellectual or a typical peasant, we would not have been that amazed or intrigued. It might be an interesting example, but nothing really more. Menocchio, however, is not typical of any of the categories (high culture, low culture, peasant culture, popular faith, etc.) that we usually apply to the past. This creates a special sensation. We get the feeling that our usual categories are not as adequate or all-encompassing as we thought them to be, that some part of the reality of the past itself breaks through and reaches us in a more direct way. We get the feeling that Menocchio is a real human being, a person of flesh and blood, precisely because his actions cannot be explained by some general category. Menocchio's thoughts seem to reach us directly, unfiltered by categorical schemes. Ginzburg himself is conscious of this fact. He explicitly states that what it is that makes Menocchio's case a special one is that the inquisitorial categories of witchcraft and satanism collide against the wall of Menocchio's bewildering belief system.[65] We as readers share the bafflement of the inquisitors as we come to the realisation that the categories by which we understand their present and our past are insufficient.[66] Because of this, the reader of *The Cheese and the Worms* gets the feeling that he or she is dealing with something authentic here, that he or she is getting a glimpse of what lies behind the veil of our conceptual scheme.

The same goes for other microhistories. Patricia Cohen writes extensively about the oppression of women in Victorian New York, but Helen Jewett is the subject of her book not because she is typical, but precisely because she, as well as some other prostitutes, was able to somewhat escape from these oppressive structures and even turn them into her advantage. Precisely because of this, we get a feeling of the contingency of historical reality, of the fact that Helen Jewett was a real person and not just a mindless puppet or a straw woman of some general categories, be they those of her contemporaries or those we as historians use to understand her time. Something similar holds for the peasants of Montaillou, Romans Carnival or the Great Cat Massacre. All of these people are not typical of any category, and precisely because of this we get a special feeling of amazement about the richness of historical reality itself.

Besides the trade-off between knowing and feeling the past, a second important aspect of Huizinga's and Ankersmit's view is the idea that historical experience is never *merely* a feeling of the past itself. It is always accompanied by the idea of *historical distance*, the idea that although the past may seem ready at hand at certain moments, there will always be an irreducible gap between the present and the past.[67] Although we may get a glimpse of the past itself, it will never be more than a glimpse, always limited by historical distance. Huizinga in this respect describes historical experience as a dreamlike experience in which the past seems at the same time ready at hand and infinitely far away.[68] This combination of proximity and distance, of the feeling of being able to touch historical reality itself and at the same time experiencing the irrevocable rupture between past and present, gives rise to the specific nature of historical experience, or historical sensation.

All of this may seem a bit abstract now, but it will be clear enough when we apply it to some peculiar phrases and figures of style we encounter throughout most microhistories. Many microhistorians love to stress that the sources they use are extraordinary, that we are very lucky to have them, and that it could just as well have been otherwise. Even within the sources, they still repeatedly emphasise the otherness of the people in the past, our inability to capture their ways of living and thinking completely and the often tentative and speculative nature of their own writing. Robert Darnton and Natalie Zemon-Davis, for example, are explicit about this:

> But one thing seems clear to everyone who returns from field work: other people are other. They do not think the way we do. And if we want to understand their way of thinking, we should set out with the idea of capturing otherness [. . .] We constantly need to be shaken out of a false sense of familiarity with the past, to be administered doses of culture shock.[69]

> What I offer you here is in part my invention, but held tightly in check by the voices of the past.[70]

Of course, statements such as Zemon-Davis's are indeed a consequence of the fact that a responsible historian is always aware of the limitations of his or her sources and the difficulties of interpreting other people's mind. In this sense, this is an epistemic point. But these seemingly innocent comments also have a strong literary effect. Natalie Zemon-Davis, for example, uses a whole array of speculative terms and sentences. Examples are the uses of 'perhaps'[71] and tentative formulations such as 'one can imagine what it was like between the insistent father Sanxi and his reluctant son Martin',[72] 'she must have realized the difference'[73] and 'Bertrande de Rols must have been delighted with this turn of events'.[74] Speculative turns like these, loaded with perhapses, probablies and must-have-beens, are present throughout the genre of microhistory.[75] Such statements have the effect of blurring and obscuring the story (Giovanni Levi literally speaks of the '*nebulous* institutional world of the ancient régime'[76]), which makes it much more like to generate a real historical 'feeling'. Carlo Ginzburg dramatises this effect in the very last sentence of *The Cheese and the Worms*, which also contains many more statements of the we-do-not-know-this-but-wouldn't-it-be-great-if-we-did kind:[77] 'About Menocchio we know many things. About this Marcato, or Marco – and so many others like him who lived and died without leaving a trace – we know nothing.'[78] Natalie Zemon-Davis writes something similar in the final pages of *The Return of Martin Guerre* as do Brucker in the final pages of *Giovanni and Lusanna* and Levi somewhere in the beginning of *Inheriting Power* on the fate of his main protagonist, Giovan Battista Chiesa:

> I think I have uncovered the true face of the past – or has Pancette done it once again?[79]

What was her fate after the invalidation of her marriage to Giovanni? [. . .] Lusanna's last years are cloaked in obscurity, but for a brief moment she achieved celebrity status.[80]

We do not know his date of death, nor what became of him, nor what new ties he may have forged.[81]

One of the most dramatic (although the event in itself couldn't be less dramatic) figures of style in which this has been done is in *Montaillou*:

Perhaps we could have learned more about Pierre's thoughts on marriage from the continuation of this dialogue . . . if Fabrisse's pot had not begun to boil, cutting short the rhetorical efforts of the mistress and forcing her to run off to the kitchen. Cursed pot.[82]

There is also a variation on this theme. Besides stressing those aspects or parts of the past we do not know, it is also possible to stress that the parts we do know have come to us purely by chance. This at the same time creates a fascination for the subject in question (since we are lucky to see it) and a fascination with all those maybe even more interesting things we are missing out. Gene Brucker's arrival story, of how he accidentally found the document that made him discover the story of Giovanni and Lusanna, is a clear example (see above). Ginzburg's remarks on how difficult it is to find sources on popular culture[83] is another example, as are these two remarks from *Montaillou*:

All of a sudden, we find ourselves right in the middle of a tragedy. A beautiful dialogue, worthy of the antiques, confronts young Guillaume with his friend Guillaume Belot and his mother Allemand Guilhabert: she loves her son with all her heart; but the future of her *domus* is constantly on her mind as well. That future would be compromised if the inquisitors would find out about the *consolamentum* of her son.[84]

What I tried to do was find other sources, even more specific and introspective, which could give me an image of peasants made of flesh and blood. By sheer luck for us, and to their own great misfortune, the inhabitants of Montaillou, the whole village even, was given an occasion to speak by one man in the fourteenth century.[85]

As I stated previously, I do not mean to say that microhistorians use these kinds of formulations and expressions for literary effect alone.[86] It still is a direct consequence of their epistemic situation, of the sources they have at their disposal. But this does not mean that publicly announcing the limitations of their sources does not have an effect on the reader. First of all, it convinces the reader that what he or she is reading is real, proper and serious history. The historian seeks to create a kind of 'reading pact', a state of trust between the reader and the writer/historian. If the historian is open about his or her limitations, the reader is assured that he or she did not try to fill in the gaps, and that everything that is being told is the real thing.[87] Second, it also creates, as we have said, a sense of historical distance, a sense that the past will never be completely at our disposal.

Now let us recall the importance of outsiders in microhistory, the fact that the people and events studied by microhistory typically fall out of mainstream historical discourse. Now, we have the different elements constitutive of a historical sensation, according to Huizinga and Ankersmit. On the one hand, we as readers have the feeling that we can experience something of the past itself and that what we are experiencing is really truthful, not just the imagination of the writer (thanks to the reading pact). On the other hand, we also have a sense of historical distance, the feeling that we will never know the past completely, and that we are lucky enough to catch some nebulous glimpses. It is this combination of presence and absence which, according to Ankersmit and Huizinga, gives rise to the sublime feeling of historical experience.

THE ETHICAL LEVEL

In the previous section, I have argued that microhistory aims at the creation of an effect and the arousal of emotions rather than the establishment of a cognitive claim. An obvious next question then is: to what end? What is the point of letting the reader identify with historical characters or creating a feeling of 'being there'? One could simply say that the feeling itself is reason enough. Huizinga certainly thinks so, stating that historical experience is a lot like aesthetic experience.[88]

However, I do not believe this to be the case, at least not for microhistory. I argue that microhistorians do aim at something else as well. This 'something else' is best described as an ethical agenda. Moreover, I will argue that they do so in a double way. First, microhistorians have an ethical agenda with respect to their contemporaries. They want to change the society they themselves live in in some way. Second, however, microhistorians also have an ethical relationship to the past itself, as an ideal of historical justice and historical responsibility.

A hint of the first of these two points is already present when we look at the biography of the most important microhistorians themselves. Carlo Ginzburg, for example, describes himself as something of a leftist and as being very aware of the political implications of his work.[89] Furthermore, his father was active, in the 1930s, in an anti-fascist group called *Giustizia e Libertá*, and he himself was strongly involved with *Lotta Continua*, a more or less informal student and working-class movement, after 1968.[90] Emmanuel Le Roy Ladurie was a member of the French communist party from 1949–56 and the secretary of a local department of the *Parti Socialiste Unifée* from 1960–3.[91] Natalie Zemon-Davis as well was politically very active in her student days and states that this political activism was deeply influential on the way she approached history. Besides this, because of the McCarthy regime in the 1960, she lost her passport, her husband was in prison for a while, and both partners had to move to Canada.[92] And this even leaves out Zemon-Davis's feminism, a political theme which is equally important for Patricia Cohen.

This leftist orientation of microhistory is clearly noticeable in most of our examples. As already said, Emmanuel Le Roy Ladurie's *Montaillou* sets the free spirit and benevolent shepherd Pierre Maury up against the perverted, elitist and power-hungry priest Pierre Clergue. A similar opposition arises in the course of *Carnival in Romans* between the popular rabble-rouser Paumier (whom Le Roy Ladurie calls 'our man'[93]) and the manipulative and ruthless upper-class judge Guérin ('He showed himself to be cruel and intransigent',[94] 'We have already observed his cunning, secretly murderous attitude . . .',[95] 'He was the sort of main who likes to punch below the belt';[96] not surprisingly, the index has an entry 'Guérin, evil genius of Romans'[97]). We have already seen how Ginzburg wants us to root for Menocchio and how Patricia Cohen portrays Helen Jewett as a feminist heroine. Likewise, in Natalie Zemon-Davis's *The Return of Martin Guerre*, there is a heroine, Bertrande de Rols, Martin's wife, who stands up for her own happiness against Martin's father Sanxi and half of the village of Artigat (she has a 'stubborn independence' and a 'shrew realism',[98] and she is 'obstinate and 'honorable'[99]). In *Giovanni and Lusanna*, it is Lusanna who is the heroine, following what her heart tells her instead of submitting to social conventions of widowhood.[100] And even in Darnton's short essay 'The Great Cat Massacre', there is a certain implicit sympathy for the resourceful workers who are able to take revenge on their employers by means of popular traditions of symbolic re-enactment. In all of these stories, we find the same theme: an independent working-class hero or heroine who takes on the powers that be and eventually succumbs to them. The moral of all of this is clear: microhistorians show us that resistance against dominant structures is always a possibility. Individuals can stand out and do what their heart or conscience dictates. In short, microhistories have an essentially emancipating agenda, arguing against submission and rooting for independency and freedom, particularly in the lower classes.

Yet this is not the only ethical aspect of microhistory, and maybe not even the most important one. The fact that the heroes of microhistory are mostly tragic (Paumier and Helen Jewett are murdered, Bertrande de Rols and Lusanna lose their trials, Menocchio is executed, etc.) is a hint at this. If Ginzburg, Le Roy Ladurie & co. had simply wanted to promote an emancipating agenda, they would have chosen people who eventually succeeded in what they were trying to do. So I believe there is something else that drives microhistorians: a sense of historical justice. The idea is that by saving them from oblivion, the historical wrongs these people have suffered are somehow, maybe only in a minimal way, righted. This means that microhistorians, and maybe all of us, have a responsibility towards the dead, or, in other words, that there is an ethical appeal coming from the past. This basic idea is not new. Antoon De Baets has already made a forceful case for the ethical treatment of the dead.[101] Carlo Ginzburg himself once said that historians should tell the truth because of an ethical obligation towards the dead, and not because of historians' (would-be?) status as scientists.[102]

Of course, this is only a hypothesis, but it does explain two things. First, it explains why microhistorians pick out the losers of history. Second, it explains why microhistorians are historians and not writers of fiction, why they have a yearning towards the reality of the past itself. After all, if the only aim were to tell inspiring stories about working-class heroes in the past, they could just as well use fictional characters.

In the utilitarian world we live in, pleading for an ethical attitude towards the dead is not an easy thing. Indeed, in a utilitarian ethics, the moral status of the dead is not an issue. The dead are dead, and that's it. They cannot benefit from anything we do, so no moral considerations should be at stake here. The same goes for, among others, social contract theories: how can the dead be part of our ethical community that engages in social contracts if they cannot contribute to society in any way? Nevertheless, there are some important alternatives in ethical theory which fit nicely with how microhistory is done. We could group these under the banner of *ethics of recognition and representation*. In broad strokes, this view has been defended by philosophers such as Martin Buber, Emmanuel Levinas and Charles Taylor, as well as the ethicists active in the domain of *care ethics*.[103] The general idea is that the aim of ethics and morality is not to maximise the total amount of well-being in a community, but rather to maximise *recognition* as well as *care*. A good person is not someone who is very good at calculating the effects of his or her actions on other beings or at knowing many law-like rules of moral conduct by heart. Rather, a good person is he or she who is able to recognise the other as a concrete human being, with needs and wishes which might be different from those of him- or herself or of the rest of the community. He or she will care for the other and take care of him or her, as well as engaging in constructive dialogue while still trying to respect the otherness and autonomy of the person he or she cares for as much as possible. Most importantly, he or she will do so in a *personal* way, without reducing the other to a conceptual scheme, an instance of a general principle, a pawn on a chess board or a number in a statistic.

This does indeed seem to be the kind of thing microhistorians have in mind. The preference of care ethicists and recognition ethicists for feeling rather than knowing runs parallel with that of microhistorians. Jill Lepore has nicknamed the latter 'historians who love too much', and this seems right.[104] Reading microhistories, it is surely striking how much people like Ginzburg or Cohen care about the people they write about. The sympathy they try to arouse in us as readers is not just a literary trick; it reflects a genuine care for the characters (or rather real people) they describe and the will to tell their story to an audience as large as they can get. Furthermore, they will try to get their audience to care for and identify with their characters. Of course, this a fallible enterprise. A too one-sidedly positive description might have the opposite effect, or an all too generous use of literary techniques might make a textual representation seem artificial. And of course, every reader still has the freedom to disagree with the author and identify with or root for the 'wrong' character. Nevertheless, the fact that microhistorians do everything in their power to make their readers care for their characters points to their ethical engagement with the past.

E. P. Thompson, who although not a microhistorian himself has had a lot of influence on (especially) microhistory,[105] forcefully bears witness to an ethical mission of this kind in the classic opening statement of *The Making of the English Working Class*:

> I am seeking to rescue the poor stockinger, the Luddite cropper,
> the 'obsolete' hand-loom weaver, the 'Utopian' artisan, and even
> the deluded follower of Joanna Southcott, from the enormous
> condescension of posterity. Their crafts and traditions may have
> been dying. Their hostility to the new industrialism may have been
> backward-looking. Their communitarian ideals may have been
> fantasies. Their insurrectionary conspiracies may have been foolhardy.
> But they lived through these times of acute social disturbance, and we
> did not. Their aspirations were valid in terms of their own experience;
> and, if they were casualties of history, they remain, condemned in their
> own lives, as casualties.[106]

In this view, microhistory becomes a kind of ethical tightrope walk between the responsibility to tell the truth about the dead and the will, equally ethical in nature, to 'bring them back to life' and to create a kind of historical justice by letting their story be known among as many people as possible. So the challenge for a microhistorian then is to tell their story as attractively as possible, without violating the responsibility to tell the truth.

At this stage, one might ask the question: what is the general point of microhistory? Is there one single trait which links Ginzburg's and Jones's remarks on 'being there', Ankersmit's and Huizinga's notions of historical sensation and historical distance, and the ethics of recognition present in microhistory? Is there some common agenda which links these three layers of meaning? In this chapter, I do not make any sweeping claims on this point. Rather, I stress the multiplicity of meaning in microhistory, on the cognitive, experiential and ethical layer, with the emphasis on the latter two more so than on the first. Furthermore, I also do not make a claim about the relation between microhistory and more traditional forms of historical writing. It may well be that many of the features I have highlighted above are present in more mainstream forms of historiography as well. Or it may be that microhistory is really very distinct as a genre, and that the experiential and ethical dimensions of the writing of history are largely absent in other works. Both options are possible; I do not intend to find out which one is true for now.

NOTES

1. Patrick Boucheron, 'Le Dossier Montaillou', *L'Historie*, 259 (2001), 46–7; Michael Roberts, 'The Annales School and Historical Writing', in Peter Lambert and Philipp Schofield (eds), *Making History: An Introduction of the History and Practices of a Discipline*, London: Routledge, 2004, p. 85.
2. Charles Tilly, 'Anthropology, History and the Annales', *Review*, 1: 3/4 (1978), 211.
3. Giovanni Levi, 'On Microhistory', in Peter Burke (ed.), *New Perspectives on Historical Writing*, Cambridge: Polity Press, 1991, p. 100.
4. Ibid. pp. 101–2; see also Giovanni Levi, *Inheriting Power: The Story of an Exorcist*, Chicago: University of Chicago Press, 1988, pp. 67–99.
5. Emmanuel Le Roy Ladurie, *Montaillou: Cathars and Catholics in a French Village, 1294–1324*, Harmondsworth: Penguin, 1980; Emmanuel Le Roy Ladurie, *Montaillou, Village Occitan de 1294 à 1324*, Paris: Gallimard, 1975; Carlo Ginzburg, *The Cheese and the Worms: The Cosmos of a Sixteenth-Century Miller*, Harmondsworth: Penguin, 1982.
6. Levi, *Inheriting Power*, pp. 121–2.
7. Robert Darnton, *The Great Cat Massacre and Other Episodes in French Cultural History*, New York: Vintage Books, 1984, pp. 75–106.
8. Emmanuel Le Roy Ladurie, *Carnival in Romans: A People's Uprising at Romans 1579–1580*, Harmondsworth: Penguin, 1981.
9. Natalie Zemon-Davis, *The Return of Martin Guerre*, London: Harvard University Press, 1983.
10. Patricia Cohen, *The Murder of Helen Jewett: The Life and Death of a Prostitute in Nineteenth-Century New York*, New York: Alfred A. Knopf, 1998.
11. Darnton, *The Great Cat Massacre*, pp. 5–6.
12. Clifford Geertz, *The Interpretation of Cultures*, New York: Basic Books, 1973, pp. 6–7, 412–54.
13. Ibid. p. 6.
14. Ibid. pp. 414–17.
15. Ibid. from p. 417, but from p. 432 in a higher gear.
16. See Ronald Walters, 'Clifford Geertz and Historians', *Social Research*, 47: 3 (1980), 537–56; Levi, 'On Microhistory', pp. 100–8; Roger Chartier, 'Texts, Symbols and Frenchness', *Journal of Modern History*, 57: 4 (1985), 683–5.
17. See Darnton, *The Great Cat Massacre*, p. xiii.
18. Ibid. pp. 78–82.
19. Ibid. pp. 98–9.
20. Ibid. p. 89.
21. Ibid. pp. 96–9.
22. Geertz, *The Interpretation of Cultures*, p. 452.

23. Dominick LaCapra, *History and Criticism*, Ithaca: Cornell University Press, 1985, pp. 60–2.

24. Cohen, *The Murder of Helen Jewett*, pp. 61–76.

25. Ibid. pp. 166–79.

26. Ibid. pp. 198–200.

27. Adrian Jones, 'Reporting in Prose: Reconsidering Ways of Writing History', *The European Legacy*, 12 (2007), 311–36.

28. Clifford Geertz, *Works and Lives: The Anthropologist as Author*, Stanford: Stanford University Press, 1988, pp. 4–5.

29. Hayden White, 'Figural Realism in Witness Literature', *Parallax*, 10: 1 (2004), 113–24, 119.

30. For an overview of different types of explanation in historical writing, see Bert Leuridan and Anton Froeyman, 'On Lawfulness in History and Historiography', *History and Theory*, 51: 2 (2012), 172–92; Anton Froeyman, 'Concepts of Causation in Historiography', *Historical Methods*, 42: 3 (2009), 116–28.

31. Le Roy Ladurie, *Carnival in Romans*, p. 108.

32. Le Roy Ladurie, *Cathars and Catholics*, p. 356.

33. Zemon-Davis, *The Return of Martin Guerre*, p. 74.

34. Raymond Firth, *We, the Tikopia: A Sociological Study of Kinship in Primitive Polynesia*, London: Allen & Unwin, 1936, qtd in Geertz, *Works and Lives*, pp. 11–13.

35. Mary Louise Pratt, 'Fieldwork in Common Places', in James Clifford and George Marcus (eds), *Writing Culture: The Poetics and Politics of Ethnography*, Berkeley: University of California Press, 1986, pp. 31–2; Christine Hine, *Virtual Ethnography*, London: SAGE, 2000, p. 45.

36. Cohen, *The Murder of Helen Jewett*, pp. 3–7.

37. Maury is not the first character introduced in *Montaillou*. That part is played by the corrupt and treacherous priest, Pierre Clergue. Clergue, however, is described in such negative terms that he is nigh impossible to identify with.

38. Darnton, *The Great Cat Massacre*, p. 7.

39. Zemon-Davis, *The Return of Martin Guerre*, p. 4.

40. Gene Brucker, *Giovanni and Lusanna: Love and Marriage in Renaissance Florence*, Berkeley: University of California Press, 1986, p. vii.

41. Le Roy Ladurie, *Village Occitan*, pp. 118, 132; but not in the English version. Sadly, many features of Le Roy Ladurie's *Montaillou*, as well as from *Le Carnaval de Romans*, have not survived translation. As a general rule, I will cite and refer to the English translations if possible, but I will turn to my own translations of the French version if necessary.

42. Le Roy Ladurie, *Village Occitan*, p. 132.

43. Emmanuel Le Roy Ladurie, *Le Carnaval de Romans*, Paris: Seuil, 1979, p. 306.

44. Darnton, *The Great Cat Massacre*, pp. 107, 145.
45. Ibid. pp. 109, 116, 124.
46. Ibid. pp. 109, 113, 130.
47. Ibid. p. 145.
48. Ginzburg, *The Cheese and the Worms*, p. 70.
49. Ibid. p. 71.
50. Ibid. pp. 101–2.
51. Ibid. pp. 109–10.
52. Cohen, *The Murder of Helen Jewett*, pp. 234–5.
53. Ibid. p. 73.
54. Ibid. p. 342.
55. Zemon-Davis, *The Return of Martin Guerre*, pp. 118–19.
56. Ibid. p. 44.
57. Brucker, *Giovanni and Lusanna*, pp. 16, 57, 63, 85–6, 92–3; Zemon-Davis, *The Return of Martin Guerre*, pp. 15, 17, 24, 28, 39, 44, 55, 58, 60, 69, 70, 76, 79, 81, 84–6, 89–90, 99, 100, 102, 103.
58. Cohen, *The Murder of Helen Jewett*, pp. 310, 338–40; Darnton, *The Great Cat Massacre*, pp. 147, 157–8, 173–6.
59. Zemon-Davis at *The Return of Martin Guerre*, pp. 83–4, is an exception
60. Ibid. p. 90.
61. For some clear examples, see Ginzburg, *The Cheese and the Worms*, pp. 9–12, 70–1, 77, 106; Darnton, *The Great Cat Massacre*, pp. 130–3, 168, 176; Zemon-Davis, *The Return of Martin Guerre*, pp. 28, 53–4, 66, 70, 74–5, 80, 90–1, 103; Le Roy Ladurie, *Cathars and Catholics*, pp. 80, 103; Le Roy Ladurie, *Village Occitan*, pp. 592–611; Brucker, *Giovanni and Lusanna*, pp. 35, 57; Cohen, *The Murder of Helen Jewett*, p. 141; Le Roy Ladurie, *Le Carnaval de Romans*, pp. 69–70, 144, 153, 162, 175; Le Roy Ladurie, *Carnival in Romans*, pp. 115, 190.
62. Johan Huizinga, *Verzamelde werken, Vol. II*, Haarlem: Tjeenk Willink, 1948, pp. 559–69; Frank Ankersmit, 'The Sublime Dissociation of the Past: Or How to Be(come) What One Is No Longer', *History and Theory*, 40: 3 (2001), 310–11.
63. Le Roy Ladurie, *Village Occitan*, p. 612.
64. Brucker, *Giovanni and Lusanna*, p. 84.
65. Ginzburg, *The Cheese and the Worms*, pp. xix–xx.
66. Ibid. pp. 91–3.
67. This kind of historical distance should be distinguished from the way I have used it above. In that sense, it refers to a textual representation in which the author (and the reader) tries to take an apathic, unemotional and neutral stance, something like a bird's-eye view. What I mean under the term 'historical distance' is something else, namely, the unavoidable gap between past and present, which can be a deeply emotional affair. Frank Ankersmit's *Sublime Historical Experience*, Stanford: Stanford University Press, 2005, makes a strong case for this point. On the different use

of notions of 'distance' in history, see Mark Salber Phillips, *On Historical Distance*, New Haven, CT: Yale University Press, 2013.

68. Johan Huizinga, *Verzamelde werken, Vol. VII*, Haarlem: Tjeenk Willink, 1948–53, pp. 69–73.

69. Darnton, *The Great Cat Massacre*, p. 4.

70. Zemon-Davis, *The Return of Martin Guerre*, p. 5.

71. Ibid. pp. 7, 16, 19, 37, 51–3, 68, 71, 95.

72. Ibid. p. 21.

73. Ibid. p. 44.

74. Ibid. p. 52.

75. For example, see Le Roy Ladurie, *Cathars and Catholics*, pp. 121–2; Cohen, *The Murder of Helen Jewett*, p. 182; Le Roy Ladurie, *Carnival in Romans*, pp. 169–77; Ginzburg, *The Cheese and the Worms*, pp. 53–4, 57, 70; Darnton, *The Great Cat Massacre*, pp. 18, 108, 119; Levi, *Inheriting Power*, p. 30.

76. Levi, *Inheriting Power*, p. 38; my emphasis.

77. Ginzburg, *The Cheese and the Worms*, pp. xxvi, 5, 66.

78. Ibid. p. 128.

79. Zemon-Davis, *The Return of Martin Guerre*, p. 125.

80. Brucker, *Giovanni and Lusanna*, p. 120.

81. Levi, *Inheriting Power*, p. 19.

82. Le Roy Ladurie, *Village Occitan*, p. 227; my translation.

83. Ginzburg, *The Cheese and the Worms*, p. xix.

84. Le Roy Ladurie, *Village Occitan*, p. 341; my translation.

85. Ibid. p. 9; my translation.

86. In comparison, see White, 'Figural Realism', p. 116.

87. Of course, this does not mean that the reader will be a positivist and believe that the story he or she reads is the only true one. Neither will he or she assume that the text is perfectly objective and free of ideology, since it is usually quite clear that microhistorians do have a personal engagement with the past they describe. But the reader will assume that the text at least *refers* to a historical reality, even if this reality is described in an engaged and partial way.

88. Huizinga, *Verzamelde werken, Vol. II*, pp. 559–69.

89. Keith Luria and Romulo Gandolfo, 'Carlo Ginzburg: An Interview', *Radical History Review*, 35 (1986), 89–111.

90. Ibid. pp. 90–2.

91. Hélène Chaubin, 'Le Roy Ladurie Emmanuel', *Le Midi Rouge*, 13 (2009), 13–16.

92. Roger Adelson, 'Interview with Natalie Zemon-Davis', *Historian*, 53: 3 (1991), 410–14.

93. Le Roy Ladurie, *Le Carnaval de Romans*, p. 306; my translation.

94. Le Roy Ladurie, *Carnival in Romans*, p. 115.

95. Ibid. p. 214.

96. Le Roy Ladurie, *Le Carnaval de Romans*, p. 274; my translation.

97. Le Roy Ladurie, *Carnival in Romans*, p. 405.

98. Zemon-Davis, *The Return of Martin Guerre*, p. 28.

99. Ibid. p. 44; see also Zemon-Davis's criticism on pp. 116–19 on the traditional reception of the story.

100. See Brucker, *Giovanni and Lusanna*, pp. 84, 121.

101. Antoon De Baets, 'A Declaration of the Responsibilities of Present Generations Toward Past Generations', *History and Theory*, 43: 4 (2004), 130–64.

102. Trygve Riiser Gundersen, 'On the Dark Side of History', *Eurozine*, 11 July 2003, available at <http://www.eurozine.com/articles/2003-07-11-ginzburg-en.html> (last accessed 14 December 2016).

103. See Martin Buber, *I and Thou*, New York: Touchstone, 1996; Emmanuel Levinas, *Totality and Infinity*, The Hague: Martinus Nijhoff, 1979; Emmanuel Levinas, *Otherwise than Being*, Pittsburgh: Duquesne University Press, 1998; Charles Taylor, *Multiculturalism: Examining the Politics of Recognition*, ed. Amy Gutmann, Princeton: Princeton University Press, 1994; Carol Gilligan, In a Different Voice: Psychological Theory and Women's Development, Cambridge, MA: Harvard University Press, 1982; Nel Noddings, Caring: A Feminine Approach to Ethics and Moral Education, Berkeley: University of California Press, 1984; Michael Slote, *The Ethics of Care and Empathy*, New York: Routledge, 2007.

104. Jill Lepore, 'Historians Who Love Too Much: Reflections on Microhistory and Biography', *The Journal of American History*, 88: 1 (2001), 129–44.

105. David Sabean, 'Reflections on Microhistory', in Gunilla Budde, Sebastian Conrad and Oliver Janz (eds), *Transnationale Geschichte. Themen, Tendenzen und Theorien*, Göttingen: Vandenhoeck & Ruprecht, 2006, pp. 275ff.

106. Edward P. Thompson, The Making of the English Working Class, London: Penguin, 1991, p. 12.

CHAPTER 7

Writing Fiction, Making History: Historical Narrative and the Process of Creating History

Christine Berberich

Where there is no narrative, there is no history.

Benedetto Croce (qtd in White 1987: 28)

How do we learn 'history'? When do 'memories' become 'history' and, as such, change from something that is individual, personal, to something that is a collective property, part of general knowledge or a history curriculum? These are questions that have occupied historians for decades; but they are also issues that have been dealt with in literature over many years, and increasingly so from the 1990s onwards. Particularly noteworthy in this context is the rise of historiographical metafiction that self-consciously problematises the very processes of history writing and that has highlighted a certain overlap between the writing of history and the writing of fiction. Linda Hutcheon has pointed out the seemingly paradoxical juxtaposition of the 'self-reflexive and the historically grounded' (Hutcheon 2003: 2) in postmodern historical fiction that distinguishes itself through an obsession 'with the question of how we can come to know the past today' (2003: 44). This chapter offers an assessment of historiographical thinking and its potentially very close links to the processes of fiction writing. It briefly introduces key figures involved in the debate – such as Hayden White and Linda Hutcheon – and then offers a more detailed reading of the historiographical theories proposed by the Dutch historian Frank Ankersmit. The chapter concludes with a detailed discussion of two recent examples of 'factional/fictional' writing on the Holocaust and its aftermath – Patrick Modiano's *The Search Warrant* of 1997 (first English translation 2000) and Laurent Binet's novel *HHhH* of 2009 (first English translation 2012). The Holocaust, as will be shown, further challenges theories of historiography and narrative as it still is an emotionally and ethically highly charged topic with historians, critics and writers alike walking a fine and closely observed line between pushing the boundaries of scholarship on the one hand, and being accused of dealing with a sensitive topic in an unethical manner on the other. Both Modiano and Binet, I shall argue, do indeed push the boundaries of conventional writing on the events of the Shoah by producing highly self-reflexive pieces of work that continuously question their respective research, their motivation for writing, and their narrative strategies.

To start with, however, I would like to briefly look at a novel that is *not* a historical one per se – but one that admirably serves to highlight the inherent problems involved in teaching, writing and interpreting history. Julian Barnes's *England England* of 1998 ostensibly focuses on nation building and the creation of national identity. Yet it starts with its protagonist Martha Cochrane recalling her history lessons as a series of rhythmic chants, learnt by heart and recited endlessly in class:

> 55BC (clap clap) Roman Invasion
> 1066 (clap clap) Battle of Hastings
> 1215 (clap clap) Magna Carta
> 1512 (clap clap) Henry the Eighth (clap clap)
>   Defender of Faith (clap clap)
> [. . .]
> 1940 (clap clap) Battle of Britain
> 1973 (clap clap) Treaty of Rome (Barnes 1998: 11)

This rhyme has inscribed itself deeply into her memory and, many years later, the adult Martha ponders that it was, in particular, its combination of rhyming and clapping that made it easier to memorise the historical dates and events in the rhyme. Ultimately, though, these history lessons, with their straightforward 'date/event' approach, were a failure. They admittedly taught her, and seemingly indelibly so, important 'facts' – but the rhythmic intonation when reciting them did not leave time to query, or space to think what these dates and events actually represent. For Martha, this becomes an issue years later, when she realises that she and her Spanish flatmate have 'different' versions of history about Sir Francis Drake: for Martha, still intoning her school-learnt 'date/event' rhymes, he was a hero and a gentleman; for her Spanish friend, he was 'a pirate'. Martha realises that 'one person's plundering privateer might be another person's pirate' (Barnes 1998: 7), and that history writing, by extension, depends on circumstances, on background, on cultural and political outlooks. Barnes's novel thus reflects the very questions that historians had, at that point, been debating for some time: how should historical events be represented? How should they be taught?

According to the historian Hayden White, there are 'three basic kinds of historical representation – the annals, the chronicle, and the history proper' (White 1987: 4) – the annals presenting a year-by-year account of events, the chronicle the attempt of a 'story' about events, and the 'history proper' an additional measured narrative and, importantly, interpretation of the events depicted. For White, both annals and chronicle can only ever offer an incomplete account of history as they fail 'to attain to full narrativity of the events of which they treat' (1987: 4). Similarly, Peter Gay has commented that 'Historical narration without analysis is trivial, historical analysis without narration is incomplete' (Gay 1974: 189). Comments such as these suggest that successful history writing needs to involve a narrative that interprets the depicted events for the reader. According to White, 'History proper' can only ever be achieved through a combination of annals, chronology and respectful handling of sources – and an additional narrative component, an attempt to provide the mere facts and events with a 'structure, an order of meaning, that they do not possess as mere sequence' (White 1987: 5).

However, history, to White, does generally not happen like a story (see White 1987: 4) and while the narrative of any historical discourse 'transforms . . . a list of historical events that would otherwise be only a chronicle' into a story, this transformation can only be achieved through inserting potentially problematic 'story elements' (1987: 43). The result is, according to White, that 'any historical object can sustain a number of equally plausible descriptions or narratives of its processes' (1987: 76). This very attempt to structure historical events and turn them into a more graspable narrative invests them, inevitably, with a personal interpretation. Turning historical events into 'stories' narrativises them and blurs the line between the idea of history as a strictly fact-based 'science' on the one hand, and 'narrative', often associated with the creative, the fictional, on the other. If we refer back to the example from Barnes's *England England*, we can see that Martha learns the mere 'annals' in school, a chronological listing of important dates and events. The different approaches to Sir Francis Drake that she and her friend argue over represent the chronicle – the attempt to narrativise a historical figure or event. What is consequently required, in order to fully engage with history, is the critical narrative assessment of the 'facts' and 'historical evidence', the interpretative evaluation of various sources; a version that, in the case of the Drake example, takes in both sides of the story and allows for the fact that the national hero actually also *was* a plundering privateer.

While White has been among the forerunners in academic debate about the link between history writing and narrative, the following discussion will focus on the work of the Flemish historian and philosopher Frank Ankersmit whose work not only responds to White's but takes it further. In groundbreaking works such as *The Reality Effect in the Writing of History* (1989), *History and Tropology: The Rise and Fall of the Metaphor* (1994) and *Historical Representation* (2001), Ankersmit has extended White's debate on the importance of narrative in the writing of history to the point of actively challenging traditional conceptions of history writing. Ankersmit's provocative statement 'the past is how we represent it' (Ankersmit 1988: 222) serves as a thought-provoking opening for this debate: it challenges long-held beliefs that history is objective, impartial and always providing a detached overview and, instead, focuses on the fact that the past can be – and is – manipulated through the very narrative used to depict it: the historian's background, political outlook or social engagements will, inevitably, colour his or her presentation of historical events. Meticulous research of what there is of historical evidence is still a given, and established 'facts' are scrupulously adhered to; but the accompanying narrative, the evaluation of them, is more subjective, and openly acknowledges that. For Ankersmit, this is best summed up with the term 'narrative substance':

> [a] set of statements that together embody the representation of the past that is proposed in the historical narrative in question. Thus, the statements of an historical narrative not only describe the past: they also individuate, or define, the nature of such a narrative substance. (Ankersmit 1988: 219)

This brings the individual into the writing of history: history writing becomes more subjective and personalised, which, ultimately, leads to not just one, overarching metanarrative of the past but a variety of narratives, a variety of pasts. Not *the* historical truth but historical *truths* that can, and do, contradict each other and that do, in the process, engage in dialogue with each other. For Ankersmit, 'historical representations are not so much contradicted by historical reality itself but by other historical representations' (Ankersmit 1988: 222) – which leads us back, neatly, to the various interpretations of Sir Francis Drake in Julian Barnes's *England England*: different sides of the same story.

But while we might consider these statements and ideas logical and seemingly commonsensical, they also harbour inherent dangers. As Ankersmit himself points out in his article 'Historiography and Postmodernism', 'we no longer have any texts, any past, but just interpretations of them' (Ankersmit 1989: 137). For some critics, this might be seen as opening the past up to an ever-increasing variety of interpretations which might, ultimately, lead to a side-lining of the 'real' events reminiscent of Baudrillard's postmodern hyperreality. Pre-empting this critique, the postmodern literary theorist Linda Hutcheon points out that 'it is not that representation now dominates or effaces the referent, but rather that it now self-consciously acknowledges its existence as representation – that is, as interpreting (indeed as creating) its referent, not as offering direct and immediate access to it' (Hutcheon 2003: 32). Hutcheon thus acknowledges the possibility of various accounts and interpretations of the same historical events, and for Ankersmit it is this very diversity of historical narrative and interpretation that enriches historiography. In line with postmodern thought that rejects one overarching truth or metanarrative in favour of many different truths and narratives, Ankersmit, too, finds that 'historical interpretations of the past first become recognizable, they first acquire their identity, through the contrast with *other* interpretations; they are what they are only on the basis of what they are *not*' (Ankersmit 1989: 142). The historical researcher, consequently, offers his or her own interpretation of a past event based on historical sources and evidence and by carefully comparing and contrasting alternative narratives of the same events. In this approach to history, 'the past', a seemingly stable entity, becomes destabilised and is no longer a firm referent because, as Ankersmit points out, we can 'never test our conclusions by comparing the elected text with "the past" itself' (Ankersmit 1990: 281). The past is gone; all that is left are competing narratives of it.

What some historians welcome and celebrate, others find disturbing and problematic, however. Some readers and critics might still persevere that this approach to history writing harbours some problems: and even Ankersmit himself is quick to query what we should do if 'we have two or more historical texts on roughly the same historical topic and we wish to decide between them' (Ankersmit 1990: 281). What are readers supposed to base their judgements on? Can a convincing historical narrative not simply 'seduce' its readers and potentially, and very dangerously, mislead through a blatant *mis*interpretation of the past?

This potential for misinterpretation has been particularly hotly debated in the context of Holocaust historiography, scholarship and narrative. The deeply traumatic events of the Shoah are still within living memory and, as such, need to be covered ethically and sensitively in order to avoid upsetting survivors and their families or relatives of victims. For years, leading historians such as Berel Lang, Saul Friedlander, James E. Young and many others have argued over the 'correct' way of depicting the history of the Holocaust – which also, incidentally, extends into fictional engagement with the events of the Shoah. Berel Lang, one of the most outspoken critics of *narrative* engagement with the Holocaust in any form or shape (which, for him, includes over-narrativisation of historical accounts), refers to 'the Holocaust's special representational status' (Lang 1995: 85) as an event that defies all attempts to suitably describe, let alone narrate it. For him, only a very detached and objective stating of 'facts' is appropriate when talking about the Holocaust. Other historians and critics, by contrast, emphasise the role of personal memory in writing on the Shoah. Both groups of scholars speak out *against* more creative, or even fictional narratives of the Holocaust, fearing that they might open the door for Holocaust deniers. Ankersmit himself is acutely aware that

> writing about the Holocaust requires tact and a talent for knowing when and how to avoid the pitfalls of the inappropriate. Each discussion of the Holocaust is in danger of getting involved in a vicious circle where misunderstanding and immorality mutually suggest and reinforce each other. (Ankersmit 1997: 62)

Nevertheless, he also warns that a traditional historical discourse is not effective in writing about the Holocaust. He explains that

> history, and the discourse of history aim at describing and explaining the past. . . . The historian typically realizes this aim by reducing what was initially strange, alien and incomprehensible in the past to what was known to us already. (Ankersmit 1997: 63)

In the case of the Shoah, however, there is no 'already well-known and well-established pattern of human behaviour from which we can derive the Holocaust' (Ankersmit 1997: 63): in an event so outside of what is deemed 'normal human behaviour', traditional modes of description fail and, in the words of Saul Friedlander, the 'limits of representation' are reached (see Friedlander 1992a). In the words of Holocaust survivor Elie Wiesel (otherwise a staunch supporter of the need for personal memory in Holocaust historiography), this results in the need to 'invent a new language' (Wiesel 2008: viii–ix).

For Ankersmit, these 'limits of representation' are particularly problematic because, in his opinion, historians have constructed 'complex linguistic signs . . . for relating words to things in the case of . . . specific part[s] of the past' (Ankersmit 1990: 282). The examples he lists include '"the Industrial Revolution" or "the Cold War"' (1990: 280), terms that have been developed out of historical interpretation with hindsight, 'semantic convention[s] *proposed* by the historian . . . for connecting things with words' (1990: 282). We could add here that these 'linguistic signs' or 'semantic conventions' were introduced in order to make a historical period or series of interlinking events more graspable; adding a label to something makes it more tangible, easier to talk about and compartmentalise. It almost becomes a code that, 'in historical narrative . . . tend[s] to act as a "substitute" or "replacement" for (part of) the past *itself*' (1990: 290). Add to this list of semantic conventions the term 'the Holocaust', however, and we immediately see the danger inherent to this 'codification' of the past. According to the Israeli political sociologist Ronit Lentin, '"holocaust", with capital H . . . [is a euphemism], standing for something that one does not want to hear mentioned' (Lentin 2004: 6). For Lentin, this kind of code 'does not help us remember the Shoah and its victims, but rather erases that memory, as do other representations . . . but also history itself' (2004: 6). What is required, consequently, are new forms of engagement with the events of the Holocaust that do not aim to provide the 'bigger picture', the grand, overarching historical metanarrative, but that, instead, focus on the smaller scale, the more personal, offering a variety of perspectives and assessments.

For Friedlander, the success of such new forms of representation lies in the fact that they 'test implicit boundaries and . . . raise not only aesthetic and intellectual problems, but moral issues, too' (Friedlander 1992b: 2). For Ankersmit, one such way forward could be the *narrativist* approach to history writing: the clear recognition that 'the historians' narrative had its foundations in the results of historical research' and their honest acknowledgement that 'these results had to be integrated in some way or other into a historical text' (Ankersmit 2000: 292). This is where, for Ankersmit, there is a clear link between history writing and postmodern literary theory, and especially the work of critics such as Linda Hutcheon. In *The Politics of Postmodernism*, Hutcheon points out that in postmodern historiographic writing,

the narrativization of past events is not hidden; the events no longer
seem to speak for themselves, but are shown to be consciously
composed into a narrative, whose constructed – not found – order is
imposed upon them, often overtly by the narrating figure. (Hutcheon
2003: 63)

Hutcheon refers to this kind of writing as 'historiographic metafiction' and
explains that it does not only represent 'just a world of fiction, however self-
consciously presented as a constructed one, but also a world of public experience' (Hutcheon 2003: 34). Progressive historians and postmodern literary
critics alike thus stress the importance of self-reflexive (history) writing that
highlights the very problematics involved in the writing process and where
'writing history' comes close to 'making history' – to structuring the past into
a narrative that is aware of its own constructed narrativity.

In recent fiction writing on the Second World War, the Holocaust and their
aftermaths, this is a particularly prominent trend. The best-known writer in
this tradition is probably W. G. Sebald with his genre-defying accounts of exile
and emigration, with his attempts to create and perpetuate memories of those
who would have remained name- and faceless in the 'bigger picture' of and
'grand-narrative' approach to history. Sebald's intricate narratives that avoid
direct speech in favour of multi-levelled indirect speech show up the difficulty
inherent in constructing historical narratives when the witnesses of history
can no longer speak out for themselves. Another example is Jonathan Littell's
hugely controversial *Les Bienveillantes* of 2006 (published in English as *The
Kindly Ones* in 2009). Littell's novel offers nearly a thousand pages of fictionalised narrative from the perspective of an SS perpetrator that is, however,
deeply steeped in meticulous historical research, often referencing specific texts
of established Holocaust historiography, such as, for instance, Christopher
Browning's *Ordinary Men*. Littell's novel pushes the boundaries of traditional
Holocaust writing through its unflinching, graphic accounts of violence and its
seemingly unapologetic perpetrator-narrator whose repeated claims that 'I am
a man like other men, I am a man like you. I tell you, I am just like you' (Littell
2009: 24) immediately alienate the reader. Yet, simultaneously, they also serve
to, in the words of Emily Miller Budick, 'hold up a dark, distorted, and yet
frighteningly revealing mirror to the field of Holocaust studies itself' (Budick
2015: 15). Texts such as *The Kindly Ones* thus further the field of Holocaust
studies by providing new, albeit very challenging, insights, offering new perspectives and, in particular, by making readers question their own motivations
behind reading such texts.

The following debate, however, will focus on two different texts: Patrick
Modiano's *The Search Warrant* and Laurent Binet's *HHhH*. Both texts deal
with the Holocaust and its aftermath – but in an indirect way. Rather than
focusing on the 'bigger picture' of the Final Solution, or perpetuating images of
camps and persecution that have almost become 'staples' in Holocaust writing,

both authors focus on the small scale, on, in Ankersmit's words, 'micro-stories' that stand out through their 'anecdotal character' (Ankersmit 1988: 227ff.). Modiano's narrative opens with the reproduction of a missing person notice found in a copy of *Paris Soir* from 31 December 1941 that seeks information on the disappearance of fifteen-year-old Dora Bruder. The unnamed first-person narrator makes it clear that, ever since first setting eyes on this notice it has stayed with and preoccupied him, interweaving with his own life and, ultimately, resulting in an increasingly obsessive search to find out more information about Dora Bruder who, the final pages of the book reveal, was deported from the detention camp of Drancy to Auschwitz on 18 September 1942, and who perished there. *HHhH*, by contrast, focuses on a similarly obsessive search: Laurent Binet's self-confessed aim in writing his novel is to provide a history of the often-overlooked heroes of Czechoslovak resistance, Jozef Gabčík and Jan Kubiš, who assassinated the Reich Protektor Reinhard Heydrich in Prague in 1942. However, during the course of the account, Heydrich, the 'Blonde Beast', the 'Butcher of Prague', increasingly takes over the narrative. Binet explains that 'Heydrich is the target, not the protagonist' but simultaneously admits that 'in literary terms Heydrich is a wonderful character' (Binet 2012: ch. 88). Binet thus problematises the actual scope of his book: he *wants* to write a historical narrative, and *not* a novel. In fact, he starts his account with a condemnation of 'the veneer of fiction' (Binet 2012: ch. 1) but also shows his awareness of the narrativity of history: 'The story, I mean. History' (Binet 2012: ch. 2). The word 'story' is thus shown to be an integral and vital component of the word 'history' itself – no official *history* without the multifarious *stories* that make it up. Both texts are admirable examples of historiographical metafiction, and both authors make it very clear from the outset of their accounts that the historical events they are trying to piece together have affected them personally – that they are trying to base their narratives on historical evidence painstakingly pieced together but that this evidence, inevitably, will be affected by their subjective interpretation of it. Importantly, their self-reflexive agonising over their respective research and writing strategies forms an integral part of their narratives that highlights the problems involved in *any* form of history writing and that suggests, ultimately, that history *writing* equates history *making*.

Modiano's search for the history of Dora Bruder is one deeply steeped in his contemporary Paris where he obsessively walks the same neighbourhoods she would have spent parts of her life in, and where he tries to find traces of her in former residences or schools. This approach to history might be useful in the case of a famous person, somebody who has entered the official historical discourse: blue plaques on houses, for instance, announce to the world which famous resident once used to live there, and how long for; streets might be renamed in historical hindsight to honour birthplaces of national heroes. Not so, however, in the case of a perfectly ordinary person who has not entered the history books. Modiano ponders that Dora Bruder and her parents 'are the sort of people who leave few traces. Virtually anonymous' (Modiano 2014: 23). He is again and again confronted with a dearth of evidence about Dora: school registers have disappeared, or he is confronted with bureaucratic red tape that refuses him access because he is not a family member. Modiano's response is pragmatic:

> It takes time for what has been erased to resurface. Traces survive in registers, and nobody knows where these registers are hidden, and who has custody of them, and whether or not their custodians are willing to let you see them. Or perhaps they have simply forgotten that such registers exist. (Modiano 2014: 9)

'Patience' and 'persistence' thus become the key words for the historical researcher and the writer of historical narratives who both want to unearth previously unknown *truths* about the past – 'It took me four years to discover her exact date of birth', Modiano writes, and 'I am a patient man' (Modiano 2014: 10).

His attempts to situate Dora Bruder within the topography of wartime occupied Paris have a further dimension: the locations of where she lived are *real*, are tangible, they are places that he can access, and they thus juxtapose his lack of knowledge in other respects. In Modiano's words, 'such topographical precision contrasts with what we shall never know about their life – this blank, this mute block of the unknown' (Modiano 2014: 23). His search for details about Dora Bruder's life thus becomes a detective's quest for historical jigsaw pieces – but, in this case, a jigsaw that cannot ever be complete. Certain elements, certain facts, will always remain missing, having been lost, irrevocably. Modiano asks 'How can one know?' (2014: 18), or repeatedly admits, 'I don't know' (2014: 36, 78, 82), 'I have no means of knowing' (2014: 19), 'we have no idea' (2014: 83) and 'I am reduced to conjecture' (2014: 36), thus acknowledging the fact that, no matter how hard he tries, he will never know for certain what exactly happened in Dora's life. Historical evidence can clearly tell *a* part of *a* story. But it can never fill all the gaps.

Laurent Binet's *HHhH* is similarly punctured by his personal frustration of not being able to know the exact order of events and all the facts connected to the historical events he wants to present. 'I haven't been able to find out', he points out early on in his novel (Binet 2012: ch. 23), and he repeatedly admits, 'I don't know' (2012: chs 34, 84, 140) and 'I have been talking rubbish' (2012: ch. 35). Interestingly, *HHhH* is also presented to the reader without traditional pagination but consisting, instead, of 257 chapters, some of them comprising just a few words or lines, others spanning several pages. The lack of page numbers and the seemingly idiosyncratic 'chapterisation' (for want of another word) might thus be a subliminal message from Binet that historical chronology is not straightforward and 'naturally' given, as might be assumed, but always a result of careful (read here: subjective) construction. And although he tries to offer a reasonably straightforward narrative account of the events leading up to Heydrich's assassination, his narrative is interspersed with retrospective insertions, seemingly unnecessary tangents and self-reflexive accounts on the benefit of historical hindsight and the problem of ascertaining historical 'facts'.

In his quest to provide a factually accurate account of not only the assassination but the run-up to it, Binet, like Modiano, tries to situate himself in the location where the events took place: he lives and researches in Prague, he repeatedly returns to the City during the course of writing his book. Like Modiano, whose claim, 'I had long been familiar with the area around the Boulevard Ornano [where the Bruder family lived when Dora disappeared in December 1941]' (Modiano 2014: 3) starts *The Search Warrant*, Binet likewise opens his narrative with the statement 'I know Prague well' (Binet 2012: ch. 1). Yet, in the long run, these certainties do not help to fill all the gaps in his knowledge. Cities change over the years; new research findings lead to his revisiting Prague with 'new eyes', discovering new evidence in streets or buildings he had previously not noticed. Yet both Modiano and Binet use their respective topographical knowledge to imbue their narratives with a sense of realism, of certainty to assure their readers that, although they might not know *all* the facts, they *do*, at least, know the locations of their described events well.

For Binet, 'realism' plays an important part in historical writing. Early on in his account, he triumphantly announces that 'the good thing about writing a true story is that you don't have to worry about giving an impression of realism' (Binet 2012: ch. 20). What this means is that, in the initial stages of writing his account, he still believes that the very 'facts' he presents also convey a sense of reality, that they do, effectively, speak for themselves. Yet, in the course of his research, Binet begins to realise that historical 'certainties' are open to subjectivity and interpretation and thus shift and change in meaning. One pertinent example for this is his repeated reference to Heydrich's 'black Mercedes' (2012: chs 6, 44, 108) which he has also seen on display in Prague's Army Museum (2012: ch. 8). During his research, however, he comes across two historical novels on the assassination – David Chacko's *Like a Man* and Alan Burgess's *Seven Men at Daybreak* – that both claim the colour of the Mercedes was green. What might, effectively, be an entirely irrelevant historical detail becomes an obsession for Binet who 'suddenly . . . start[s] questioning' himself (2012: ch. 155). His research-based certainty – 'But this Mercedes – it was black, I'm sure. Not only in the army museum at Prague . . . but also in the numerous photos that I checked' (2012: ch. 155) – is suddenly confronted with differing historical interpretations: both Chacko and Burgess, historical novelists just like Binet himself, have interpreted the historical evidence differently, or unearthed a historical source unknown to Binet that specifies the colour as green rather than black. As Ankersmit points out, 'Texts are all we have and we can only compare texts with texts' (Ankersmit 1990: 281) – but this can bring with it its very own problems if texts differ substantially in content. In Binet's case, this constant and obsessive comparison with other historical texts and assessment of personal interpretations of evidence complicates his own research and his commitment to providing a fact-based, realist, dispassionate account of the assassination of Heydrich; effectively, it also hampers his account's progression and highlights that, at some point, he will have to make a decision as to how to depict the Mercedes: black or green.

This seemingly insignificant detail, however, is, in fact, part of a larger discussion as to the differences between historical and fictional writing, the different styles and narrative registers required. Binet consistently blurs the line between the two genres he tries to straddle – producing a straightforward historical account one moment ('It's July 31, 1941, and we are present at the Birth of the Final Solution' (Binet 2012: ch. 108)), and a highly narrativised and imagined one the next ('That scene . . . is perfectly believable and totally made up' (2012: ch. 91)). His initial belief that 'to begin with, this seemed a simple enough story to tell' (2012: ch. 175) begins to waver.

Throughout *HHhH*, there are distinct and very different narrative registers that clearly seem to reflect Hayden White's differentiation of history writing into annals, chronology and history proper. The 'annals' are represented through a number of quasi-paratextual insertions: a speech by Hitler about the Sudetenland from 26 September 1938 (Binet 2012: ch. 61); a proclamation made by him from 16 March 1939 (2012: ch. 86); the verbatim authorisation for the Final Solution of 31 July 1941 (2012: ch. 108); an 'article appearing in the specialist magazine *Gymnastics and Physical Education*' (2012: ch. 110); and a press release issued by the Czech press agency from 27 September 1941 (2012: ch. 114) among others. These text fragments convey mere facts and/or dates, without any kind of elaboration. In some cases, Binet offers a brief explanatory sentence – which could be seen as an attempt at a chronicle, providing a brief explication for these inclusions: when quoting from a programme for a musical soirée that Heydrich himself had written, he contextualises this programme and highlights the poor style it is written in (2012: ch. 209).

However, things become problematic for Binet when trying to attempt the 'history proper', the assessment, evaluation and narrativisation of real historical events. At those points, his narrative register changes completely – he builds suspense, language becomes flowery. Chapter 105 ends with Heydrich's plane crash behind enemy lines in Russia; the following chapter starts with the evocative words 'Himmler looks like someone's just smacked him in the face. The blood rises to his cheeks and he feels his brain swell inside his skull' (Binet 2012: ch. 106). Gone are Binet's declaration about factuality and realism – the assumption that Himmler turned purple is pure conjecture on his part. Yet, in the obsessively self-reflexive manner of his writing, Binet immediately confronts his own slip in style in the following chapter that sees his girlfriend chastise him for 'making [things] up' (2012: ch. 107). His response to her criticism is worth quoting in full as it illustrates the problems faced by writers of history but also those of 'factual' fiction:

> I have been boring her for years with my theories about the puerile, ridiculous nature of novelistic invention, and she's right, I suppose, not to let me get away with this skull thing. I thought I'd decided to avoid this kind of stuff, which has, a priori, no virtue other than giving a bit of colour to the story, and which is rather ugly. And even if there

are clues to Himmler's panicked reaction, I can't really be sure of the symptoms of this panic: perhaps he went red (that's how I imagine it), but then again, perhaps he turned white. This is quite a serious problem. (Binet 2012: ch. 107)

Binet juxtaposes his commitment to 'factuality' with his – in his opinion, lamentable – inability to refrain from producing a captivating story (read here: a story with fictionalised elements and elaborate language). Although he labels his own conjecture – the red face, the swelling brain of Himmler – as 'ugly', he knows that, ultimately, they help to create suspense.

Binet's obsessive preoccupation with his own writing style might, in the long run, simply irritate those readers who expect a more straightforward, factual account of events surrounding the assassination of Heydrich. In fact, the critic Leyla Sanai, writing in *The Independent*, complained that 'his interjections [obstruct] the flow of a mesmerizing true story' (Sanai 2012). But it is these very interjections that add value to Binet's account and elevate it from a mere historical narrative to a text problematising the nature of history writing: what is the best language to use? Is there such a thing as a straightforwardly historical discourse? In *The Politics of Postmodernism*, Hutcheon points out the 'overt self-consciousness about language and (his)story' (Hutcheon 2003: 6) to be found in postmodern historiographical metafiction, and this obsession with language and its effects can be seen clearly in Binet's dedication of another full page to his attempts to resolve the dilemma about his depiction of Himmler's face: 'The next day, I delete the sentence. Unfortunately, that creates an emptiness that I don't like. . . . I feel obliged to replace the deleted sentence with another, more *prudent* one' (Binet 2012: ch. 107). My emphasis here is on the word 'prudent', which highlights Binet's acute awareness (and fear?) of the fact that these more fictionalised passages in his text might detract from its overall factuality. Yet they are, in my reading, a confirmation of Hutcheon's claim that self-reflexive historical fiction that involves the author's actual writing process 'focuses attention on the act of imposing order on that past, of encoding strategies of meaning making through representation' (Hutcheon 2003: 63). For Binet, it is an important component of the actual story to highlight Himmler's shock at Heydrich's crash. A sentence such as 'Himmler was upset' does not do justice to how Binet himself imagined the scene. As he cannot know the exact facts of this moment, his 'tyrannic imagination', as he terms it (Binet 2012: ch. 107), takes over – and, after much deliberation, he retypes the words 'The blood rises to his cheeks and he feels his brain swell inside his skull' (2012: ch. 107). In some cases, only imaginative elaboration can bring historical moments to life.

Binet's narrative slowly builds towards the actual assassination of Heydrich, an event he looks towards with considerable trepidation. Once again, he is aware that over-narrativisation of the event can ruin his account. Early on, he confides:

that night, I dreamed that I wrote the chapter about the assassination, and it began: 'A black Mercedes slid along the road like a snake.' That's when I understood that I had to start writing the rest of the story, because the rest of the story had to converge at this crucial episode. By pursuing the chain of causality back into infinity, I allowed myself to keep delaying the moment when I must face the novel's bravura moment, its scene of scenes. (Binet 2012: ch. 46)

This quote is noteworthy for a number of reasons: it highlights Binet's obsessive preoccupation with his topic that even pursues him into his dreams. It illustrates the fact that, like most researchers, he is prone to delay the actual writing in the quest for yet more – and often only tangible – information: 'Everything I read takes me farther and farther away from the curve in Holešovice Street' (Binet 2012: ch. 215). But, importantly, it also shows a linguistic slip as this is one of the few instances when Binet openly refers to his book as a 'novel' rather than a historical and purely factual account. These fictional additions and stylistic elaborations increase as the novel works towards its climax – the day of the assassination.

Chapter 206 sees yet another shift in narrative register to include evocative language such as 'the moment is getting closer, I can feel it. The Mercedes is on its way. It's coming . . . I hear the engine of the Mercedes as it glides along the road' (Binet 2012: ch. 206), comments that are echoed repeatedly later on: 'Heydrich's Mercedes snakes along the thread of its knotted destiny' (2012: ch. 215); 'A black Mercedes glides along the road – I can see it' (2012: ch. 215). Binet knows that this is the crucial scene of his novel, depicting an event that was witnessed by many bystanders and that has already attracted many rival accounts. For him, the black (or dark green?) Mercedes serves as a metaphor to build suspense, to guide his reader towards this all-important moment.

The closer Binet gets to the events of the assassination, the more he slips into an overtly fictionalised narrative. Gone is the mere listing of historical events. Instead he utilises a variety of narrative ploys in order to build and maintain suspense; the 'gliding' or 'snaking' Mercedes is just one of them. The actual moment of the assassination is a case in point. After meticulously setting the scene in the preceding chapters – Gabčík and Kubiš waiting initially in vain and increasingly anxious in their designated spots, Heydrich's Mercedes actually speeding (rather than 'snaking') along the road – he opens a new chapter with the melodramatic words 'He fires and nothing happens', which are immediately followed by 'I can't resist cheap literary effects' (Binet 2012: ch. 218). This sentence shows, in Hutcheon's words, 'postmodern fiction in its paradoxical confrontation of self-consciously fictive and resolutely historical representation' (Hutcheon 2003: 63): Gabčík did, indeed, fire and his English-made Sten gun really did jam. These are the 'resolutely historical facts'. But Binet's narrative register is anything but purely factual; instead he uses language often found in sensation fiction, keeping his readers on tenterhooks. This is representative of what Hutcheon refers to as the habitual crossing of 'the borders between high art and mass and popular culture and those between the discourses of art and the discourse of the world (especially history)' (Hutcheon 2003: 33). Binet's language fluctuates between traditional historical *de*tachment and deeply personal *at*tachment; it merges the official propaganda language of Nazi speeches with the sensationalist language of a penny dreadful. The result is a carefully constructed narrative that manages to convey many different angles, perspectives, assessments and interpretations all at once.

The biggest problem for both Binet and Modiano appears to be the fact that they cannot ask their historical characters for authentication or verification of their respective narratives. Binet, for instance, notes on several occasions: 'I would pay dearly to feel what they felt then' (Binet 2012: ch. 206) and 'If only I could have been inside his head at this precise instant. I am absolutely convinced I would have enough material to fill hundreds of pages. But I wasn't, and I don't have the faintest idea what he felt' (2012: ch. 218). Merging historical facts with his own creative interpretations, however, allows him certain liberties: in what is by far the longest and most openly narrativised chapter in his book (2012: ch. 222) he imagines himself, in turn, in the heads of Gabčík, Kubiš and Heydrich during the actual moments of the assassination. And while these presented 'thoughts' might not correspond to a historical reality we will never know about, they at least offer *one possible interpretation* of events.

Modiano, by contrast, ends his narrative on this very note of historical uncertainty, on the very 'not knowing' of the precise movements of Dora Bruder prior to her deportation. His final paragraph reflects:

> I shall never know how she spent her days, where she hid, in whose company she passed the winter months of her first escape, or the few weeks of spring when she escaped for the second time. That is her secret. A poor and precious secret which not even the executioners, the decrees, the occupying authorities, the Dépôt, the barracks, the camps, history, time – everything that corrupts and destroys you – have been able to take away from her. (Modiano 2014: 137)

Unlike Binet, Modiano does not imagine, nor interpret. Instead, though, he ends on a typically postmodern open-ended note that rejects all notion of omniscient narration and final closure. He recounts the 'facts' as he unearths them; he philosophises about his search processes; he offers interpretations of the few facts he finds. But where he finds 'nothing', he does not invent, or elaborate. Instead, just as Binet in other instances, he occasionally tries to merge his own life with that of his historical character. He compares his own teenage attempts at running away to those of Dora Bruder decades earlier (see Modiano 2014: 52) in order to provide a potential explanation for Dora's act, and professes that he feels 'haunted' by her:

ever since, the Paris wherein I have tried to retrace her steps has remained as silent and deserted as it was on that day. I walk through empty streets. For me, they are always empty, even at dusk, during the rush-hour, when the crowds are hurrying towards the mouths of the metro. I think of her in spite of myself, sensing an echo of her presence in this neighbourhood or that. (Modiano 2014: 137)

His obsessive search for details about Dora's largely unchronicled life leads him to see clues and hints of her existence wherever he looks. But it also leaves him feeling empty and dissatisfied, aware that his search has only been partially successful and that Dora is one of all too many forgotten victims of history who do not have a memorial to their suffering.

What both authors ultimately do is push the boundaries of existing Holocaust writing – both fictional and historical – in that they both offer highly personalised and partly fictionalised accounts of events that did not affect them personally when they happened and that they have no familial connection to. Their challenges to the genre of postmodern historiographical metafiction lies in their constant blurring of the fine line between fact and fiction – which, in the eyes of Holocaust scholars, is a potentially dangerous thing. Importantly, for both authors, writing their texts has become a mission. Modiano declares: 'In writing this book I am sending out signals' (Modiano 2014: 37) – signals, perhaps, for other writers to imaginatively create histories for those people who did not survive the horrors of the Holocaust to speak for themselves; signals to his readers to come forward should they have historical information they previously considered unimportant. Binet, in turn, philosophises:

I hope I can be forgiven. I hope they can forgive me. I am doing all of this for them. I had to start up the black Mercedes – that wasn't easy. I had to put everything into place, take care of the preparations. I had to spin the web of this adventure, erect the gallows of the Resistance, cover death's hideous iron fist in the sumptuous velvet glove of the struggle. (Binet 2012: ch. 206)

The historical facts, for him, are at the heart of his narrative, his aim is to do justice to the often overlooked heroes Gabčík and Kubiš. But he realises that his means of creating a 'monument' to his heroes are different from a purely historical account, that, for him, the way towards depicting their story, the very writing processes and narrative elaborations, is part of the journey. Both authors thus engage with, as Hayden White terms it, 'the problem of the relation between narrative discourse and historical representation', openly acknowledging the fact that 'narrative is not merely a neutral discursive form that may or may not be used to represent real events in their aspect as developmental processes but rather [a form that] entails ontological and epistemic choices' (White 1987: ix). In the process, both *The Search Warrant* and *HHhH* highlight the, in Hutcheon's words, 'uneasy and problematising tension that provokes an investigation of how we make meaning in culture, how we "de-doxify" the systems of meaning (and representation) by which we know our culture and ourselves' (Hutcheon 2003: 18). Both Modiano's and Binet's texts – be they called 'novels', or 'faction', 'documentary fiction' or 'historiographic metafiction' – challenge the ways we perceive the past, how we often assume the past to be a coherent entity. They highlight the fact that narratives of the past are always constructed and, as such, coloured by personal opinion, personal choices, personal agendas. They highlight not only the processes of meaning making, but the very processes of making history, or rather, making histor*ies*: not one coherent metanarrative of the past, but a series of possible micro-stories of a myriad of past*s*.

   With the final words of this chapter I would like to return to the work of Frank Ankersmit who emphasises that what we have left of the past are a plethora of clues – to be found in museums, in archives, in private attics, in excavations; to be discovered in ancient buildings, in personal correspondences, in photo albums. But these clues 'do not provide us with an experience of the past itself'; rather, they 'enable us to formulate hypotheses with regard to what the past has actually been like'. Importantly, these clues provide an 'experiential basis for constructions of the past but not for a *re*-construction of the past (as it actually has been)' (Ankersmit 1996: 48). The work of the historian – or, as in the case of the two texts under discussion here, the postmodern historical novelist – is to use the clues the past has left us and weave them into a 'plausible hypothesis' (1996: 48), into one possible interpretation of the events of the past. In the process, these different interpretations, or 'micro-stories' of the past (1996: 51) contribute to a wider, and, in the long run, more comprehensive understanding of the past.

WORKS CITED

Ankersmit, Frank (1988), 'Historical Representation', *History and Theory*, 27: 3 (October), 205–28.

Ankersmit, Frank (1989), 'Historiography and Postmodernism', *History and Theory*, 28: 2 (May), 137–53.

Ankersmit, Frank (1990), '[Historiography and Postmodernism: Reconsiderations]: Reply to Professor Zagorin', *History and Theory*, 29: 3 (October), 275–96.

Ankersmit, Frank (1996), 'Can We Experience the Past?', in Rolf Torstendahl and Irmeline Veit-Brause (eds), *History-Making: The Intellectual and Social Formation of a Discipline. Proceedings of an International Conference*, Stockholm: Kungl. Vitterhets, pp. 47–77.

Ankersmit, Frank (1997), 'Remembering the Holocaust: Mourning and Melancholia', in Pirjo Ahokas and Martine Chard-Hutchinson (eds), *Reclaiming Memory: American Representations of the Holocaust*, Turku: University of Turku Press, pp. 62–87.

Ankersmit, Frank (2000), 'The Linguistic Turn, Literary Theory and Historical Theory', *Historia*, 45: 2 (November), 271–310.

Barnes, Julian (1998), *England England*, London: Jonathan Cape.

Binet, Laurent [2009] (2012), *HHhH*, London: Vintage.

Budick, Emily Miller (2015), *The Subject of Holocaust Fiction*, Bloomington: Indiana University Press.

Friedlander, Saul (1992a), *Probing the Limits of Representation: Nazism and the 'Final Solution'*, Cambridge, MA: Harvard University Press.

Friedlander, Saul (1992b), 'Introduction', in *Probing the Limits of Representation: Nazism and the 'Final Solution'*, Cambridge, MA: Harvard University Press, pp. 1–21.

Gay, Peter (1974), *Style in History*, New York: Basic Books.

Hutcheon, Linda (2003), *The Politics of Postmodernism*, 2nd edn, London: Routledge.

Lang, Berel (1995), 'Is It Possible to Misrepresent the Holocaust?', *History and Theory*, 34: 1 (February), 84–9.

Lentin, Ronit (2004), 'Postmemory, Unsayability and the Return of the Auschwitz Code', in Ronit Lentin (ed.), *Re-Presenting the Shoah for the 21st Century*, New York: Berghahn Books, pp. 1–24.

Littell, Jonathan (2009), *The Kindly Ones*, London: Chatto & Windus.

Modiano, Patrick [1997] (2014), *The Search Warrant*, London: Harvill Secker.

Sanai, Leyla (2012), '*HHhH*, by Laurent Binet (trans. Sam Taylor)', *The Independent (Online)*, 26 May 2012, available at <http://www.independent.co.uk/arts-entertainment/books/reviews/hhhh-by-laurent-binet-trs-by-sam-taylor-7791200.html> (last accessed 14 December 2016).

White, Hayden (1987), *The Content of the Form: Narrative Discourse and Historical Representation*, Baltimore: Johns Hopkins University Press.

Wiesel, Elie (2008), *Night*, London: Penguin.

CHAPTER 8

Witnessing, Recognition and Response Ethics

Kelly Oliver

For at least the last twenty years, philosophers have attempted various strategies for reviving the Hegelian notion of recognition and redeploying it in discourses around social justice, including multiculturalism, feminism, race theory and queer theory. Hegel's master–slave dialectic may seem like an obvious place to start to analyse the oppression of one group by another. Given that Hegel is not literally talking about slaves, however, but a stage of consciousness, indeed the onset of self-consciousness, we might wonder why his notion of recognition has become so important to these contemporary discourses on oppression. One reason is that the Hegelian model of recognition proposes that self-consciousness, or in more contemporary discourse, *subjectivity*, is not autonomous and self-contained within an individual, but rather develops through relationships with others. Subjectivity is inherently inter-subjective.

Twenty years ago, theorists such as Charles Taylor, Axel Honneth, Judith Butler and Nancy Fraser used notions of recognition against liberal ideas and ideals of the autonomous individual as a starting place for social and political theory. If our subjectivity is dependent upon relations with others, then autonomy is an illusion at worst, and a construct at best. For example, Axel Honneth believes that we see ourselves as autonomous only by virtue of relations of positive recognition with others, whereas Judith Butler argues that we must give up the illusion of autonomy for survival (Butler 1997: 196). Regardless of their stand on autonomy, they both insist that subjectivity is dialogic because the subject is a response to an address from an other (Honneth 1996: 92; Butler 1993: 225). Here, I want to focus on subjectivity as a form of address and response, with and beyond recognition.

If subjectivity is fundamentally inter-subjective because it is formed through mutual recognition, then many of the assumptions of liberalism, based as they are on the notion of individual autonomy, are unfounded. Indeed, in light of mutual recognition as the basis for subjectivity, we must reconceive of what it means to decide, to act, to be free. Reinventing the very concept of freedom has been the project of some post-Hegelian theorists of recognition, especially most recently Axel Honneth (Honneth 2015).

In spite of its promise, I begin this chapter by sketching some of the possible limitations of recognition for grounding both politics and ethics. While the ideal of mutual recognition is admirable, my central argument is that in practice, recognition is experienced as conferred by the very groups and institutions responsible for withholding it in the first place. In other words, recognition is distributed according to an axis of power that is part and parcel of systems of dominance and oppression. Next, I take up more recent attempts to link recognition to vulnerability rather than to self-consciousness. I both challenge the concept of vulnerability as exclusive to, or constitutive of, humanity, on the one hand, and criticise the concept for levelling differences in levels of vulnerability, on the other. I argue that rather than constitute uniquely human subjectivity or humanity as some theorists suggest, vulnerability is shared with nonhuman animals – and this may be its advantage over recognition based on self-consciousness. Furthermore, like recognition, vulnerability is distributed according to political and social power. Some are more vulnerable than others. Making vulnerability, or recognition of vulnerability, constitutive of human subjectivity risks levelling differential vulnerability that is the result of political or social oppression (Sheth 2009). In this regard, vulnerability could be seen as the flip side of political recognition. Some people or animals are given political recognition while others are made vulnerable. And while starting with the vulnerable may be better than starting with the beneficiaries of political power, it too has its risks.

In the second part of this chapter, I propose witnessing, grounded in response ethics, as a supplement to recognition models of political and ethical subjectivity. Witnessing takes us beyond recognition to the affective and imaginative dimensions of experience, which must be added to the politics of recognition. Perhaps this is why Butler talks about recognition in terms of 'seeing as'. Seeing as requires not only re-cognition but also imagination. Avowing the suffering of others caused by my own privilege, however, requires more than cognition or even imagination. It requires pathos beyond recognition. It requires a commitment to what Jacques Derrida calls *hyperbolic ethics*, an ethics of impossible responsibilities for what we do not and cannot recognise.

Intellectual, epistemological or even political recognition is not enough to move from politics to ethics. If politics is about general principles and universal laws for the good of the whole, ethics is about the singularity of each. The question for politics today is how to bring the ethical concern for the singularity of each living being into politics. This tension between ethics and politics is at the heart of justice. The tension at the heart of this radical notion of ethics is echoed in the tension between the concrete social, historical context of situated subjects, on the one hand, and the witnessing structure of subjectivity constituted through address and response, on the other. The tension in witnessing between eyewitness testimony and bearing witness to what cannot be seen – or even seen as – is productive for thinking about the relationship between ethics and politics.

In the third part of this chapter, I argue that witnessing is a process of address and response that radicalises Hegel's insight that subjectivity is constituted inter-subjectively. Discussing the double meaning of witnessing as both eyewitness testimony and bearing witness to what cannot be seen, I develop a tension at the heart of subjectivity that opens up the possibility of considering both the social-political context, on the one hand, and the inter-subjective constitution of subjectivity, on the other. In conclusion, I relate witnessing and response ethics to an ethics of earth grounded on our shared bond to our singular home, planet earth. Rather than start with our recognition of ourselves as self-conscious human beings, or recognition of our shared vulnerability as human beings, I ask what happens when we see ourselves as earthlings who exist by virtue of our ability to respond to the call of others, including our environments. Moving beyond the humanism of most theories of mutual recognition of either self-consciousness or vulnerability, I argue for a response ethics grounded on our singular shared bond to the earth. Witnessing as ongoing address and response between earthlings and their environments cannot be reduced to recognition, mutual or otherwise.

SOME LIMITATIONS OF RECOGNITION

While I appreciate the critique of liberalism involved in contemporary theories of recognition, and while I endorse the inter-subjective nature of subjectivity, I find the notion of recognition problematic on several levels. First, it is imperative to consider the political and social context of recognition, something that Hegel himself did not do in the *Phenomenology of Spirit* when he developed the notion of mutual recognition. And while his followers have attempted to consider social context, especially thinkers like Honneth, Butler and Fraser, adherence to the concept of recognition can limit the flexibility of a theory to accommodate the complexities of inter-subjectivity, especially the interrelationships between subjects and their environments. For example, Alessandro Ferrara criticises Honneth for focusing on only the family and political institutions rather than on educational institutions or churches, which he contends are as important in the formation of values (Ferrara 2015). Second, in practice, recognition rarely, if ever, attains the ideal of mutual recognition. Rather, it is conferred by one individual, group or institution on another individual or group. And, as such, it can become a symptom of oppression rather than its cure. This means that marginalised individuals or groups must seek recognition from the very people or institutions responsible for their oppression. Even if political recognition is won, the power structure that made it necessary to fight for recognition is still in place.

Some, such as Charles Taylor (1994), have attempted to use recognition to describe multiculturalism, and in so doing endorse the idea of one culture recognising another such that one culture confers recognition as a judge and jury in relation to the other (Oliver 2001). Axel Honneth also suggests that social struggles for recognition are struggles to be recognised within the dominant norms of a society. The problem with these theories is that recognition by the dominant group not only reinforces the power structure of dominance insofar as those in power control who is recognised and who is not, but also, recognition so conferred is part and parcel of a pathology of recognition inherent in colonisation and oppression (Oliver 2001, 2004). In other words, marginalised groups struggle for recognition from dominant groups or institutions wherein both the criteria for that recognition and its conferral are controlled by the dominant groups or institutions. This notion of recognition makes oppressed peoples beholden to their oppressors for recognition, even if that recognition is the beginning of their political rights and improved social standing. While political recognition benefits marginalised peoples, within theories of recognition, there is still a lingering sense that recognition is bestowed by some people upon others. And, the risk is that this power dynamic continues even in the struggle for recognition.

Third, the concept of recognition suggests a moment rather than a process. The culminating moment, or *telos*, of Hegel's master–slave dialectic is mutual recognition, and his followers embrace mutual recognition as an ideal, if never completely possible in practice. Recognition seems to be something one has or one doesn't, without anything in between. And, even the ideal of mutual recognition becomes suspect unless we acknowledge the impossibility of ever achieving it. In other words, we must be vigilant in our efforts to reach beyond recognition towards those whom we may not recognise, and even those who do not actively engage in a struggle for recognition. We cannot rest assuming that recognition has been won. Rather, ethics requires that we go beyond recognition and take responsibility for the possibility of witnessing, the possibility of address and response, whether in words, moans, cries, whispers, grunts, whinnies or birdsong. Recognition is but a stage in an ongoing process, one that continually requires re-evaluating. Or, more accurately, recognition itself is an ongoing process in which mutual recognition is never actualised.

In spite of the various productive ways in which contemporary theorists attempt to revive and expand Hegel's notion of recognition, it is difficult to get beyond the connection between recognition and cognition. Because of this, the notion of recognition lends itself to the sense of an *aha* moment wherein recognition happens. This is to say, recognition seems to be an either–or proposition. Either you have it or you don't. In this regard, recognition seems too much like flipping a switch. This may be apt when describing political recognition, which requires policy changes or new laws. Even so, it risks covering over the process that makes those changes possible. The risk is twofold. First, if we consider just epistemological or political recognition, the affective and imaginative dimensions of political life are missing. Second, and more problematic, if we consider recognition as a moment or a goal that can be reached, then we risk resting easy that justice has been served. If we think that recognition is something that can be attained, or given, the risk is that once we feel it has been, then we can be confident that we have satisfied the conditions of justice. Following Emmanuel Levinas and Derrida, I will argue that justice requires holding open the possibility of something beyond recognition.

RECOGNITION OF VULNERABILITY

Feminist theorists such as Judith Butler, Rosemarie Garland-Thomson, Ann Murphy and Julia Kristeva have suggested that recognition involves not merely recognising self-conscious, but also recognising vulnerability. In various ways, these theorists argue that ethical norms result from our shared vulnerability and not our shared rationality or self-consciousness. Contrary to traditional liberal theory, they argue that it is not our autonomy and rational will that ground politics, but rather their opposites, dependence and vulnerability. Modifying the Hegelian notion of recognition, they suggest that what is acknowledged in the struggle for mutual recognition is mutual vulnerability – namely, that we can both wound and be wounded by the other. They ask us to rethink politics starting from mutual vulnerability rather than from liberal contract theory. One issue is that insofar as vulnerability and dependence are just the flip sides of the autonomous individual, then the binary logic of liberal theory has not been changed by endorsing the underside rather than the traditional one. Furthermore, vulnerability is not only something that we share with all life forms, but also variously experienced depending on one's position in social and political hierarchies.

Take, for example, Judith Butler's argument in *Precarious Life* that there is a primary vulnerability that comes with being human, and more specifically, it comes with being born as a human infant completely beholden to others for survival. She argues that this primary vulnerability, associated with infants, is constitutive of humanity (Butler 2004: especially xiv, 31). She concludes her reflections on violence by insisting:

> the task at hand is to establish modes of public seeing and hearing
> that might well respond to the *cry of the human* within the sphere
> of appearance, a sphere in which the trace of the cry has become
> hyperbolically inflated to rationalize a gluttonous nationalism, or fully
> obliterated, where both alternatives turn out to be the same. (Butler
> 2004: 147; my emphasis)

What does it mean that the human cry has become either inflated or obliterated? In cases of oppression, torture and domination, oppressors literally do see and hear 'the cry of the human', but, presumably, the argument is that at the same time they do not *recognise* it as human. On this view, the recognition of vulnerability is the recognition of humanity and vice versa.

As important as it is to add vulnerability and dependence to our political thinking, especially as a counterbalance to autonomy and independence that have dominated political thinking for so long, however, it is also necessary to consider some possible limitations or risks of starting from shared vulnerability, or the recognition of shared vulnerability, which are not the same thing. Certainly, in situations of oppression, torture and domination, the vulnerability of others is exploited. But, it is also the case that in these violent situations, it can be the *recognition* of vulnerability, and even the *recognition* of humanity, that enables the most brutal violence. Indeed, when we treat people 'like animals' it is not because we do not recognise their humanity, but rather precisely because we do. We call people *animals* and use the rhetoric of *animality* and the *subhuman* precisely because of the need to justify treating people in violent torturous ways. In an important sense, the rhetoric of animality, or of inanimate objects, when referring to other human beings assumes recognition of their humanity in the very gesture of denying it. In other words, the fact that any justification is necessary, any categorisation or naming, suggests an underlying, if disavowed, recognition of humanity. Furthermore, recognising the humanity of others does not stop us from torturing and killing them. Recognition of the *cry of the human* is consistent with torture, oppression and violence. And, while recognition of vulnerability does not necessarily lead to violence, in an important sense, it is a prerequisite for it. We see that a body or spirit is vulnerable to being oppressed or tortured, otherwise we would not bother subjecting those bodies to our violence.

It is noteworthy that the word 'vulnerable' comes from the Latin word *vulnerabilis*, which means *wounding*. The first definition of *vulnerable* in the *Oxford English Dictionary* is 'Having power to wound; wounding'; the second is 'That may be wounded; susceptible of receiving wounds or physical injury' (*OED* 1979). *Vulnerable* means both the power to wound, or wounding, and the capacity to receive wounds, or wounded. So what exactly are we recognising when we recognise our own vulnerability and that of others? Perhaps, we are acknowledging that we can both wound and be wounded, and that others can both wound and be wounded. And further, some wounds are mortal wounds that lead to death, death of individuals, or even of entire races or species. In some sense, recognition of vulnerability is the recognition that all living beings die, that all of us are mortal. How, then, does the recognition that we are all subject to death constitute our humanity? If vulnerability is constitutive of humanity, it is so only if it is linked to self-consciousness. We might argue that the self-consciousness or recognition of our own vulnerability is uniquely human because surely vulnerability, particularly bodily vulnerability, is not. And perhaps for theorists such as Butler it is this recognition that grounds the moral community and moral obligations, a recognition that we may not share with nonhuman animals who are certainly vulnerable but may not experience their own vulnerability *as such*.[1]

If vulnerability is constitutive of humanity, then, is it not uniquely constitutive. Although infancy lasts longer in humans than in other animals, the vulnerability of newborns is not unique to humans. The fact that we can be wounded by, or wound, others is also not unique to humans. We share this vulnerability with all living creatures. Indeed, whether or not other animals have a sense of themselves as selves, whether or not they are self-conscious, they do seem to have a sense of their own vulnerability. In fact, even more than humans, nonhuman animals may be aware of their bodily vulnerability and much of their energy is spent protecting themselves and their young from harm. If vulnerability or recognising vulnerability as something we share with other humans enables ethical relationships with them, then recognising vulnerability as something we share with all creatures should enable ethical relations with nonhuman animals as well. Traditionally, at least, between humans and other animals, recognition is seen as a one-way street: we can recognise them, but they can't recognise us. In this regard, recognition of bodily vulnerability seems more promising than the mutual recognition of self-consciousness as a way to bring nonhuman animals into the moral community (given that we share vulnerability with all creatures), but this means vulnerability is not uniquely constitutive of *humanity*. Whatever we think of animals' ability for recognition or self-consciousness, and here it may depend upon which animals, it is hard to deny both that they are vulnerable and that many are also aware of their own vulnerability and that of others.[2]

Again, when discussing either recognition or vulnerability it is important to consider the ways in which recognition is conferred on some and withheld from others, human or nonhuman, and the ways in which some are made more vulnerable than others (Sheth 2009). This is true for humans as well as nonhuman animals. Indeed, many more nonhuman animals are vulnerable to human killing and violence than other human beings. Like recognition, vulnerability operates within a social political context wherein some have more power than others. Just as, in practice, recognition is withheld or conferred by those in power on those marginalised, so too vulnerability is differentially distributed. Some bodies are more vulnerable than others. Some bodies are made vulnerable for the sake of the prosperity of others. In relation to human bodies and human institutions, nonhuman animal bodies are prime examples of vulnerable bodies, particularly those raised on factory farms for human consumption. Thus, it is crucial to consider the politics of vulnerability, which can be covered over or disavowed by the notion that vulnerability is constitutive of human subjectivity (Sheth 2009). The notion that vulnerability is constitutive of subjectivity is reminiscent of older claims that violence is constitutive of subjectivity (Oliver 2001, 2004). While this may be true, it is imperative to consider different levels of violence and the ways in which violence is distributed amongst bodies. Not all people are subjected to the same levels of violence. And, arguing that violence and vulnerability are constitutive of human subjectivity risks levelling violence and vulnerability and disavowing the ways in which both are politically distributed.

Recognition of vulnerability as the foundation of ethics cannot be merely a form of knowing suggested by the etymology of the word *re-cognition*. Nor can it be merely a form of *seeing as*, for example, seeing someone *as* human. For, knowing something, or seeing, whether literally or with the mind's eye, doesn't necessarily motivate ethical relations or compassionate action. Thus, recognition alone is not enough. Along with knowing or seeing as, we need pathos or empathy to act on what we recognise. In other words, recognition, whether epistemological or political, must be accompanied by affect to become ethical.

Arguably, pathos beyond recognition is lurking behind Butler's notion of the politics of grief and mourning. In *Precarious Life* and *Frames of War*, she powerfully argues that only certain lives are grievable. She imagines a world in which we can grieve even for our enemies. She circumscribes grievability and mournability into a politics of recognition such that once again it is an epistemological problem of *seeing as* that leads to the political problem of exclusion. As we've seen, however, epistemological recognition is not enough given that human beings can torture and oppress even those they recognise as self-conscious and vulnerable, even those they recognise as human, and perhaps even those they recognise as grievable. On the other hand, just because some lives are not socially or politically grievable doesn't mean they aren't mourned. Americans may not grieve for the Iraqis killed during their invasion, but Iraqis do. And, for the most part, our society doesn't acknowledge the grief over losing animal companions, but that doesn't mean that they aren't mourned. Finally, while getting social and political recognition for the lives of those we grieve who are, or have been, deemed ungrievable is crucial, we might ask whether this happens as a matter of recognition or rather through pathos beyond recognition.

Intellectual recognition of suffering, vulnerability and mortality, while perhaps necessary are not sufficient. There has to be something that pulls us outside of ourselves and towards another. What is it that makes us not only recognise but also act on the suffering of others? What transforms recognition into compassion? Is affect the missing link between the politics of recognition and ethical regard? Ethical seeing, or what we might call ethical passion – to underscore both our passivity in bringing it on and the suffering that is its companion – is an affair of the heart and not just of the mind. What would it mean, then, to see as from the heart in addition to seeing with the mind or with the eyes? Would this change how we conceive of recognition and of *seeing as*?

What if, as Derrida suggests in *Memoirs of the Blind*, the function of the eye is not to see, but to cry? He says:

> The eye would be destined not to see but to weep . . . . The blindness that opens the eye is not the one that darkens vision. The revelatory or apocalyptic blindness, the blindness that reveals the very truth of the eyes, would be the gaze veiled by tears. (Derrida 1993: 126–7)

It is only if we 'see' vision as the proper – and perhaps only – function of the eye, that we see blindness as a defect. What if, instead, we take the function of the eye to be crying, crying for those in need or in pain? These would be tears of compassion for all other living beings. These would be tears that take us beyond epistemological or political recognition and towards our ethical obligations to them, whatever species they may be. This is a *seeing as* necessarily veiled in tears, beyond recognition.

WITNESSING PATHOS BEYOND RECOGNITION

In *Witnessing: Beyond Recognition* (Oliver 2001), I suggest that the structure of subjectivity is one of witnessing, beyond recognition. Invoking the double meaning of witnessing, I develop a theory of subjectivity that connects the historically localisable subject position of particular subjects with the infinite response-ability that makes subjectivity possible. By bringing together subject position and the structure of subjectivity as witnessing, I navigate between the extremes of conceiving of the subject as either foundation or simple effect. The notion of witnessing brings together the historical context and finite situation of particular subjects on the one hand, with the witnessing structure that makes subjectivity an infinite open system of response, on the other. By so doing, it both politicises the subject as in 'subject position' and insists on a fundamental ethical obligation at the heart of subjectivity itself.

Witnessing is defined as the action of bearing witness or giving testimony, the fact of being present and observing something; *witnessing* is from *witness*, which is defined as to bear witness, to testify, to give evidence, to be a spectator or auditor of something, to be present as an observer, to see with one's own eyes (*OED* 1979). It is important to note that witnessing has both the juridical connotations of seeing with one's own eyes and the religious connotations of testifying to that which cannot be seen, or *bearing witness*. It is this double meaning that makes witnessing such a powerful alternative to recognition in reconceiving subjectivity and thereby ethical relations. The double meaning of witnessing – *eyewitness* testimony based on first-hand knowledge, on the one hand, and *bearing witness* to something beyond recognition that can't be seen, on the other – is the heart of subjectivity. The tension between eyewitness testimony and bearing witness both positions the subject in finite history and necessitates the infinite response-ability of subjectivity. The tension between eyewitness testimony and bearing witness, between subject position and subjectivity, is the dynamic operator that moves us beyond the melancholic choice between either dead historical facts or traumatic repetition of violence. It is the tension between our social-political contexts and our ethical responsibility to imagine life otherwise.

Our experience of ourselves as subjects is maintained in the tension between our subject positions and our subjectivity. Subject positions, although mobile, are constituted in our social interactions and our positions within our culture and context. They are determined by history and circumstance. Subject positions are our relations to the finite world of human history and relations – what we might call politics. Subjectivity, on the other hand, is experienced as the sense of agency and response-ability that are constituted in the infinite encounter with otherness, which is fundamentally ethical. And, although subjectivity is logically prior to any possible subject position, in our experience, they are always profoundly interconnected. This is why our experience of our own subjectivity is the result of the productive tension between finite subject position and infinite response-ability of witnessing.

An example recounted in Dori Laub's *Testimony* illustrates the productive tension between eyewitness testimony and bearing witness to something beyond recognition. Laub, a psychoanalyst interviewing survivors as part of the Video Archive for Holocaust Testimonies at Yale, remarks on a tension between historians and psychoanalysts involved in the project (Felman and

Laub 1992). He describes a lively debate that began after the group watched the taped testimony of a woman who was an eyewitness to the Auschwitz uprising in which prisoners set fire to the camp. The woman reported four chimneys going up in flames and exploding, but historians insisted that since there was only one chimney blown up, her testimony was incorrect and should be discredited in its entirety because she proved herself an unreliable witness. One historian suggested that her testimony should be discounted because she 'ascribe[d] importance to an attempt that, historically, made no difference' (1992: 61). The psychoanalysts responded that the woman was not testifying to the number of chimneys blown up but to something more 'radical' and more 'crucial', namely, the seemingly unimaginable occurrence of Jewish resistance at Auschwitz, that is to say, the historical truth of Jewish resistance at Auschwitz. Laub concludes that what the historians could not hear, listening for empirical facts, was the 'very secret of survival and of resistance to extermination' (1992: 62). The Auschwitz survivor saw something unfamiliar, Jewish resistance, which gave her the courage to resist. She saw something that in one sense did not happen – four chimneys blowing up – but in another made all the difference to what happened. Seeing the impossible – what did not happen – gave her the strength to make what seemed impossible possible, surviving the Holocaust.

The double meaning of witness can help to theorise the Holocaust survivor testifying as both an eyewitness to the Jewish uprising at Auschwitz and as bearing witness. As an *eyewitness*, she testifies (incorrectly) to the events of that particular day when prisoners blew up a chimney. In addition, however, she *bears witness* to something that in itself cannot be seen, the conditions of possibility of Jewish resistance and survival. As an eyewitness, she occupies a particular historical position in a concrete context that constitutes her actuality as well as her possibilities. She was a Jew in the midst of deadly anti-Semitism. She was a prisoner in a concentration camp. She was a woman in the mid-twentieth century. Her position as a subject is related to the particularities of her historical and social circumstance. In order to evaluate her testimony as an eyewitness, it is crucial to consider her socio-historical subject position and not just the 'accuracy' of her testimony. Indeed, the 'accuracy' of her testimony has everything to do with her subject position. It is, in fact, her subject position that makes historians particularly interested in her testimony as a Holocaust survivor. Her testimony is unique because she was an eyewitness; she was there. But, it is not just because she was there, but why and how she was there that makes her testimony unique. The testimony of another eyewitness to the same event – a Nazi guard at the camp, or someone outside the camp who noticed flames in the air – would have a very different meaning, even if he also claimed to see four chimneys blowing up. Perhaps within the context of the Holocaust Testimonies at Yale, surrounded by mostly male professors, the fact that this witness was a woman makes a difference to how she speaks and how she is heard. Only by considering her subject position can we learn something about the 'truth' of history even from the 'inaccuracies' of her testimony.

It is also important to note that experience is constituted as such for the witness through testimony. In addition, insofar as it is the performance of testimony to which the addressee of the witness, or the witness of the testimony, responds, and through which the unseen of history is shown, our sights are directed beyond the visible world of the eyewitness. What the process of witnessing testifies to is not a state of facts but a commitment to the truth of subjectivity as addressability and response-ability. Witnessing is addressed to another and to a community; and witnessing – in both senses as addressing and responding, testifying and listening – is a commitment to embrace the responsibility of constituting communities, the responsibility inherent in subjectivity itself. In this sense, witnessing is always bearing witness to the necessity of the process of witnessing itself, the process of address and response.

From his work with Holocaust survivors, and being a survivor himself, Dori Laub concludes that psychic survival depends on an addressable other, what he calls an 'inner witness'. It is the possibility of address that sustains psychic life and the subject's sense of its subjective agency. If the possibility of address and response – whether verbal or nonverbal, grunts or whispers – is annihilated, then subjectivity is damaged. To conceive of oneself as a subject is to have the ability to address oneself to another, real or imaginary, actual or potential. Subjectivity is the result of, and depends upon, the process of witnessing – address-ability and response-ability. By attacking the very structure of address and response, oppression, domination, enslavement and torture work to undermine and destroy the ability to respond and thereby undermine and destroy subjectivity. Part of the psychoanalyst's task in treating survivors is reconstructing the addressability that makes witnessing subjectivity possible. Addressability and response-ability are the conditions for subjectivity. The subject is the result of a response to an address from another and the possibility of addressing itself to another.

If subjectivity is the process of witnessing sustained through response-ability, then we have a responsibility to response-ability, that is to say, we have a responsibility to promote the ability to respond. We have an obligation not only to respond, but also to respond in a way that opens up rather than closes off the possibility of response by others. We must be vigilant in our attempts to continually open and reopen the possibility of response. We have a responsibility to open ourselves to the responses that constitute us as subjects. Response-ability, then, is the founding possibility of subjectivity and its most fundamental obligation. We are constituted as subjects through our interactive inter-subjective address and response with others, other people, other animals and our environment. We are responsive creatures, as are all living beings. We cannot live without address and response from others. But this process of address and response is not just a matter of recognition. Our bodies are doing it without our knowledge or permission, so to speak. Moreover, our ethical obligation is not just founded on the recognition of self-consciousness, mutual or otherwise, or vulnerability, but also on witnessing to something beyond recognition.

Certainly, Butler and other recognition theorists insist on vigilance in opening up justice to those who have been disenfranchised. This is possible only by attending to the ways in which we *don't recognise* others. More radically, it is necessary to attend to the ways in which the ideal of mutual recognition is impossible, which doesn't mean that we should not continue to endorse it. Moreover, because we do not recognise the other does not make us any less responsible for him or her. To the contrary, ethics begins in the space of the impossible and unknown. It does not begin in the space of what is known or can be recognised. 'So long as there is recognizability and fellow, ethics is dormant. It is sleeping a dogmatic slumber . . . . The "unrecognizable" is the awakening' (Derrida 2009: 106).

While recognition may be necessary for politics and changing public policies, the ethical foundation of this politics must always take us beyond recognition to a realm beyond *seeing as* where our confidence as seers or knowers is shaken to its foundations. We must dwell with what Levinas calls *insomnia*. Our inability to know, to see, to recognise, must keep us awake at night. As Levinas insists, I am responsible. I cannot shirk my responsibility onto others. But, I am responsible not only for my own response, but also for that of the other. I always have one more response to give. 'The more I answer,' says Levinas, 'the more I am responsible' (1981: 93). Furthermore, I am responsible for the other's ability to respond, whether or not I recognise him or her. Indeed, for Levinas, ethics is always a movement beyond recognition. For, recognition risks turning ethics into moral rule following. While categorising and calculating may be necessary for politics, ethics requires us to dwell in the space of the incalculable, a space without moral rules or laws, a space beyond recognition.

This is what Derrida's hyperbolic ethics demands: namely, radical responsibility for my response to the other, beyond recognition. Derrida proposes a radical ethics of responsibility for justice, hospitality and forgiveness beyond recognition. Moving beyond Kant's calculable hospitality based on the limited surface of the earth, which is always a limited hospitality, Derrida argues for an unlimited, infinite hospitality. He discusses the tense, but necessary, relationship between unconditional and conditioned hospitality (Derrida 2005: 67). Perhaps in order to 'avoid the worst', as Derrida sometimes says, we need to embrace what remains a *secret*, what cannot be calculated or even anticipated, and thereby prevents us from ever thinking, or understanding, or knowing once and for all, the meanings of hospitality, justice or ethics. To think the secret is to think the impossibility of knowing, the impossibility of articulating, and perhaps even the impossibility of ethics itself. And yet, this attempt to think the impossible, to articulate the impossible, may be the very condition of possibility for ethics.

Pure or unconditional hospitality, that is to say, the impossibility of a law or habit of hospitality entering into an economy of exchange, is central to Derrida's discussions of the gift and continues through his discussions of forgiveness, and beyond. The 'pure gift' cannot be dictated by law or part of an economy of exchange. For, if you give a gift in exchange for something else, is it really a gift or more like a payment? So too with hospitality. To be pure and absolute hospitality, it cannot be given as payment for a debt or done merely out of duty to the law. It cannot become a matter of either habit or moral duty. The purity of the gift is associated with the infinite responsibility of giving, which is beyond morality insofar as morality is a matter of calculation and rules. Calculation, rules and laws turn what should be an ethical response to the singularity of the other or the event into a mere reaction or reflex determined by convention.

Like hospitality, if forgiveness is given only to get something in return, then it is not absolute. If forgiveness is given only upon certain conditions – for example, the perpetrator repent or feel remorse – then it is not true forgiveness. Once forgiveness is circumscribed within social conventions or laws, it is no longer pure (Derrida 2001a: 45). The concepts or ideals of giving, hospitality and forgiveness, in their absolute and hyperbolic forms, have an essentially limitless and infinite quality that Derrida constantly compares with what passes for giving, hospitality and forgiveness in our everyday lives. He maintains that what we do recognise as gifts have meaning only in relation to this ideal of giving that is essentially unrecognisable (Derrida 2001b: 53). Even the ideal of mutual recognition sounds too much like an exchange.

Like hospitality and forgiveness, there is a contradiction at the heart of recognition that necessarily takes us beyond positing mutual recognition as something like a Kantian ideal, a goal that we can never reach and yet must strive for nonetheless. Derridean hospitality, forgiveness and gift are more than Kantian regulative ideals precisely because there is an internal contradiction inherent within the very notions themselves (Derrida 2000: 149, 2004: 133–6). Derrida points to this contradiction when he asks: 'In giving a right, if I can put it like that, to unconditional hospitality, how can one give place to a determined, limitable, and delimitable – in a word, to a calculable – right or law?' (2000: 147–9). In other words, the principle grounding all conditional hospitality, namely, unconditional hospitality, is at odds with its practice. For, what makes hospitality unconditional not only makes hostility possible, but also inevitable insofar as ultimately there is no calculus with which we determine how to distinguish one from the other. The threat to unconditional hospitality does not come from outside, but rather from inside. Hospitality operates according to the autoimmune logic distinctive of all appeals to the self or sovereignty. In other words, if, or insofar as, hospitality is granted by one to an other, its unconditionality is already comprised. Indeed, the very terms *self* and *other* are problematic if our goal is unconditional hospitality; but these terms are required by our notion of hospitality insofar as we imagine that someone has the power to extend hospitality to another. And yet, this very power acts as a condition that prevents hospitality from being unconditional.

We could make the same argument with recognition. Mutual recognition necessarily undermines itself insofar as it assumes an exchange between two subjects, whether or not they are beholden to each other. In addition, political recognition required by our daily lives as political beings necessarily effaces the singularity of each living being. How could an ideal of recognition, mutual or otherwise, encounter the singularity of each? How could recognition be based on this encounter? In the name of what or who, then, could we claim the right to recognition? In the name of what or who would we struggle for it?

Rather than lead to inaction and indifference, Derrida suggests that this impasse between unconditional and conditional, pure and impure, is necessary for justice, if always a justice to come. Indeed, the internal tension between them is the necessary tension between ethics and politics as between singular and universal. Another way of articulating the contradiction internal to the notion of hospitality, then, is in terms of the conflict between ethics and politics. Ethics of hospitality demands that we welcome every singular being in its singularity – already the words 'we' and 'its' belie the impossibility of such a demand – and politics, even a politics of hospitality, demands that we develop a universal principle of hospitality that applies to all, effacing the singularity required by ethics. In other words, ethics demands consideration of the singularity of each unique being, while politics requires universal rules and principles that apply equally to all.

Ethics, traditionally also a realm of universals, within Derrida's thought becomes the realm of the singular, the event, what is unique to each life and each moment of that life. The demands of the ethical are impossible and unconditional and yet necessarily guide our actions. Indeed, the tension between the unconditional and the conditioned produces an urgency that takes us back to Levinasian insomnia – our decisions about what is right and what we ought to do keep us awake at night because there is no easy answer; there is no handy principle to which to appeal. Rather, we must respond to each individual and each situation anew according to its singularity. We must question the values, principles and laws with which we were raised. When ethics becomes a matter of moral rule following, then it has been reduced to mere calculation at worst and epistemology at best. In either case, ethics disappears. Ethics requires not only dwelling in the undecidable space of that Levinasian insomnia, but also reopening that space over and over again in the name of a justice 'worthy of its name'. Witnessing to what is beyond recognition is central to this impossible justice.

THE ETHICS OF SHARING A PLANET

In *Animal Lessons* (Oliver 2015), I expand the notion of witnessing to include nonhuman animals. The basis for ethical relations has moved beyond reason or recognition and towards witnessing to response-ability itself, that is to say, witnessing to the ability to respond, which is not just the domain of humankind, but all of animal-kind. In this way, witnessing ethics as response ethics can take us beyond human centrism and towards consideration of the ways in which all of the creatures of the earth, and the earth itself, respond. Within response ethics, political and moral subjects are constituted not by their sovereignty and mastery but rather by address and response. Extending my analysis of witnessing, address and response (broadly conceived) are the basis of earth ethics grounded on cohabitation and interdependence. And, the responsibility to engender response, or facilitate the ability to respond, in others and the environment, is the primary obligation of earth ethics. This earthly ethos is the result of pathos beyond rationality or recognition because it is based in our embodied relationality, which is bound to other living beings, not only through shared places and histories, but also through the larger biosphere and ecosystems that sustain us, and ultimately through our singular bond to the earth.

An ethics of earth is grounded on the affirmation of bio and social diversity that make the earth a living planet. Earth ethics emerges from the tension between the absolutely unique place of each one and the collectively shared bond to the earth, both of which necessarily constitute the life of the planet. Earth's biosphere, which cannot be separated from the earth itself, is a dynamic of individuals and communities, species and interspecies symbioses. And all life is also dependent upon nonorganic elements that also are terraforming. The earth is this complex of relationships.

To say that we are earthbound creatures is to say that we have a special bond to the earth. We belong to the earth, just as it belongs to us. Rather than ownership, this sense of belonging harkens back to a more archaic sense of the word that conjures Eros as longing and companionship. Our life on earth is a longing for home, for a home that we can love, a home that we love enough to take responsibility for. Ethos as habitat or home brings with it a sense of belonging to an ecosystem or community. This sense of belonging is not a familiarity that can be taken for granted, especially when we consider earth as home. For, as every creature 'knows', the earth is populated with strange others and foreign landscapes that can be welcoming or threatening, and everything in between. For human beings, the earth as home is fore-given and must be interpreted and reinterpreted, even as it is also a prerequisite for meaning.

Meaning both requires social bonds and emerges through social bonds, which are tied to particular spaces or places and times or histories. The relationality of social bonds, including bonds to places and histories, makes meaning possible, even while meaning emerges through relationships. The dynamic of meaning as both constituted by, and constituting, our relationships is akin to the *witnessing* structure of response-ability, the structure of address and response. Living creatures are responsive and an earth ethics promotes our responsibility to open up, rather than close off, the response-ability of others, their ability to respond.

Witnessing or response ethics maintains that even in the face of our lack of understanding, the impossibility of mastery and inherent unpredictability, we have a responsibility to act in ways that open up the possibility of response from our fellow earthlings and from the earth itself. Obviously this abstract 'principleless principle' or 'groundless ground' also opens onto the tension between ethics and politics (Willett 2014). Ethics requires that we open up response and response-ability in the face of our ignorance – for if we knew with certainty, it would no longer be ethics but rather social or even natural science – while politics requires that we negotiate relationships within our living space in order to survive and thrive, which always necessarily means killing or excluding some others (e.g. deadly bacteria, fungi and viruses). We might say that an ethical politics is one in which ethics juts through political policy and forces us to continually and vigilantly reassess and reinterpret our responsibility towards others, even if – perhaps especially if – those others are threatening.

Whether or not we share properties or capacities, whether or not we share recognition or vulnerability, we share the planet. Whether or not we share a world, we share the earth. Perhaps it is time to rethink democracy not in terms of contracts but rather in terms of proximity, not in terms of nations but in terms of the planet. Considering animals when thinking about political rights and moral responsibilities challenges traditional notions of rights and equality based in rational autonomy and forces us to go beyond rational consent or contractarian democracies, to our proximity with all of the inhabitants of the earth.

Basing democracy on proximity rather than on contracts, however, would also require us to rethink our relationship to animals, especially to companion animals with whom we live. A politics based on proximity may be more inclusive than one based on contracts implicitly signed by autonomous individuals, or even recognition given to or conferred by those in power on the marginalised or excluded. A politics of proximity does not require merely an ideal of mutual recognition. It does not require merely the recognition of vulnerability. Indeed, it may require us to go beyond recognition to consider our proximity to those whom we do not recognise.

NOTES

1. Following Derrida's engagement with Heidegger, I challenge this notion of recognition as a dividing line between humans and animals (Derrida 2008). See Oliver 2009, 2015.
2. For example, see Chloë Taylor's extension of Butler's notion of vulnerability to nonhuman animals (Taylor 2008). Taylor argues that although, as she articulates it, Butler's Levinasian ethics necessitates the exclusion of nonhuman animals, it can be extended and adapted to include animals. James Stanescu argues that fragments of concern for nonhuman animals already exist within Butler's writing. Gathering these bits together, Stanescu (2012) argues that Butler's ethics not only includes nonhuman animals, but does so necessarily. As intriguing and helpful as Stanescu's reconstitution is, nonhuman animals have not been a priority for Butler.

WORKS CITED

Butler, Judith (1993), *Bodies That Matter: On the Discursive Limits of Sex*, New York: Routledge.

Butler, Judith (1997), *The Psychic Life of Power: Theories in Subjection*, Stanford: Stanford University Press.

Butler, Judith (2004), *Precarious Life: The Power of Mourning and Violence*, London and New York: Verso.

Derrida, Jacques (1993), *Memoirs of the Blind: The Self-Portrait and Other Ruins*, trans. Michael Naas and Pascale-Anne Brault, Chicago: University of Chicago Press.

Derrida, Jacques (2000), *Of Hospitality*, trans. Rachel Bowlby, Stanford: Stanford University Press.

Derrida, Jacques (2001a), 'On Forgiveness', in *On Cosmopolitanism and Forgiveness*, trans. Mark Dooley and Michael Hughes, Hackensack, NJ: Routledge, pp. 25–60.

Derrida, Jacques (2001b), 'To Forgive the Unforgivable and the Imprescriptible', in John D. Caputo, Mark Dooley and Michael J. Scanlon (eds), *Questioning God*, Bloomington: Indiana University Press, pp. 21–51.

Derrida, Jacques (2004), *Philosophy in a Time of Terror: Dialogues with Jürgen Habermas and Jacques Derrida*, Chicago: University of Chicago Press.

Derrida, Jacques (2005), *Rogues: Two Essays on Reason*, trans. Pascale-Anne Brault and Michael Naas, Stanford: Stanford University Press.

Derrida, Jacques (2008), *The Animal That Therefore I Am*, ed. Marie-Louise Mallet, trans. David Wills, New York: Fordham University Press.

Derrida, Jacques (2009), *The Beast and the Sovereign, vol. I*, trans. Geoffrey Bennington, Chicago: University of Chicago Press.

Felman, Shoshana and Dori Laub (1992), *Testimony: Crises of Witnessing in Literature, Psychoanalysis and History*, New York: Routledge.

Ferrara, Alessandro (2015), 'Honneth and *Freedom's Right*', presented at *Philosophy and the Social Sciences* conference, Prague, 21 May 2015.

Honneth, Axel (1996), *The Struggle for Recognition: The Moral Grammar of Social Conflicts*, trans. Joel Anderson, Cambridge, MA: The MIT Press.

Honneth, Axel (2015), *Freedom's Right: The Social Foundations of Democratic Life*, New York: Columbia University Press.

Levinas, Emmanuel (1981), *Otherwise than Being, or Beyond Essence*, trans. Alphonso Lingis, Pittsburgh: Duquesne University Press.

Oliver, Kelly (2001), *Witnessing: Beyond Recognition*, Minneapolis: University of Minnesota Press.

Oliver, Kelly (2004), *The Colonization of Psychic Space*, Minneapolis: University of Minnesota Press.

Oliver, Kelly (2009), *Animal Lessons: How They Teach Us to Be Human*, New York: Columbia University Press.

Oliver, Kelly (2015), *Earth and World: Philosophy After the Apollo Missions*, New York: Columbia University Press.

Oxford English Dictionary (OED) (1979), 24th printing, Oxford: Oxford University Press.

Sheth, Felugni (2009), *Toward a Political Philosophy of Race*, Albany: State University of New York Press.

Stanescu, James (2012), 'Species Trouble: Judith Butler, Mourning and the Precarious Lives of Animals', *Hypatia*, 27: 3 (Summer), 565–82.

Taylor, Charles (1994), 'The Politics of Recognition', in *Multiculturalism: Examining the Politics of Recognition*, ed. Amy Gutmann, Princeton: Princeton University Press, pp. 25–74.

Taylor, Chloë (2008), 'The Precarious Lives of Animals', *Philosophy Today*, 51: 1 (Spring), 60–72.

Willett, Cynthia (2014), *Interspecies Ethics*, New York: Columbia University Press.

CHAPTER 9

A Norwegian Abroad: Camilla Collett's Travelogues from Berlin and Paris

Tone Selboe

The Norwegian novelist and essayist Camilla Collett (1813–95) is mainly known for her one but seminal novel, *The District Governor's Daughters* (*Amtmandens Døttre*, 1854–5) – often labelled Norway's first modern novel, her campaign for women's rights, and for being the sister of the poet Henrik Wergeland, Norway's leading romantic poet. However, she is more than a one-novel author, campaigner and sister of a famous poet; she is a leading writer in her own right: six volumes of letters, essays and travelogues appeared between 1864 and 1885, most of them first published in papers and periodicals. Her essays on city life, urban planning, literature and history are striking examples of how a writer from the margins of Europe was in dialogue with what was going on in European life and literature at the time. Camilla Collett is also a major forerunner for ideas on gender and emancipation which came to the forefront with her younger male colleagues, associated with the so-called modern breakthrough in Scandinavian literature, writers such as the critic and literary historian Georg Brandes, the playwright Henrik Ibsen and the novelists Alexander Kielland and Jonas Lie.

Liberal ideas about freedom and equality, an influence from the French Revolution, were important for the family in which Collett grew up; her father was central in the fight for Norway's independence in 1814, and instrumental in the work for a new constitution, one of the most modern and radical in Europe at the time. For Collett, however, it is the question of freedom and liberty for women, the fight for women's rights and position in society, which is the main cause. Her travelogues from Europe are motivated by a didactic intention: she compares the young nation Norway to a small boy who still hasn't learned to behave properly: he has great possibilities, he is bright, but has no *Bildung*: 'He has to stop drinking, swearing and making a fuss, just because he is always keen on fighting. He must learn to treat women better than he does' (III, 158).[1]

In the following, I will interrogate Collett's travelogues from Germany and France with a special emphasis on her Paris notes. I will discuss the interaction between urban planning, walking and city life, paying special attention to the relation between centre and periphery, or to be more precise, how a woman from the margins of Europe in the latter half of the nineteenth century confronts her impressions of Berlin and Paris with the condition in 'our own little parvenu' – the capital of Norway: Christiania or Kristiania (now Oslo). I will venture to show how this indicates a European perspective steeped in what we may call an ambivalent modernity, which in various ways prefigures contemporary debates on urban planning and feminist thinking.

*

As a young woman Camilla Collett travelled with her father to Germany and France, and as an 'older' widow she returned to Europe and lived for long periods in Berlin, Munich, Paris and Rome. In everything she writes she alludes to French and German writers and historians (she did not read English), and she takes part in the debates at the time. Thus, on the one hand, she was a European from the very start; on the other hand, the national identity had yet to be built: Norway gained its independence from Denmark in 1814 and was part of a union with Sweden until 1905.

In a letter from Berlin dated 30 October 1863, Camilla Collett praises Berlin's wide, magnificent streets: 'that ladies can walk alone along the streets ... without being addressed or offended in any way' represents a freedom she admires (II, 69). The observation leads her to a comparison with how things are in the poor Norwegian capital, Kristiania. There, Collett argues, men amuse themselves by pestering walking women, and she takes it upon herself to defend the necessity of street walking:

> Yes, we will walk. We have to walk. The women who sit in their carriages are bored to death. Those times are gone, when the woman was for the man just an object of luxury, partly a valuable toy, partly a goddess meant to be worshipped. They have themselves pushed us unto the place of action, where we have to work, acquire, fight, and move about, in one word: we have to walk. (III, 158)

Walking thus becomes a metaphor for independence, a synonym for taking part in life on an equal footing with men. The insisting, almost stubborn 'we will walk' reads like a sort of manifesto, and the way Collett connects walking with work, struggle and action gives this impression. Walking – walking the city streets alone – becomes a metaphor for independence. Sitting still is seen as synonymous with not taking part in life whereas to walk means to participate in life's struggles. It may be more convenient to be driven in a carriage, but you risk being bored to death.

The letter from Berlin is just one of many Collett wrote in her almost forty years of travelling – letters which can be read as contemporary comments on the cities she is visiting – Copenhagen, Munich, Berlin, Rome, Paris. From 1851, when her husband Jonas Collett dies, and until her death in 1895, she has no real or stable home, but spends her life travelling Europe, visiting various European cities. Streets, parks and simple rooms in hotels and guest houses become her 'home'; travelling and writing her way of living. In Copenhagen she is run over, in Paris she is stuck in a lift and as a result has to be hospitalised, in Rome she loses money – but nothing stops her. 'The eternal Jew could hardly lead a life more like a vagabond', her son Oscar comments in a letter (qtd in Steen 1954: 213).

It has been pointed out how Collett's travelling life, without a safe home to return to, in significant ways differs from the lives of her younger male contemporaries – the writers of the Scandinavian modern breakthrough with Ibsen as a leading figure – who despite their attack on the bourgeois marriage made sure they themselves had a stable family life (Steinfeld 1996: 80). In fact, Collett's writing could as well be located in the European salons of the nineteenth century as within a biographical and national context. As a young woman she is introduced to the finer circles of both Kristiania and abroad – she visits Hamburg and Paris – but she is also critical of a European culture which implies a certain superficial way of socialising. Thus, when Collett starts her travelling life as a mature woman, she shies away from the established social culture. Consequently, there is a great difference between her young self who goes to parties and balls and is celebrated as 'the Nordic Beauty', and her later, solitary self. When abroad as an older woman, she refuses most invitations to social events, and even though she keeps in touch with Ibsen in Munich and in Rome, and from time to time receives visitors (like the young writer, Alexander Kielland), she doesn't really get involved with other writers and artists – many of whom she admires and reviews. It is the solitary drifting, the distance from the established social life, that becomes her trademark. She chooses to be at the margins and speak from the margins.

Collett is nevertheless well aware of the fact that her travelogues, her 'letters home', are part of a tradition and a genre. The letters are public rather than private, written for and to a Norwegian public, for national papers and magazines. Her texts defy a conventional definition of genre: like many of the important writers at the time, she moved between genres, wrote various forms of fiction and 'faction', without always making sharp distinctions between them.

The stylistic modus of the letter cum travelogue is the *digression* – the departure from the straight line of thought – and from the straight road of walking. The various sights on offer in the city are countered by the thematic and stylistic shifts in the text – from argumentative paragraphs on the battle between the sexes to amusing details about people on the bus or angry remarks on the development of the city. This elegant way of combining wandering and thought, movement and change of view, characteristic of the essay genre, makes it possible for the writer to situate herself in an ironic position in relation to the topics she explores. She places herself as part of a larger Norwegian 'we' while at the same time distancing herself from the ordinary home-grown traveller: 'We Norwegians don't understand about travelling as a way of letting go of ourselves', she claims (II, 167), subtly indicating her difference from these 'Norwegians' by taking the reader for an amusing walk on Unter den Linden, on the Champs-Élysées or in the Tuileries Garden, instead of the expected visits to museums and monuments. Her slightly coquettish insistence on never experiencing much when out walking succeeds in pointing to the fact that her essays are full of witty and bizarre observations on daily life in the cities she visits.

Kristiania apart, Paris is the city Collett comments on most frequently. Walking the metropolis, she observes how people of all classes populate the streets and parks, and the daily life of Paris is compared with the dreariness of Kristiania. While Kristiania fails as a city when it comes to offer its inhabitants entertainment and recreation, this is not the case in Paris:

At the *Champs-Élysées* it is first and foremost the marionette-theatres that attract people; and again one is surprised on a day like this, in plain Norwegian that means being provoked, by how much time people spend on being amused. (II, 167)

Thus she writes in 1868. The tone is ironical, but there is no mistaking the message: when she substitutes 'surprised' for 'provoked', it is obvious that she is all in favour of the French worker's ability to take time off and find entertainment in the middle of a busy city life. The point is one she returns to again and again: a city, in order to earn the name of city – not to mention metropolis and capital – should be able to offer its inhabitants places for recreation. In Paris the streets themselves, and even more importantly, the great parks and gardens, fill this function. In Kristiania, however, there is nowhere a working family can enjoy itself. Consequentially, the Tuileries Garden is a favourite spot; if you walk there on any day of the week, Collett states, you get the impression that Paris is a light and festive city. Everybody will be out on the streets walking and talking; not only those entitled to walk and not work, the *flâneurs* and idlers of the city, but even 'those classes, which one at that time of the day imagines being working or slaving away at school' (II, 165).

In spite of the idealising view on Paris life, typical of the enthusiastic tourist, the argument is consistent with her view on urban planning at large: the city should be structured in a way which engenders a balance between work and play, and even more importantly, between private and public. In Norway, she argues elsewhere, there has been an increasing tendency to privatise public land, and as a consequence, social groups have been increasingly separated. Hence, by referring to Paris, Collett seeks to educate her fellow Norwegians to abolish 'this difference between behaviour and habitus' that in Kristiania emphasises rather than abolishes the difference between the classes (III, 203). She even goes as far as pointing to *private property* as the enemy, herself underlining the words. This does *not* imply that Collett is some sort of pre-Marxist class warrior; the concept of class itself she finds archaic as well as useless, although she, for lack of a better word, employs it herself. Her point is informed by her liberal-progressive background: she wants all social groups to be able to enjoy the common good on equal terms.

When it comes to class, her attitude is driven by a sense of morality and aesthetics rather than one of economy or politics; she is herself of a different social class from the ones she defends. When it comes to gender, however, her argument is socially and politically motivated: a city which excludes women from its common grounds, for instance by refusing them the right to walk alone – as we saw in the quote from the Berlin letter above – is failing as a city, not to say a modern metropolis. Public spaces should be open to all. Hence, she is also criticising the Norwegian distinction between public and private garden, or between park and garden, the former being public, the latter private:

> At home, we are very happy about having something we call our own garden, especially if it has the advantage of one being able to discover, without being seen oneself, what kind of dressing-gown the mistress next door is wearing while walking about in her garden. By this treasure we mean a patch of land between three sides of painted wood, with a bird-house, so protected that not even the sparrows may indiscreetly take a look at the family-tea-drinking-mystery. [. . .] We are all very proud and very happy that we are the owners of such a patch of blessed land. (II, 165)

While the Norwegian first and foremost protects the enclosed, private garden, this is not, according to Collett, the case for the Frenchman. Therefore, she goes on to compare the Norwegian and the Frenchman, and there is no doubt whom she sides with: if you offer a Frenchman such a patch of ground, he will say: no thanks, I have my garden, which costs me neither money nor work and irritations, but has everything I need of entertainment, social life and cultivated nature. In short, the Frenchman needs no other garden than the Tuileries Garden.

And the Frenchman is right, according to Collett: in the public garden he – she! – gets everything one can ask for; an ideal combination of nature and culture – museums, churches, park and garden all in one. City and home are in harmony. In Norway, on the contrary, the very concept of home is anti-urban; it is inextricably linked to having your own house, garden and fence where 'we', between three sides of painted fence, can keep the neighbours away.

Behind this rather polished anecdote about the Frenchman and the Norwegian, there is another argument hiding which comes to the surface in later,
more polemical essays, namely, that the division between private and public
has its gendered side: the more the public space is privatised, the more women
are confined to the home. The woman is, in other words, more likely to walk
in the private than in the public garden, and in a country with no parks, she is
more homebound than in a country which has the public garden, that is, the
park, as the family playground.

*

All of Camilla Collett's Paris notes between 1864 and 1884 circle around
what she calls the old and the new Paris, or Paris before and now. Despite
her 'modern' way of thinking and looking upon a city, she is a great nostalgic
when it comes to the development of Paris. *Le vieux* Paris changes, and Collett, like so many travellers, favours the city as it was last time she visited.
Thus, her complaints are more frequent the older she gets, and on her wanderings around the city she increasingly frets about the growing noise, traffic
and dirt. Most of all, she attacks the building of the new city, what is known
as the haussmannisation of Paris – the development and building of the boulevards led by Baron Haussmann between 1853 and 1868. Collett's letters are
contemporary comments on this radical restructuring of the French capital.
In one of her essays, 'Farewell' (first printed 1864), the focus is on how the
building of the boulevards destroys the quiet residential areas – the gardens
and houses of old Paris. 'Her' Paris, what she calls her 'paradise', has been
invaded by a snake: 'Paradise doesn't exist without a snake, and it was not
lacking here either, it was called a boulevard, a boulevard on which work is
going on' (II, 131). The point is that this modern monster called the boulevard destroys houses, gardens and narrow winding roads. What Collett terms
the aristocratic – the small, narrow road – is being overtaken by the boring
normality – the boulevard.

In the years following Haussmann's restructuring of the French capital, the
tone as well as the critique sharpens, and even her beloved Tuileries Garden
falls out of favour as she gets older. The quietness of the park is, in her opinion,
overtaken by *noise*. The streets as well as the park become vulgarised beyond
recognition. In the 1860s she is still positive to the social life she observes in
the city; in the travelogues from 1882 and 1884, on the contrary, the earlier
celebration of different groups and classes meeting in the park is absent from
her vision – and her texts. The age of the crowd is not looked upon favourably:
'Every day, when the weather is fine, I walk in the garden, my dear garden, the
Tuileries Garden, and I cry about the changes' (III, 181). The nostalgic tone
is nevertheless mixed with one of humour; the trees are being cut in order
to build barracks, one of them is placed on the spot once reserved for Marie
Antoinette and Lamballe: 'over the door there is an inscription which – I don't
understand English – sounded something like: *Watter closets*' (III, 181). Collett may not understand much English, but she does understand enough in

order to make a rhetorical point: the common crowd has taken the place of the aristocracy, the trees are replaced by human nature in its lowest form, so to speak.

One might say that while she embraces the old city – *le vieux* Paris – she benefits from the new. Thus, she seems to place herself between the pre-modern city of Balzac (whom she both admires and comments on), and the modern city of Haussmann (whom she never mentions by name). She may condemn the development of Paris, but Collett is consistent in neither her praise nor her complaints. Although she is definitely more of an observer than a woman of leisure parading the streets, she also enjoys the freedom of the crowd made possible by the modern boulevard, and she challenges the engrained prejudice that the nineteenth-century woman cannot walk the metropolis alone – unless she is a prostitute, in mourning or disguised as a man. Besides, the 'anti-haussmannic' critique of the boulevards appears as a paradoxical parallel to the celebration of the German avenues (written almost at the same time) with which I started, where she embraces the fact that it is precisely the magnificent wide streets that allow women to walk alone. Here they can see, and be seen. Even in her Paris letters, however, she sometimes lets herself go with the flow along the modern boulevard: 'And thus one can let oneself stroll with the flow of the pedestrians for how long one doesn't know, one doesn't walk, one doesn't recognize that one has feet; one is only eyes' (II, 169). Here, it is as if Collett forgets her critical perspective and simply enjoys the pleasure of walking with her eyes, in the manner of a true *flâneuse*. Whether the figure of the *flâneur* is a useful one to account for this is, however, less self-evident, as the figure is open to such a variety of interpretations – from a distinct late eighteenth- and early nineteenth-century Parisian type with a mask of pleasurable non-participation, to a metaphor for the perspective of the modern artist in general, the one who goes botanising on the asphalt, to borrow Walter Benjamin's famous expression. The main point is, however, that although the historical *flâneur* – the leisurely city walker whose principal aim was to stroll and observe city life – was a man, Camilla Collett's words confirm that female writers, like their male colleagues, have in fact given their views on the modern city as well as enjoyed walking the metropolitan streets. Her words are thus in line with the feminist appropriation of the term in recent years (cf. Wolff 1989; Parsons 2000).

*

Parks, public spaces and promenades are recurrent topics in Collett's travelogues: Copenhagen has the King's Garden, London its Hyde Park, Paris has the Champs-Élysées as well as the Tuileries Garden and Bois de Boulogne; in Berlin Unter den Linden and in Rome Monte Pincio provide entertainment for the public – 'Poor Kristiania!' has nothing of the kind. Historians have confirmed her view on the nineteenth-century Norwegian capital: after the disastrous fires in 1658 and 1686, where large parts of the city were destroyed, the city was rebuilt in bits and pieces and still, in the late nineteenth century, looked like a sort of untidy patchwork, with no proper parks or public gardens. Thus, when Collett compares Kristiania with cities like Berlin and Paris, it comes as no surprise to find that she regards Kristiania as a great village – *ce grand village*, she names it – rather than a city.

She might well criticise the development of Paris, but the freedom of the street and the park, the mixing of people regardless of class and background, and first and foremost, the freedom to walk, are nevertheless presented as an ideal when her focus is on Kristiania – 'this is what Christiania lacks the most, and before something is done about it, it has no right to be called a metropolis', she writes in 1882 (III, 201). And in her campaign for public parks she is in fact in accordance with one of Haussmann's major transformations of urban space: the creation and extension of spaces for the public good.

Collett's strange mixing of conservatism and liberal ideas, her loyalty to king and tradition combined with radical pleas for social and urban change, is part of the essays' ambiguous pattern. It is criticism and anger that are her fuel and she is often at her best when she is attacking someone or something. And if we now return to the topic we started out with – walking, or more precisely, men's contempt of women walking alone – we will see that her Berlin letter from 1863 is countered sixteen years later, in 1879, by an another essay concerned with women and walking, or to be more precise, women's position in Kristiania. She acknowledges that things are better now than back in the 1860s – a woman is no longer openly attacked when walking the streets alone – but the unpleasant feeling of being pursued only because she is on the street by herself remains. Collett calls it 'roof-dropping-sensations' (*takdrypfornemmelser*), that is, the unpleasant sensation which arises when drops of rain, or melting snow, fall from the roofs and down on women walking the streets:

> She may walk alone now, without fear. She will, however, only in
> the rarest of moments avoid bringing back home a feeling as if she
> had to be protected against nasty drippings from the roofs. Nobody
> has stopped her, nobody has dared to address her, she has only been
> reminded of – that she is walking alone. (III, 15)

The point is of course that even though the woman now may walk alone, she is constantly reminded of the price she has to pay in the form of nasty looks or sly remarks – like wet drops falling on her.

Collett brings her impressions from abroad back to the Norwegian capital in order to change 'our own little parvenu' and educate the Norwegian people. Her attack on Kristiania connects the right to walk with the right to be, and moving in the city with the question of emancipation. If a city is to earn the right to call itself a city, it must offer its inhabitants—*all* of its citizens—places where they can move freely, and if a nation is to be regarded as a civilised nation, it must offer its women the right to walk the streets alone.

NOTE

1. All quotes from Collett are from her collected works, *Mindeudgave*, vols II–III (1913), and are my translation. This chapter is based on my book *Camilla Collett: Engasjerte essays* (2013).

WORKS CITED

Collett, Camilla (1913), *Samlede verker: Mindeudgave*, vols II–III, Kristiania: Gyldendal.

Parsons, Deborah L. (2000), *Streetwalking the Metropolis: Women, the City and Modernity*, Oxford: Oxford University Press.

Selboe, Tone (2013), *Camilla Collett: Engasjerte essays*, Oslo: Aschehoug.

Steen, Ellisiv (1954), *Den lange strid: Camilla Collett og hennes senere forfatterskap*, Oslo: Gyldendal.

Steinfeld, Torill (1996), *Den unge Camilla Collett: Et kvinnehjertes historie*, Oslo: Gyldendal.

Wolff, Janet (1989), 'The Invisible Flâneuse: Women and the Problem of Modernity', in Andrew Benjamin (ed.), *The Problem of Modernity: Adorno and Benjamin*, London and New York: Routledge.

CHAPTER 10

Alfred Jarry's Nietzschean Modernism

Jean-Michel Rabaté

The most visible experimenter in French modernism was Alfred Jarry, one of the first exuberant avant-gardists who had been touched by the spirit of Nietzsche. Jarry's main invention was to transform Nietzsche's ethical energies in the sexual domain, rewriting Zarathustra's *Superman* as a phallic *Supermale*. Nietzsche's rhetoric of violence also inspired Jarry's plays. In the artistic domain, Jarry grafted late symbolism onto a specific variation of cultural anarchism. The novel *The Supermale* contains the seeds of a French modernism that took off with Guillaume Apollinaire before being relayed and transformed by André Breton and his post-Dadaist friends.

Jarry had been extremely lucky with his teachers, to the point that he never forgot any of them, beginning with the unfortunate 'Père Hébert', the ridiculous and rotund science teacher in his Rennes high school who was satirised and monumentalised in the savage parody of Père Ubu. Later in Paris it was in 1893 that Henri Bergson himself introduced Jarry to his philosophy of time and intuition.

While still a *lycéen* in Rennes, Jarry was introduced to the works of Nietzsche in 1889 by his philosophy teacher, Benjamin Bourdon. Bourdon had just come back from Germany where he had participated in Wilhelm Wundt's research on experimental psychology. Bourdon was soon to complete a dissertation entitled *The Expression of Emotions and Tendencies in Language*.[1] Bourdon followed Wundt in linking Darwinian expressive universals visible in animals and humans, and a 'popular psychology' stressing features of simplicity, intensity, stylisation and emotional empathy.[2] Wundt's psychology insisted on the pregnancy of formulaic creation when discussing gestures: gestures could be constructed as formulaic expressions of basic emotions. Wundt's 'formula' applied to the psychology of gesture helped Aby Warburg coin his favourite expression, *Pathosformel* (formula of pathos). Warburg not only coined the expression *Pathosformel* but also systematised a theory of thinking via images and symbols. The 'formula of pathos' combines the expressivity of strong or violent affects and a systematic comparison of universal forms. The essay in which the term was introduced dates from 1905 and was devoted to Dürer's classical models, especially his early modern rendering of the 'Death of Orpheus' topos. The language used by Warburg implies that 'pathos' is not reducible to 'emotion', no more than *Formel* can mean 'form' or 'formalism'. *Formel* corresponds to a series of formulaic expressions developing matrices of encoded sequences in specific visual languages. Dürer adapted a formal vocabulary of expressive forms and thus initiated a process of intensification that culminated with the Baroque. Jarry accelerated this process until it exploded in parody and caricature.

Jarry's creation of Ubu as a terrifying puppet, a schoolboy's bogey condensing the laughable power of adults, their omnipotence experienced as random and pathetic displays of violent sadism by children, owes a lot to Wundt and Bourdon's psychology of emotions. The barely caricatured figure of Bourdon appears as Ubu's 'Conscience' – easily identifiable because of his mannerism, the regular interjection of '*et ainsi de suite*' in all his sentences – in *Ubu Cocu*. It is astonishing to think that Bourdon introduced French high-school students to untranslated works of Nietzsche eleven years before the philosopher's demise. Bourdon would 'explain' Nietzsche, as Jarry writes in memories of his youth.[3] In 1893, the future poet Léon-Paul Fargue, Jarry's close friend, one-time lover and soon bitter enemy, wrote to Jarry from Germany, confessing that he wished that Bergson could talk more about Nietzsche; if he did, his lectures would truly be beyond good and evil![4] Soon, Jarry blended Nietzsche's self-proclaimed persona of the 'Anti-Christ' with Bergson's theory of Intuition in his 'pataphysical' or 'anarchist' version of 'César-Antechrist'. And indeed, King Ubu appears for the first time in *César-Antechrist*, a long prose text published in several instalments in 1984.[5]

Besides being a cultural anarchist tending to nihilism and a gifted literary provocateur, Jarry was a fervent disciple of Mallarmé. Mallarmé had congratulated him on the success of *Ubu Roi*, and after that wrote to the young writer several times. When Mallarmé died in 1898, Jarry attended the funeral. His obituary evoked the 'island of Ptyx' in a warm and moving homage to the most esoteric and obscure sonnet of the master's production, the famous 'Sonnet in X'.[6] Jarry was a living bridge between late symbolism and early Futurism. Marinetti, a futurist who is rarely linked with symbolism, had been impressed by the Ubu cycle of plays. He met Jarry several times; in 1906, we see Jarry thanking Marinetti, who had sent him *Roi Bombance*, a proto-futurist play inspired by the Ubu cycle.[7]

I will concentrate on two novels by Jarry: *Messaline, Roman de l'ancienne Rome* (1901) and *Le Surmâle, Roman moderne* (1902). While the former novel takes imperial Rome as its setting, the latter is situated in the future of 1902, for it takes place, by a neat inversion, in 1920. Given the deliberate manner in which the future and the past are intertwined, the conditions are gathered for the creation of a specific French modernism. This is confirmed by a term not translated in the English version, the subtitle of the second novel: *The Supermale: A Modern Novel*.[8] Indeed, this novel flaunts its modernity by heaping up real and fantastic machines, bicycles, locomotives, fast cars, phonographs and dynamos. At the end, a terrifying machine-to-inspire-love explodes and kills the hero. *The Supermale*'s plot is similar to that of *Messalina*: in both novels, a character seeks a paroxystic sexual pleasure and dies after having beaten world records in love-making. The feminine half of the diptych is situated in the histories of the debaucheries of the Roman emperors, whose vignettes had been narrated by Suetonius and Tacitus. The future of 1920 is marked by mostly American inventions and delirious machines. Jarry's conceit presupposes an almost total identification of technology and sexuality. In both novels, sexual excess leads to new wisdom, but it flirts so much with the Absolute that it leads to an explosive and apocalyptic demise.

Jarry's modernism was constituted by the splicing of the 'modern' text of *The Supermale* with *Messalina*, a historical novel evoking Flaubert's *Salammbô*. Both novels display narrative techniques that are daringly innovative, which is more visible with *The Supermale*. The two main 'events' of the plot – a bicycle race of ten thousand miles won by the hero, André Marcueil, against a racing locomotive and a team of five cyclists fuelled by 'perpetual-motion-food', and the sexual contest in which Marcueil, disguised as an Indian, has sex for a whole day before reaching the sum of eighty-two orgasms – are narrated by several filters like the voice of a journalistic report, the account provided by a doctor records the sexual prowess while speculating on God and 'pataphysics', the pseudo-science invented by Faustroll, another character of Jarry's. *The Supermale* is a modernist novel because it splices the present and the past seamlessly. Even though it is shot through with science-fiction speculations about a futurist intermixing of men and machines, it keeps harking back to the past. Marcueil's wish to make love indefinitely is based upon his reading of a Latin poem. His curiosity is roused when he reads about Messalina in Juvenal's satire that describes how when the Emperor Claudius was asleep, Messalina, disguised, would go to a brothel and sell herself to the clients; she would be the last to leave reluctantly, and with 'her taut sex still burning, inflamed with lust', she would return to the Emperor's bed.[9]

Marcueil is a super-athlete and a fine Latinist. The point of departure for his sexual fantasies is the word *rigidae* used by Juvenal to depict the Empress Messalina's insatiable appetite (TS, 30):

> *adhuc ardens rigidae tentigine vulvae,*
> *Et lassata viris nec dum satiate recessit.* [10]

The epigraph for *Messalina*[11] is not translated – those who do not know Latin need to follow Marcueil's gloss in the third chapter of *The Supermale* (TS, 29–31). Marcueil explains to the doctor and the general that lines 128–30 of Juvenal's sixth satire present us with a woman 'still ardent', but he refuses to translate more. A Latinist can reconstruct the sense. Messalina leaves her 'cell' in the 'House of Happiness', her brothel in Suburra, feeling 'still ardent with the tension of her rigid vulva, and tired of men but not satiated yet'. The events evoked in the first chapter of *Messalina* become the object of a heated discussion in *The Supermale*.

The doctor reduces Messalina to a pathological case of nymphomania, to which he adds hysteria, priapism and satyriasis (TS, 32). Defending her, Marcueil states, 'The only real women are Messalinas' (TS, 30), and assures his listeners that her case proves that women can also experience what men happen to experience, that is, a case of ithyphallicism: 'There is no reason why there should not be produced in men, once a certain figure is reached, the very same physiological phenomenon as in Messalina' (TS, 31). In short, men and women are entitled to experience shattering, absolute and overwhelming paroxysms of sexual jouissance. When the doctor expresses scepticism in the face of this literalist interpretation of *rigidi tentigo veretri'* (the rigid tension of the penis), Marcueil complicates his position by asserting that the line was an interpolation that he retranslates: 'still ardent or kept ardent by the tension of her rigid vulva' (TS, 30).

The sexual vertigo experienced by Marcueil hinges around infinite series: he is as fascinated by the fact that women carry all their ova in their organs (eighteen million) as by the fact that repeated sexual congress can induce a state of sexual 'rigidity' for a woman like Messalina. This condition can then be repeated endlessly, for it 'becomes permanent, and even more pronounced, as one moves beyond the limits of human strength toward numerical infinity; and that it is consequently advantageous to pass beyond as rapidly as is possible, or if you prefer, as is conceivable' (TS, 31). This states the main ithyphallic fantasy of the novel – by playing on infinite numbers, immortality is at hand, or at least a variation on the eternal return of the same. Marcueil asserts: '[I]t is possible that a man capable of making love indefinitely might experience no difficulty in doing anything else indefinitely' (TS, 34). The boast transforming a 'Supermale' into a 'Spermale' will trigger the ire of the doctor. Marcueil is accused of not being scientific, of wallowing 'in the department of the impossible' (TS, 34) when he claims that sexual excess leads to a superhuman transformation of women and men into rigid, turgid, ever-ready phalluses. Jarry did not wallow in the department of the Impossible, and appears here as a predecessor of Georges Bataille.

The futurist fantasy is the counterpart of Messalina's quest. Messalina's deepest wish is to be united with Phales, the god of erect phalluses. Phales, she thinks, has fled her brothel, to her despair. She then keeps invoking the god of phalluses, Pan, Priapus, Phallus, Phales, Love – the various names of her multifaceted god. A passage describes its emblem in a way that would have attracted Freud's attention, precisely because he was writing about the 'Thing' (*das Ding*) in his 'Project for a Scientific Psychology'. Freud attempted to pinpoint the irreducible exteriority or intractable otherness of libidinal objects that cannot be processed by consciousness.[12] In the novel, the phallus is similarly called the 'Thing' (*Chose*):

But the Thing is more monstrous, strange and enticing, for it has meaning.

This divine emblem, the great Phallus carved from a fig-tree, is nailed to the lintel like a night-owl to a barn-door, or a god to the pediment of a temple. (MNIR, 10)

If one could only catch and keep the priapic 'Thing', one would feel an endless immersion in love. This outpouring of jouissance is compared to the union of the Emperor and his whore: 'A man is the husband of Messalina during the moment of love, and then for as long as he is able to live an uninterrupted series of such moments' (MNIR, 10–11). This sentence generates the entire narrative and the first sentence of *The Supermale*: 'The act of love is of no importance, since it can be performed indefinitely' (TS, 3). In the end, what happens is the reverse: the act of love is of supreme importance because it can be performed indefinitely.

Why this parallel debasement and exaltation? *Messalina* provides a clue to what is at stake by showing that one of the rare positive characters is Claudius. Although he is weak, a cuckold and a stutterer, he keeps on writing poetry and playing with dice, with repeated allusions to Mallarmé's 'ancient master' losing himself in abstruse calculations in *Un coup de dés* . . . Indeed, when by a curious bigamy Messalina marries her lover, the virile Silius, a Roman consul, the only obstacle to their sexual bliss comes when he discovers one of Claudius's dice in the bed where they have just had sex: 'Silius searched, fumbled feverishly [. . .] and captured what was it that was causing his discomfort – had an insect bitten him? Livid, angular, crystalline, sharp, senile, obscene, naked to the bone. A die' (MNIR, 56–7). The diminutive die is 'that thing' (MNIR, 57) preventing Messalina from loving him 'absolutely'. Because of this obstacle, Silius will never possess the phallic 'Thing'. When he grasps this, he screams all of a sudden, quite surprisingly: 'MESSALINA IS VIRGIN!' (MNIR, 57). How can this be, given her record of more than twenty-five lovers per night? It all becomes clearer if we see Messalina as a Mallarméan heroine like Hérodiade, who in *Igitur* stands for Salome, a name evoking castration or beheading. However, the Christian Virgin lurks behind her.

Hérodiade obtained the decapitation of the prophet John in the same way as Messalina manipulates Claudius who forces Asiaticus to commit suicide, whereas he is innocent. The impure Messalina announces the Christian Saint Messalina mentioned in the fanciful almanac of Père Ubu for the month of January 1901. Next to '*Décervelage*' ('Debraining', the punishment meted out for the nobles under King Ubu's despotic rule), given for 1 January, we find 'Saint Messalina' as the patron saint for 23 January (JOCI, 575). The Christian meaning of 'real presence' refers to the Eucharist, a symbol endowed with the reality of divine presence, in Roman Catholic rituals at least. In conformity with the logic elaborated at the end of *L'Amour Absolu*, and the Mallarméan logic of abolition, the divine absolute kills whoever experiences it. The only chance of an encounter with excessive jouissance will have to be mediated through art.

The outcome of Messalina's relentless quest for the 'real presence' of a phallic god will, of course, cause her death, which comes at the end, once Claudius has seen her for what she is. While he reluctantly condemns her to death, she welcomes the centurion's sword, for in her delirium she mistakes it for an ivory phallus. She wants to be penetrated by it. She falls in front of the soldier. When he plunges the weapon into her naked breast, she exclaims: 'O how you are a god, PHALES! Phalès, I knew nothing of love; I knew all men but you are the first Immortal I have loved! Phalès, at last, and so late!' (MNIR, 69). The centurion has to assert that his sword is a blade, not his penis. She keeps asking Phalès to take her away, and thus dies – of love. As she dies, the god Phalès vanishes for good: the great Pan of phallicism has gone.

In this *fin-de-siècle* fantasy of *Liebe und Tod*, the ithyphallicism sought by Messalina and Marcueil betrays a hyperbolic fantasy of bisexual enjoyment. Jarry's pataphysics depicts men and women as having the possibility of attaining a superhuman energy and sexual bliss, even if their ultimate erection always spells death. At the last minute, Messalina gazes at her own reflection in the sword that will dispatch her. The phallus is a mirror but also a sharp stake, such as those used for impalement. By a loaded Latin pun, the *phallus* turns into *palus*, an association made explicit in *César-Antichrist*:

The Templar: Uprooted phallus, do not bounce around so much.

Fasce: Tail or head [Jarry puns on '*Pile ou face*' ('heads or
                tails')], reflection of my master, in you I gaze at my
                reflection. [. . .] Phallus perpendicular to the smile of
                the Ithyphallic in your laterality. (JOCI, 289)

Jarry's own ithyphallicism was not devoid of humour. When Apollinaire visited the small apartment in which Jarry lived (the rooms had been cut in two, and only a small man like Jarry could stand upright in it), he saw a huge stone phallus made in Japan, a gift of the painter Félicien Rops. As all the objects in the room looked diminutive, Jarry retorted to a visiting lady who had asked playfully whether the object was a plaster cast of his organ: 'No, this is a reduction.'[13]

Jarry's mixture of laughter and tragedy, of heresy and saintliness, tapped an old doctrine that Joyce would apply to *Finnegans Wake*, the doctrine of the unity of the opposites. Joy and Sadness combine to heighten each other. Fasce continues:

Axiom and principle of identical contraries, the pataphysician, clinging
to your ears and retractable wings, flying fish, is the dwarf climax of
the giant, beyond all metaphysics; thanks to you, it is the Antichrist
and God too, horse of the Spirit, Less-in-More, Less-that-is-More,
cinematics of the zero remaining in the eyes, infinite polyhedron.
[. . .] You are the owl, Sex and Spirit, hermaphrodite, you create and
destroy. (JOCI, 289–90)

A similar pun on a lethal *phallus* underpins several scenes in *Messalina*. At one point, Messalina wonders why she cannot find any 'lingam or ithyphallus silhouetting its tall pale' (MNIR, 32) when she visits the stately garden of Asiaticus. The recurrent phallicisation of the objects of desire derives from an obvious wish to compensate for the wobbly nature of emotions. Feminine sexuality is bounded with a hard and rigid pole. It is from such a vantage point that one can then jump into infinity, as we see at the end of *Absolute Love*, when we are introduced to 'The right to lie'. The sex or gender of lies is feminine, we learn (JOCI, 949). Truth is to be found in a masculine God; however, God would prostitute Himself if He gave access to the truth He embodies. The way out of this contradiction is to affirm human desire above all.

Jarry would have agreed with Freud's contention that libido, all libido, is male; if a feminine pole is necessary for the transmutation into an infinite power to affect, this pole will be firmly controlled. The love scenes between Marcueil and the young passionaria Ellen in *The Supermale* are curiously fraught with tension, marked by aggression. After Marcueil's exertions make Ellen reach the impressive number of eighty-two orgasms, she feels mostly hostile to Marcueil and comments dryly: 'That wasn't the least bit funny.' Then, instead of being thankful, she tries to blind him with her hatpin, so that he has to hypnotise her to prevent this (TS, 104–5). When he believes (wrongly, it turns out) that Ellen, exhausted, has died, suddenly Marcueil expresses an immense tenderness. It is conveyed in a love poem that he recites over her inert body, concluding with 'I adore her.' In fact, she has just passed out and we discover that this surprising and highly lyrical profession of love had in fact been generated by a 'love machine'. In the end, this love machine goes too fast in super-drive mode, which makes it explode and kill Marcueil. With these anarchic and self-destructive machines, we enter the world of futurist modernism. Jarry singlehandedly invented both Italian Futurism and the desiring (and bachelor) machines popularised by Deleuze and Guattari.

It is no coincidence that the best essay on Jarry's philosophy was written by Gilles Deleuze, who understood the links between Jarry's anarchism and Heidegger's meditation on the disappearance of Being and the domination of technology. Technology is the modern danger, but a form of salvation can come from it:

> The bicycle is not a simple machine, but the simplest model of a
> Machine appropriate to the times. [. . .] The Bicycle, with its chains
> and its gears, is the essence of technology: it envelops and develops, it
> brings about the great Turning of the earth. The bicycle is the frame,
> like Heidegger's 'fourfold'.[14]

What Deleuze did not say, because he was reluctant to use Freudian terms, is that Jarry's textual and allegorical Bicycle connects desiring subjects with the ontology of the drive. Jarry calls up the specific Freudian term of *Trieb*, a term that should not be confused with 'instinct' even under its form of 'death drive'.

Freud saw in the drive a general force accounting for the upsurge of erotic energy in human beings. He defined it in 1915 according to its force, source, object and aim. Jarry anticipated Freud's later invention of the 'death drive' as Thanatos, an ultimate allegory in which Lacan saw the model for the structure of all drives. Jarry's particular hardness, intensity and eccentricity derive from his intimate familiarity with a death drive whose increased speed he was hoping to harness and that he magnified until it reached infinity.

The same symbol of infinity is hidden in the speeding bicycle drafted by Marcel Duchamp in 1914. His mysteriously titled 'Having the apprentice in the sun' (*'Avoir l'apprenti dans le soleil'*) represents a man pedalling up a slope towards the sun, sketched on yellowing music paper. Inverting the common expression of *'Avoir le soleil dans l'oeil'* ('To be blinded by the sun'), Duchamp evokes Jarry's cyclist, Marcueil. His title puns on *'à voir: l'empreinte dans le sol'* and *'avoir la pente dans le soleil'* ('to be seen: the imprint in the ground' and 'to have the slope in the sun'). A speeding 'apprentice', a learner sublimely fighting against a sun blinding him: this is Duchamp's homage to Jarry who was known as a notoriously fierce cyclist. We can learn in our *apprentissage* by toiling upwards and fighting against a paternal and domineering sun.

Like the wheels of a bicycle, Jarry's novels form a diptych of sexual excess. The 'novel of ancient Rome' and the 'modern novel' combine like two wheels spinning together; by reading, re-reading and pedalling, readers create a lemniscate, the symbol of infinity; if sexual excess leads to a superhuman transformation of women and men into rigid phalluses, textual excess ushers in the pathos of the new. The frantic ithyphallicism sought by Messalina and Marcueil recycles Nietzsche's religious parody in *Zarathustra* while pointing to the future, heralding Bataille's orgiastic and lethal 'accursed share', a dark drive that would exceed even modernism.

NOTES

1. Benjamin B. Bourdon, *L'Expression des emotions et des tendances dans le langage*, Paris: Felix Alcan, 1892.

2. Wilhelm Wundt, *Elements of Folk Psychology* (1900), trans. Edward Leroy Schaub, Project Gutenberg, 2013, pp. 59–64.

3. Alfred Jarry, *Oeuvres complètes*, vol. III, ed. Henri Bordillon, Patrick Besnier, Bernard Le Doze and Michel Arrivé, Paris: Gallimard, Pléiade, 1988, p. 531.

4. Léon-Paul Fargue à Alfred Jarry, 5 mai 1893, from Coburg, available at <http://www.alfredjarry.wordpress.com/1893/05/> (last accessed 15 December 2016).

5. See 'César-Antechrist', in Alfred Jarry, *Oeuvres complètes*, vol. I, ed. Michel Arrivé, Paris: Pléiade, 1972, pp. 271–332. Hereafter in the text abbreviated as JOCI, followed by page number. César-Antechrist says: 'I am the infinite Intuition . . .' (Jarry, *Oeuvres complètes*, vol. I, p. 330).

6. 'Gestes et opinions du docteur Faustroll, pataphysicien', in Jarry, *Oeuvres complètes*, vol. I, pp. 685–6. See also Marieke Dubbelboer, *The Subversive Poetics of Alfred Jarry: Abusing Culture in the Almanachs du Pere Ubu*, London: Legenda, 2012, pp. 35–7.

7. See their exchange in Jarry, *Oeuvres complètes*, vol. III, pp. 635–6.

8. Alfred Jarry, *The Supermale*, trans. Ralph Gladstone and Barbara Wright, Cambridge: Exact Change, 1999. Hereafter in the text abbreviated as TS, followed by page number.

9. Juvenal, Satire VI – 'Don't Marry', in *The Satires*, trans. A. S. Kline, 2011, available at <http://www.poetryintranslation.com/PITBR/Latin/JuvenalSatires6.htm> (last accessed 15 December 2016).

10. See Alfred Jarry, 'Messaline, roman de l'ancienne Rome', in *Oeuvres complètes*, vol. II, ed. Henri Bordillon, Patrick Besnier and Bernard Le Doze, Paris: Gallimard, Pléiade, 1987, p. 75.

11. Alfred Jarry, *Messalina: A Novel of Imperial Rome*, trans. John Harman, London: Atlas Press, 1985, p. 9. Hereafter in the text abbreviated as MNIR, followed by page number.

12. Sigmund Freud, 'Project for a Scientific Psychology' (1895), in *The Invention of Psychoanalysis: Letters to Wilhelm Fliess*, trans. Eric Mosbacher and James Strachey, New York: Basic Books, 1977, p. 441.

13. Guillaume Apollinaire, 'Feu Jarry' (1909), in *Oeuvres en prose complètes*, vol. II, ed. Pierre Caizergues and Michel Décaudin, Paris: Gallimard, Pléiade, 1991, p. 1040.

14. Gilles Deleuze, 'An Unrecognized Precursor to Heidegger: Alfred Jarry', in *Essays Critical and Clinical*, trans. D. W. Smith and M. A. Greco, Minneapolis: University of Minnesota Press, 1997, p. 93.

CHAPTER 11

On First Looking into Derrida's *Glas*

J. Hillis Miller

> Then felt I like some watcher of the skies
> When a new planet swims into his ken;
> Or like stout Cortez when with eagle eyes
> He star'd at the Pacific – and all his men
> Look'd at each other with a wild surmise –
> Silent, upon a peak in Darien.
> John Keats, 'On First Looking into Chapman's Homer'[1]

My current work is on the question of what actually happens when some-one (you or I, dear reader) opens up a book or a journal and starts reading a novel, a poem, a short story, a critical essay, a critical book or a philosophical work. My claim is that what happens is extremely strange. Moreover, it differs from person to person and for a given person from one time to another. What happens in reading can by no means be limited to just making rational sense of the words, as pedagogues and reading specialists sometimes claim should be the primary goal of reading. Cognitive science and brain scans are of little use in this project, since they can tell me which parts of my brain light up when I read a given text, but do not generally pay attention to my report of my sub-jective experience. 'It's not scientific.' A report of my subjective experience in a given case, however, untrustworthy as it may be, is the only evidence in support of carrying out my quixotic project.

I have already written essays working on this project about passages in an illustrated novel by Anthony Trollope (*Framley Parsonage*), a poem by Yeats ('The Cold Heaven'), a poem by Wallace Stevens ('The Motive for Metaphor') and a passage in a book by Derrida (*Otobiographies*).[2] In this present essay, here and now, I shall try to identify from memory as best I can what happened in my mind and feelings when in 1974 I first picked up Derrida's *Glas*[3] in Bethany, Connecticut, and read. *Tolle, lege!* Doing that certainly produced 'wild surmise'.

Or, rather, I shall perforce compare what happened then (a first reading) with what happens here and now, in Deer Isle, Maine, from 13 October to 2 November 2015, in a much later reading. The latter unavoidably stands as a screen between now and then. I now have long since read the whole of *Glas*, carefully, word by word. All during the fall of 1974 and beyond I read a few pages early each morning while doing my running in place. I read it, of course, necessarily in the original French, since no translation as yet existed. My French was pretty good, and I had read earlier work by Derrida in French, but I quickly discovered that to read *Glas* requires more than understanding sentences like 'Je vais au tableau noir' or 'Je prends ma place'. Not that such an elementary level of French was good enough for Derrida's *De la grammatologie* either![4] I started out with *Glas* trying to read just the Hegel column on the left, planning to come back later to the Genet column. I soon found, however, that Derrida's layout was too much for me. My eye kept drifting to the right towards the Genet column. So I gave in and read both columns of a given page at the same time, with binocular vision, looking for resonances and, usually, not finding any, but having my intellectual and affective confusion exacerbated.

My reading the first page of *Glas* now is quite different, partly because it is a second reading and has, for starters, as a presupposition all that I remember of my first reading, especially my conviction that it is a truly amazing book, a masterwork of postmodernism. I now have at hand, moreover, all the help in reading *Glas* that was not available then. That includes especially the English translation by John P. Leavey, Jr. and Richard Rand,[5] as well as the big book of commentary and annotation, *Glassary*, by Gregory L. Ulmer and John P. Leavey, Jr., with a valuable 'Foreword' by Derrida himself.[6] In 1974, by contrast, I was pretty much on my own, even though I had read carefully most of Derrida's previously published work and had heard his seminars at Johns Hopkins and (I think) already the first annual ones at Yale.

The printing of *Glas* was completed on 27 September 1974, according to the legal notice at the end of the book. On a day in late September or early October of that year, I think it must have been, I went out in all innocence from my house at 28 Sperry Road in Bethany, Connecticut, to get my daily mail from our rural roadside mailbox. I had moved from Johns Hopkins to Yale in 1972. There among the bills and ads was a sizable package from France. I carried it inside and opened it. Behold! It was a book about the size of a small telephone book with *Glas* in big letters on the cover and the name Jacques Derrida in small print plus the name of the publisher, Éditions Galilée, in slightly larger print. Here is a scan of what remains of that cover, in somewhat battered condition and separated from the book itself by all those months of reading the book (Figure 11.1). At some point over the years I tried unsuccessfully to glue it back onto the rest of the book.

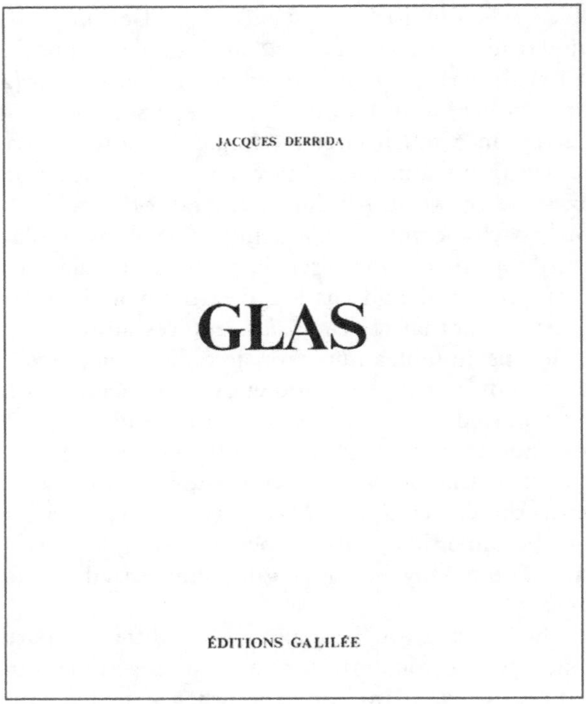

JACQUES DERRIDA

GLAS

ÉDITIONS GALILÉE

Figure 11.1

Galilée! Of course. That is French for the astronomer and mathematician Galileo (1564–1642). It could also refer to the region of Israel called Galilee. I don't know which, or both, the founding editors of Galilée had in mind. Joanna Delorme, who runs Galilée's permissions department now, would probably know, but the allusion to Galileo, deliberate or not, would in any case remain. Galileo was famous, among other things, for discovering the satellites around Jupiter and for observing the planet Neptune. The lines quoted from Keats in my epigraph, 'Then felt I like some watcher of the skies / When a new planet swims into his ken', apply especially well to Galileo.[7]

If the publisher of *Glas* is named for that watcher of the skies who observed a new planet, then the book is published under that aegis. Its name commits it to new discoveries. My experience on first opening *Glas* was certainly like discovering a new planet. I had never seen anything like it. So to my mental image by way of a fortuitous association of stout Cortez 'discovering' the Pacific must be added the imaginary scene of Galileo looking through a telescope at a new planet. Derrida once mentioned to me soon after *Glas* was published that doing so had nearly bankrupted Galilée, so costly was it in those pre-computer days to get the typefaces and the arrangement of the words on the pages right. Derrida said, with a gesture of his outstretched hand, palm down about three feet from the floor, that the proofs were 'This high.' That mental image from my memory bank must be added to all the others *Glas* generates in my mind. Galilée, finally, is another of the words in 'gl', or almost in 'gl', that are so important in *Glas*. They are glottal stop words that mimic stran*gul*ation when they are uttered.

The word 'galactics' (*galactique*) (another 'gl' word) is used in the inserted 'Blurb' (of which more later) to name the arrangement of the elements of the right, or Genet, column. 'Galactics' is opposed to the 'dialectics' of the left, or Hegel, column and may allude obscurely to Derrida's publisher: 'Une *dialectique* d'un côté, une *galactique* de l'autre.' Galilée went on to publish many books by Derrida and now owns the rights to his unpublished 'remains', so they have got their investment back and then some, but they have served him well.

When I opened the book, I found the title page had a handwritten dedication to me by Derrida (Figure 11.2). He already had the touching generosity of sending me inscribed copies of his books as they came out. I have a lot of

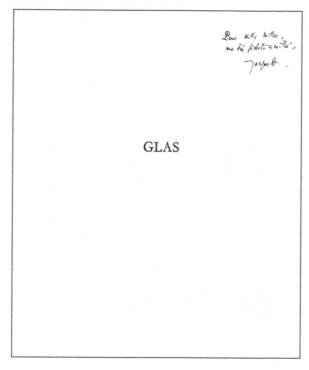

Figure 11.2

them from over the years until his death. They have monetary as well as much sentimental value. I used to tell him that I would support myself and my wife in our old age by selling my inscribed Derridas one by one. I have not had to do that yet.

In addition, the book had a separate insert of a smaller page size, the sort of self-explanation, aids to reading, by the author that often is printed on the back cover of a book but in France was commonly printed on a loose sheet. Derrida used one form or another of these pre-orientations habitually. Since the 'Blurb' provides invaluable directions for how to read *Glas*, here are scans of both recto and verso of my yellowed and torn copy, with the corner torn off in some accident over the years (Figures 11.3 and 11.4).[8]

With all that preliminary digitation and deciphering as context, I must finally have opened *Glas* to the first page. It is numbered 7 in the book, though it is actually the first page of the text proper. I will call it in this essay 'the first page' or 'page one'. Here it is, again scanned from my original battered copy (Figure 11.5).

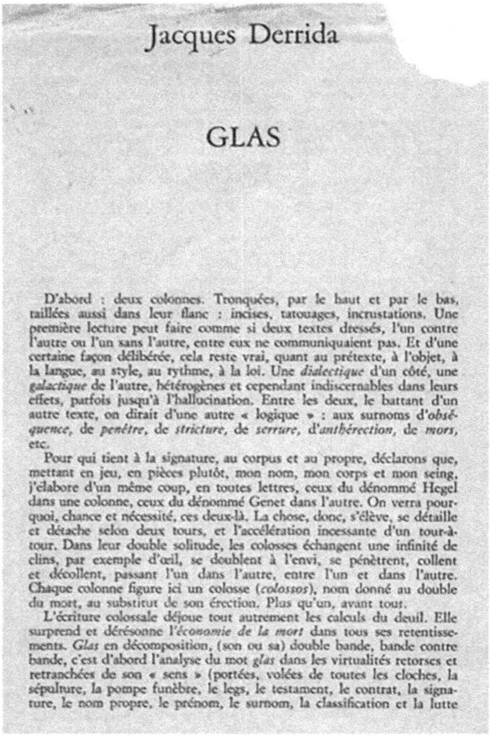

Jacques Derrida

GLAS

D'abord : deux colonnes. Tronquées, par le haut et par le bas, taillées aussi dans leur flanc : incises, tatouages, incrustations. Une première lecture peut faire comme si deux textes dressés, l'un contre l'autre ou l'un sans l'autre, entre eux ne communiquaient pas. Et d'une certaine façon délibérée, cela reste vrai, quant au prétexte, à l'objet, à la langue, au style, au rythme, à la loi. Une *dialectique* d'un côté, une *galactique* de l'autre, hétérogènes et cependant indiscernables dans leurs effets, parfois jusqu'à l'hallucination. Entre les deux, le battant d'un autre texte, on dirait d'une autre « logique » : aux surnoms d'*obséquence*, de *penêtre*, de *stricture*, de *serrure*, d'*anthérection*, de *mors*, etc.

Pour qui tient à la signature, au corpus et au propre, déclarons que, mettant en jeu, en pièces plutôt, mon nom, mon corps et mon seing, j'élabore d'un même coup, en toutes lettres, ceux du dénommé Hegel dans une colonne, ceux du dénommé Genet dans l'autre. On verra pourquoi, chance et nécessité, ces deux-là. La chose, donc, s'élève, se détaille et détache selon deux tours, et l'accélération incessante d'un tour-à-tour. Dans leur double solitude, les colosses échangent une infinité de clins, par exemple d'œil, se doublent à l'envi, se pénètrent, collent et décollent, passant l'un dans l'autre, entre l'un et dans l'autre. Chaque colonne figure ici un colosse (*colossos*), nom donné au double du mort, au substitut de son érection. Plus qu'un, avant tout.

L'écriture colossale déjoue tout autrement les calculs du deuil. Elle surprend et dérésonne l'*économie de la mort* dans tous ses retentissements. *Glas* en décomposition, (son ou sa) double bande, bande contre bande, c'est d'abord l'analyse du mot *glas* dans les virtualités retorses et retranchées de son « sens » (portées, volées de toutes les cloches, la sépulture, la pompe funèbre, le legs, le testament, le contrat, la signature, le nom propre, le prénom, le surnom, la classification et la lutte

Figure 11.3

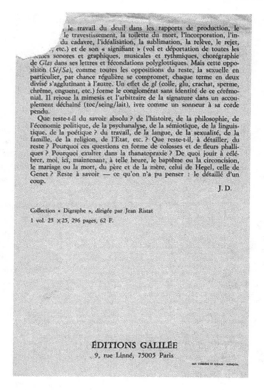

le travail du deuil dans les rapports de production, le
le travestissement, la toilette du mort, l'incorporation, l'in-
du cadavre, l'idéalisation, la sublimation, la relève, le rejet,
etc.) et de son « signifiant » (vol et déportation de toutes les
...mes sonores et graphiques, musicales et rythmiques, chorégraphie
de *Glas* dans ses lettres et fécondations polyglottiques. Mais cette opposition (*Sé/Sa*), comme toutes les oppositions du reste, la sexuelle en
particulier, par chance régulière se compromet, chaque terme en deux
divisé s'agglutinant à l'autre. Un effet de *gl* (colle, glu, crachat, sperme,
chrême, onguent, etc.) forme le conglomérat sans identité de ce cérémo-
nial. Il rejoue la mimesis et l'arbitraire de la signature dans un accou-
plement déchaîné (toc/seing/lait), ivre comme un sonneur à sa corde
pendu.
       Que reste-t-il du savoir absolu ? de l'histoire, de la philosophie, de
l'économie politique, de la psychanalyse, de la sémiotique, de la linguis-
tique, de la poétique ? du travail, de la langue, de la sexualité, de la
famille, de la religion, de l'Etat, etc. ? Que reste-t-il, à détailler, du
reste ? Pourquoi ces questions en forme de colosses et de fleurs phalli-
ques ? Pourquoi exulter dans la thanatopraxie ? De quoi jouir à célé-
brer, moi, ici, maintenant, à telle heure, le baptême ou la circoncision,
le mariage ou la mort, du père et de la mère, celui de Hegel, celle de
Genet ? Reste à savoir — ce qu'on n'a pu penser : le détaillé d'un
coup.

                                                                J.D.

Collection « Digraphe », dirigée par Jean Ristat
1 vol. 23 ×25, 296 pages, 62 F.

                  ÉDITIONS GALILÉE
                  9, rue Linné, 75005 Paris

Figure 11.4

I give all these details in part to remind my readers that beginning to read
a book has all sorts of physical contexts that involve hands, fingers and other
parts of the body as well as looking at the words on the page. As many other
people have argued, this means that reading a printed book is quite different
from reading an e-text version of the same text.

*

When I began to try to read the first page of *Glas* I was certainly like stout
Cortez (actually stout Balboa, Keats's mistake) discovering the Pacific Ocean,
'silent, upon a peak in Darien'. I had great difficulty even beginning to understand what was going on. Remember that I had no translation and no commentary beyond that 'Blurb' to help me. I knew Derrida's previous work quite
well, but nothing in that work except 'Tympan', the prefatory essay to *Marges*,
published in 1972, two years before *Glas*, at all prepared me for the typograph-
ical high jinks of *Glas*.[9] Though I read French quite well, as I have said, that
first page was full of words I did not know. This included the word *Glas* itself,

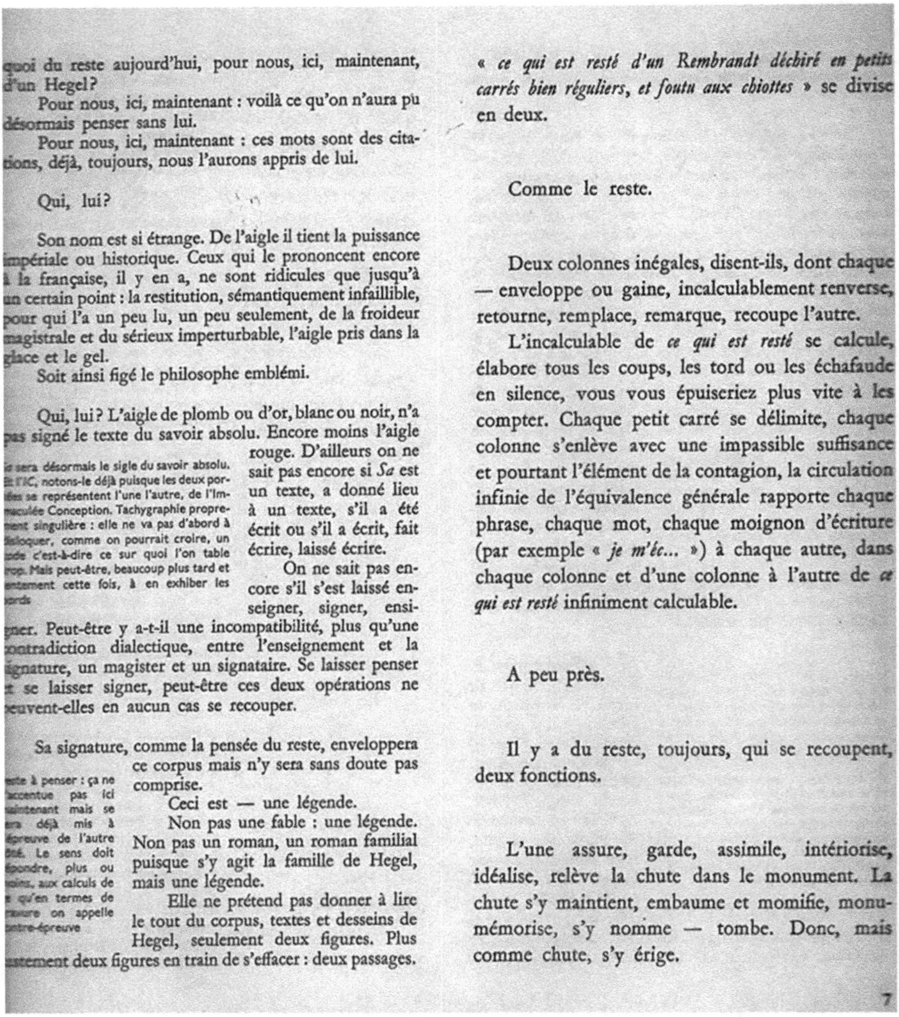

quoi du reste aujourd'hui, pour nous, ici, maintenant, d'un Hegel?

Pour nous, ici, maintenant : voilà ce qu'on n'aura pu désormais penser sans lui.

Pour nous, ici, maintenant : ces mots sont des citations, déjà, toujours, nous l'aurons appris de lui.

Qui, lui?

Son nom est si étrange. De l'aigle il tient la puissance impériale ou historique. Ceux qui le prononcent encore à la française, il y en a, ne sont ridicules que jusqu'à un certain point : la restitution, sémantiquement infaillible, pour qui l'a un peu lu, un peu seulement, de la froideur magistrale et du sérieux imperturbable, l'aigle pris dans la glace et le gel.

Soit ainsi figé le philosophe emblémi.

Qui, lui? L'aigle de plomb ou d'or, blanc ou noir, n'a pas signé le texte du savoir absolu. Encore moins l'aigle rouge. D'ailleurs on ne sait pas encore si *Sa* est un texte, a donné lieu à un texte, s'il a été écrit ou s'il a écrit, fait écrire, laissé écrire.

On ne sait pas encore s'il s'est laissé enseigner, signer, ensigner. Peut-être y a-t-il une incompatibilité, plus qu'une contradiction dialectique, entre l'enseignement et la signature, un magister et un signataire. Se laisser penser et se laisser signer, peut-être ces deux opérations ne peuvent-elles en aucun cas se recouper.

Sa signature, comme la pensée du reste, enveloppera ce corpus mais n'y sera sans doute pas comprise.

Ceci est — une légende.

Non pas une fable : une légende. Non pas un roman, un roman familial puisque s'y agit la famille de Hegel mais une légende.

Elle ne prétend pas donner à lire le tout du corpus, textes et desseins de Hegel, seulement deux figures. Plus exactement deux figures en train de s'effacer : deux passages.

(marginal notes, left)
la sera désormais le sigle du savoir absolu. E l'IC, notons-le déjà puisque les deux portées se représentent l'une l'autre, de l'Immaculée Conception. Tachygraphie proprement singulière : elle ne va pas d'abord à disloquer, comme on pourrait croire, un code c'est-à-dire ce sur quoi l'on tablerop. Mais peut-être, beaucoup plus tard et entament cette fois, à en exhiber les bords.

(marginal notes)
note à penser : ça ne accentue pas ici maintenant mais se sera déjà mis à l'épreuve de l'autre côté. Le sens doit répondre, plus ou moins, aux calculs de ce qu'en termes de clôture on appelle contre-épreuve

« *ce qui est resté d'un Rembrandt déchiré en petits carrés bien réguliers, et foutu aux chiottes* » se divise en deux.

Comme le reste.

Deux colonnes inégales, disent-ils, dont chaque — enveloppe ou gaine, incalculablement renverse, retourne, remplace, remarque, recoupe l'autre.

L'incalculable de *ce qui est resté* se calcule, élabore tous les coups, les tord ou les échafaude en silence, vous vous épuiseriez plus vite à les compter. Chaque petit carré se délimite, chaque colonne s'enlève avec une impassible suffisance et pourtant l'élément de la contagion, la circulation infinie de l'équivalence générale rapporte chaque phrase, chaque mot, chaque moignon d'écriture (par exemple « *je m'éc...* ») à chaque autre, dans chaque colonne et d'une colonne à l'autre de *ce qui est resté* infiniment calculable.

A peu près.

Il y a du reste, toujours, qui se recoupent, deux fonctions.

L'une assure, garde, assimile, intériorise, idéalise, relève la chute dans le monument. La chute s'y maintient, embaume et momifie, monu-mémorise, s'y nomme — tombe. Donc, mais comme chute, s'y érige.

7

Figure 11.5

which means, my *Petit Robert*[10] tells me, a trumpet call as well as the tolling of a church bell for a funeral and, figuratively, the end of a hope (for example, 'That rang the knell on my hope to make it to Maine that summer'). The word *glas* comes from medieval Latin *classum*, 'class', and *classicum*, 'sonnerie de trompette', so it involves classification as well as the tolling of a church bell and a trumpet call, as Derrida himself signals. His list of meanings – what he calls in the 'Blurb' 'les virtualités retorses et retranchées de son "sens"' ('Blurb', *recto*) ('the twisted and cut out virtualities of its "sense"' (*Glassary*, 28)) – of the word *glas* is outrageously long. I give the English translation:

staffs, peals of all the bells, the burial place, the funeral pomp, the legacy, the contract, signature, proper name, forename, surname, classification and the class struggle, the work of mourning in its production relations, fetishism, transvestism, the 'toilette' of the deceased, incorporation, introjection of the corpse, idealization, sublimation, relief, vomit, the remain(s), etc. (*Glassary*, 28)

'Etc.'?! Come on, Jacques, surely the word cannot mean all those diverse things! So much for dictionary meanings. But yes (*Mais oui*), for Derrida, 'virtualities of its sense' covers all those things and more ('etc.').

It is easy to see, once you have read the whole book, that Derrida's list of virtual meanings for the word *glas* covers all the salient themes of *Glas*. The volume must be seen as an untangling and elaborate commentary on all those virtual senses of the word. A word means for Derrida all its possible uses and these are typically, for him, limitless, 'infinitely calculable', as the right column of the first page says explicitly about the word *reste*. This infinite calculability means, among other things, that anything like an even modestly comprehensive commentary on *Glas*, line by line and page by page, would be of enormous length. When I get around later on in this essay to saying something about the meaning of the first page of *Glas*, I shall, perforce, limit myself to a few incomplete remarks about one key word in *Glas*, in this case *reste*, remain(s), as a noun and as a verb. Otherwise, my essay would be interminable.

*

One of Derrida's targets in *Glas* is the assumption that a word has a definite set of meanings that can be given in a dictionary and that allows for a verifiable identification of page one's meaning. This would be one form of 'absolute knowledge', in Hegel's phrase, given on page one by Derrida as *sa*, for *savoir absolu*. This is the meaning that scholars and students are supposed to identify and specify. Derrida asks what follows from that dismantling of absolute knowledge in a complex question in the 'Blurb':

What remains of absolute knowledge? of history, philosophy, political economics, psychoanalysis, semiotics, linguistics, poetics? of work, language, tongue [mostly in the sense used in a phrase like 'foreign tongue' –JHM.], sexuality, family, religion, State, etc.? (*Glassary*, 28)

The implied answer is that nothing remains except fragments, morsels, that cannot be reassembled into the kind of 'absolute knowledge' Hegel promised could be attained. The multiple meanings of such a word as *glas* 'deconstructs', if I may dare to use that word, all those disciplines. Make no mistake: Derrida's target through all the fascinating exuberance of *Glas* is the whole edifice of Western intellectual assumptions.

One of Derrida's most powerful tools for dismantling that edifice is those lists of apparently heterogeneous entities that are said somehow to be the same, to be validly put in apposition. Here are two examples from the foot of the right-hand column of *Glas*, page one. Derrida is talking about the first of two functions of 'the remain(s)':

> The first [function] assures, guards, assimilates, interiorizes, idealizes, relieves [in the contradictory sense, in part, of the final stage of the three stages of the Hegelian dialectic. That stage is reached by an act of *aufheben*, meaning abolish and preserve, sublate, cancel and lift up.[11] *Relève* is the common French translation of the German word *aufheben* –JHM.] the fall [*chute*] into the monument. There the fall maintains, embalms, and mummifies itself, monumemorizes and names itself – falls (to the tomb(stone)) [*tombe*]. (E1/G7)

Wow! Are the words in these lists synonyms or do they make some kind of progression? It is not possible to be sure.

I met up on that first page with other words the meaning of which I did not know, like *seing* (signature), as well as words whose meaning I more or less knew, like *reste* (remainder, remains), but that are used in *Glas* in odd ways, in strange syntactical combinations or in a series of different senses. That exemplifies Saussure's claim that the meaning of a word depends on the sentence in which it is used.

*

Paul de Man, in a notable passage in 'Conclusions: Walter Benjamin's "The Task of the Translator"', distinguishes, with some help from Walter Benjamin, between 'Hermeneutics' and 'Poetics', *das Gemeinte* and *die Art des Meinens*, what is meant and the way that meaning is said.[12] De Man argues that these two ways of reading interfere with one another, or may be incompatible, or impossible to do at the same time. That first page of *Glas* and all the rest (remainder!) of the book tend to place poetics over hermeneutics. This happens by way of such things as typeface, the placement of assemblies of words on the page, the constant use of ellipses, sentence fragments, and the interference of outrageous wordplay over clear paraphrasable meaning: puns, alliteration, polysemantics, polyglottism, assonance, consonance, lists of not quite synonymous words or phrases, such as all those words beginning in *gl*, etc. It was then and is now my habit and training to seek out what is meant, *das Gemeinte*. In *Glas*, *die Art des Meinens* keeps me to an amazing degree from getting on with *das Gemeinte*.

One could define all this wordplay in either or both of two ways: either as a magnificent exploitation of the richness of the French language or as a revengeful deconstruction, once and for all, of the vaunted clarity of French. If the latter, this is because the rich multiple meanings of words in French (as in English or other languages, too) make it impossible to mean one thing without at the same time inadvertently meaning a lot of other things. So much for any clear statement of *savoir absolu*! The French language (tongue) was imposed on the child Derrida as an Algerian Jew, victim of French colonial imperialism. That imperialism is alluded to in the passages about Hegel (*aigle* [eagle] as pronounced by the French) in the left column of *Glas* page one: 'His name is so strange. From the eagle it draws imperial or historic power. Those who still pronounce his name like the French (there are some) are ludicrous only up to a certain point' (E1/G7).

The French language will never be the same again after *Glas*, just as the English language will never be the same again after Joyce's *Finnegans Wake*. Derrida read the *Wake* carefully during his year on an *école normale* fellowship at Harvard during the 1950s. *Finnegans Wake* was undoubtedly one of his models for *Glas*. Joyce too, like Derrida, was a victim of colonialism and was forced to use the tongue of the conqueror, just as I am in a different way. We Americans went on using English and basing our ethos on British literature long after we won the War of Independence, right down to the present. We still are taught that all Americans should read Shakespeare. Why? My ancestors were chiefly German immigrants. Why would not Goethe or even Hegel do as well for me as Shakespeare? Hegel, by no means French, was after all the basis of French university intellectual life in Derrida's youth, in Sartre's time. Derrida was on official record as at work writing a habilitation dissertation on Hegel, of which *Glas* is a sardonic, belated and defiant fulfilment.

*

Two things happened at once and happen again now when I try to 'read' that first page of *Glas*: (1) I made, and now make again, a heroic and on the whole unsuccessful attempt to figure out just what Derrida is saying, just what the words mean. I shall return to this effort at the end of this essay. (2) A strange inner space opened up then and opens up again within me. That imaginary space is generated partly by the arrangement of the words on the page and partly by what that 'Blurb' says, as well as by what the text itself says. This space is made up of two tall columns side by side in a sandy desert and encrusted with inscriptions that interact in complex ways. These columns are also *colossi*, that is, like enormous memorial statues of kings and the like. The words on the page are, after all, in parallel columns that are covered with inscriptions of various sorts, with strange inserts on the sides in smaller typeface, as you can see from my scan above of page one (Figure 11.5). Derrida gives these inserts striking names drawn from windows in walls: 'Judases' and 'Jalousies'. A Judas window is an aperture enabling a prison guard to see into a cell without being seen by the prisoner, a peephole. The allusion is to the way Judas betrayed his pretended friendship for Jesus.[13] *Jalousies* is the French word for what in English we call louvred windows.[14]

I have found that what actually happens when I read a poem, a novel, a philosophical text or a critical text is the spontaneous generation of a quite definite imaginary space with appropriate feelings as well as a visual vividness not entirely justified by the words on the page. *Glas* is no exception. There before my mind's eye are those two inscribed columns standing side by side in a desert solitude. They are a scary and forbidding sight. This imaginary vision reminds me of those 'two vast and trunkless legs of stone' standing in the desert in Shelley's sonnet 'Ozymandias'.[15] This is an example of those irrelevant and fortuitous associations that are one of the (perhaps distressing) things that happen, to me at least, in reading. Can I be the only person for whom this occurs? I doubt it.

*

The generation of an imaginary image of two vast columns in the desert is perhaps primarily brought about by the way the words are arranged on the pages of *Glas*, but three actual passages near the beginning powerfully endorse that mental and affective image. I give a citation from each in the order in which I encountered them, first a passage in the inserted 'Blurb', then a passage on the first page of *Glas*, then one of the two passages from Hegel that are given on the following pages. For the convenience of the reader I give these 'passages', somewhat reluctantly, in the English translations, with some of the French interpolated. The French versions of the first two are in any case given in my scans above.

Derrida, by the way, plays on the innocent-looking word 'passage'. He makes it mean a movement towards disappearance, as we speak of someone's death as a 'passing'. He speaks at the bottom of the left-hand column of *Glas* on page one of the two passages from Hegel on which he will focus as 'two figures in the act of effacing themselves, two passages' (E1/G7).

The first 'passage', caught in the act of effacing itself, I would have read uncomprehendingly, *en passage* to *Glas* itself, since I did not yet know just what he meant by 'two columns'. This is the first paragraph of the 'Blurb', in the English translation in *Glassary*, with some key words in French interpolated. I also insert some commentary in brackets along the way. I do this for brevity's sake, rather than appending my commentary separately and therefore necessarily at greater length. I have quailed before the idea of putting my commentary in as Judas windows:

> First of all [*D'abord*]: two columns. Truncated at the top and the
> bottom, also carved [*taillées*] in their flank: interpolated clauses,
> tattooings, incrustations. A first reading can act if the two erected
> [*dressés*] texts, one against the other or one without the other, do not
> communicate between themselves. [That was the way I tried at first
> to read *Glas* – JHM.] And in a certain, deliberate way, that remains
> true, concerning pretext, object, language, style, rhythm, law. [He
> means, I guess, that the two columns seem at first to be separate texts
> in different styles, one about Hegel, the other about a greatly different
> writer, Genet. This is still a shocking juxtaposition –JHM.] A *dialectics*
> on one side [How can anyone write about Hegel without engaging
> in dialectical reasoning? – JHM.], a *galactics* on the other [I suppose
> that is an allusion to Walter Benjamin's idea in *The Arcades Project*[16] of

gathering together passages that are not sequential but arranged in an imaginary spatial array, like a galaxy or like the stars in a constellation. Or it may be an obscure allusion to Galilée, the name of the publisher of *Glas*, as discussed above –JHM.], heterogeneous and yet indiscernible [*indiscernables*: the French word has a somewhat different meaning from the English homonym. The French has the double senses of 'inseparable' and 'impossible to be distinguished or differentiated from one another' – JHM.] in their effects, at times up to hallucination. [Why is this hallucinatory? I suppose because such a similarity in effects of two such different columnar texts seems crazy, like a hallucination – JHM.] Between the two the clapper [*le battant*: I should have thought 'beating' or 'vibrating' might have been a better translation, but my *Petit Robert* gives the noun and the adjective three additional meanings: the clapper of a bell, the beating of a heart, and the pelting of a heavy rain – JHM.] of another text, one would say of another 'logic': with the surnames [*surnoms*: nicknames] obsequence, *pénêtre*, strict-ure, lock, antherection, bit [*mors*], etc. [Here is another of Derrida's bewildering lists of words. What in the world, for example, is an 'antherection' (*anthérection*)? Erections in various senses appear often in *Glas*, both in the sense of the erection of a tower and in the sexual sense. Derrida sees all towers, including his two columns, as phallic, but what about the prefix 'anth-'? It can hardly just mean 'anti', in the sense of detumescence, or Derrida would have written 'anti'. The answer to my question requires reading carefully the whole Genet column of *Glas*, with its treatment of homosexuality in Genet's writings. Sartre's big book on Genet hovers somewhere in the background.[17] Genet's homosexuality is placed in juxtaposition with Hegel's family life, treated in the left column. What, moreover, is the word for a morsel (*mors*) doing at the end of the sequence, and what in the world is an 'obsequence' (*obséquence*)? It must have something to do with exaggerated marks of politeness, but what that has to do with the third text beating between the two columns and generated by their interaction beats me. Maybe the two columns are obsequious to one another by figuratively bowing with exaggerated *politesse*. The defeat of my comprehension makes my heart beat faster. Just where on the page, by the way, is that *autre texte* to be found? It must be a hallucinatory or ghostly text that exists and does not exist, but is generated virtually by the interaction between the words in the two columns. I certainly had no idea what those words in this list meant and what they were doing there when I first read the 'Blurb'. One answer to my questions, I suppose, is, 'Read the whole of *Glas*, all 291 pages of it, carefully and thoughtfully, word by word and line by line, with one eye on each column, and you will find out.' Good luck. I'll see you in a couple of years or maybe more. Let me know when you are ready – JHM.] (*Glassary*, 28)

*

In any case, the passage about the two columns in the 'Blurb' encourages me further to do what I already do spontaneously when I look at page one. I see it in my mind's eye as a strange spatial scene of two physical inscribed or incised columns standing side by side. A passage on the right column of page one reinforces that mental image but also greatly complicates it or even makes it impossible to imagine it as a coherent visual scene. My earlier essay on a passage in Derrida's *Otobiographies*[18] similarly discovers that the passage in question also is not imaginable in the way the description of a drawing room in a novel by Anthony Trollope can be successfully imagined to look. This success occurs in Trollope's case even if that subjective image goes beyond the actual details Trollope gives and imports something from my memories of actual drawing rooms from 'real life', or from films and television.

*

Here is my second pillars passage, this time given in the English translation of *Glas* by Leavey and Rand. It is a pretty bewildering series of notations, in English or in French. Again, I give glosses in parentheses along the way:

> Two unequal [Why are they 'unequal' (*inégales*)? Because they are
> in different typefaces and have a different number of total words,
> though they fill the same space on the page? – JHM.] columns, they
> say distyle [*disent-ils*] [The similarity in sound is the justification
> for translating a phrase which means 'they say' as 'distyle'. It adds
> to my mental image of those two columns in that 'distyle'. 'Distyle'
> means 'a temple having two columns in front' – JHM.], each of
> which envelop(e)(s) or sheath(es) [*enveloppe ou gaine*: *gaine* in
> French has a bewildering number of meanings, including, as a
> noun, the cover for an umbrella or even (no doubt somewhere in
> Derrida's mind) 'vagina', which means 'sheath' in Latin – JHM.],
> incalculably reverses, turns inside out [as one might turn the
> finger of a glove inside out, a figure Derrida elsewhere forcefully
> uses, under the name of 'double invagination'.[19] The fingers of a
> glove are already vagina-like sheaths. To push one finger of the
> glove inside itself makes another vagina-shaped container. Hence
> 'double invagination'. You will note that Derrida's phrase does not
> necessarily name a static fact but by way of the '-ion' at the end
> of 'invagination' may name an ongoing action. Part of the reason
> for my failure to imagine the scene Derrida's words name in this
> citation is that, unlike my mental image of the drawing room in
> a Trollope novel, it is in constant dynamic movement like a glove
> finger constantly turning to outside in and then back to outside out
> – JHM.], replaces, remarks, overlaps [*recoupe*] the other. [. . .] each
> column rises with an impassive self-sufficiency, and yet the element

of contagion, the infinite circulation of general equivalence relates each sentence, each stump [*moignon*: I suppose this is a synonym of the enigmatic *mors* (morsel) in the insert, but 'stump' obscurely implies what remains after an emasculation – JHM.] of writing (for example, '*je m'éc. . .*') ['I gag. . .', later important in *Glas*, is a play on what happens when you say 'gl. . .' or 'cl. . .' as the first letters of any of the many words that Derrida lists that begin with 'gl' or 'cl' – JHM.]) to each other, within each column and from one column to the other of *what remained* [*ce qui est resté*] infinitely calculable. (E1/G7)

Wow! If you can follow all those parentheses and lists you are a highly adept reader. The bottom line is that Derrida is now describing these two columns not as solid pillars but as two strange entities (strange because they are made of words not stones, as I imagined them to be) that constantly and dynamically interact in weird ways that are unimaginable as a static mental visual image. Each column envelops the other, turns itself and its fellow column inside out, like a glove or a sheath. What Derrida is, in my view, attempting to describe is the way the words, each with its own multiple and contradictory meanings, as put down in each column and in the interaction between each column with the other, violently subvert one another or contaminate one another by an irresistible contagion. This happens in a way that is 'infinitely calculable'. That means, I take it, that you would never come to the end of calculating or specifying this interaction among the words just on page one of *Glas*. The final implication of this second passage is that you can name something in words that cannot be coherently imagined as a physical visual image, even though the reader is invited both by the format and by the spatial images in the words (for example, 'Each column rises with an impassive self-sufficiency') to struggle, though unsuccessfully, to see some encompassing coherent imaginary visual image generated by page one of *Glas*.

*

After the somewhat hallucinatory effect, on me at least, of my second passage, the third and final one is straightforward and simple, or almost. That may be because it is not by Derrida. It is a citation from Hegel's *Aesthetik*. At the bottom of the left-hand column of page one, Derrida says his 'legend' does not 'pretend to afford a reading of Hegel's whole corpus, texts and plans [*desseins*], just of two figures. More precisely, of two figures in the act of effacing themselves, two passages' (E1/G7). The following page indicates that one 'passage' from Hegel's *Aesthetik* is about the 'religion of flowers', the other about 'the phallic columns of India'. It is the second one that interests me, since it is an invitation to view the two columns of *Glas* in imagination in a certain way. The passage, Derrida tells the reader, comes in Hegel's *Aesthetics* in the chapter on 'Independent or Symbolic Architecture'. The passage is primarily a translation of what Hegel says, as the inserted long citation in Hegel's German, not re-cited by me, demonstrates. We are reading in the version I cite the translation of a translation:

> [The phallic column of India] is said to have spread toward Phrygia, Syria, and Greece, where, in the course of Dionysiac celebrations (according to Herodotus as cited by Hegel), the women were pulling the thread of a phallus that thus stood in the air, 'almost as big as the rest of the body.' [When I was in grade school in a very small town in upstate New York, my father was President of a tiny Baptist women's college of two hundred students, Keuka College. Every May Day students from the college would dance in a circle around a maypole, two groups going in opposite directions and interweaving, each holding a ribbon attached to a pole. If it was done right, the pole would gradually be covered from the top down by the interwoven ribbons. I had no idea of the phallic significance or antiquity of this charming folk ritual, nor do I think the dancing girls did. It was just something you do on May Day. A maypole dance also appears in Hardy's *The Return of the Native*. That dance's meaning is made more or less explicit by Hardy. Hardy's girls wreathe the pole in flowers from the top down[20] – JHM.] At the beginning, then, the phallic columns of India, enormous formations, pillars, towers, larger at the base than at the top. Now at the outset – but as a setting out that already departed from itself – [A long exegesis would be required to unravel this observation. It fits Derrida's assertions in many places in his work that the origin is always already self-divided. Difference or differing (*différance*) goes all the way down[21] – JHM.] these columns were intact, unbreached [*inentamés*], smooth. And only later (*erst später*) are notches, excavations, openings (*Offnungen und Aushöhlungen*) made in the columns, in the flank, if such can be said. These hollowings, holes, these lateral marks in depth would be like accidents coming over the phallic columns at first unperforated or apparently unperforatable. Images of the gods (*Götterbilder*) were set, niched, inserted, embedded, driven in, tattooed on the columns [another of Derrida's lists of synonyms that are not quite synonyms – JHM]. Just as these small caverns or lateral pockets on the flank of the phallus announced small portable and hermetic Greek temples, so they broached/breeched [*entamaient*] the model of the pagoda, not yet altogether a habitation and still distinguished by the separation between shell and kernel (*Schale und Kern*). A middle ground hard to determine between the column and the house, sculpture and architecture. (E2–3/G8–9)

Well! That gives me a lot of new different mental images to have at once when looking at those two columns on the first page of *Glas*. They are columns that are also phalluses. These phalluses are bare but are also encrusted with painful (to me at least, in imagination) incisions that are almost, but not quite, also habitations, like pagodas. They are also, as Derrida observes in the 'Blurb', like colossuses, huge statues of dead royalty, reminding me once more of those remains of a colossus in Shelley's 'Ozymandias'. The columns are also innocent, but not quite innocent, maypoles. What a lot of mental images to think of at once, in superimposition! The mind boggles.

*

A final question about those columns. Why are there two of them, side by side, each with the characteristics of Hegel's mature phallic column from India? You will remember that 'erections', in all senses of the word, are a big topic in *Glas*. We know that this is to set Hegel against Genet in a scandalous juxtaposition, but other ways to do this can be imagined. The answer, in my judgement, is that the doubling of the columns on the page is an echo of what Freud (a big source for *Glas* throughout) says about the way the doubling in dreams of the phallus, or some penis symbol, equals its disappearance, the castration we men so (mostly unconsciously), Freud says, fear,[22] and as all those incisions on Hegel's phallic columns from India so painfully threaten. It hurts to think of it. The loss of the phallus, the head signifier, is of course one way to express the loss of systematic coherent meaning, the loss of the *savoir absolu* that gives certain comprehensive knowledge of 'history, philosophy, political economics, psychoanalysis, semiotics, linguistics, poetics [. . .] of work, language, tongue, sexuality, family, religion, State, etc.' (*Glassary*, 28). As Wallace Stevens puts it: 'exit the whole/Shebang!'[23]

Please remember that I am still on page one. Think what a commentary on all 291 pages of *Glas* would be like. Interminable!

*

I conclude with a few words about Derrida's use of the word *reste* (remains) as a noun or a verb. The word appears repeatedly in the 'Blurb' and on page one, as in the beginnings in mid-sentence of the two columns: 'what, after all, of the remains(s), today, for us, here, now, of a Hegel?' [Why *a* Hegel? To call attention to the homology in the French pronunciation, developed a moment later, of Hegel and *aigle* (eagle)? – JHM.]; '"*what remained of a Rembrandt torn into small, very regular squares and rammed down the shithole*" is divided in two. / As the remain(s) [*reste*]' (E1/G7). Other appearances of 'reste' on page one are 'remains(s) to be thought'; 'The incalculable of *what remained* calculates itself '; 'the infinite circulation of general equivalence relates each sentence, each stump of writing [. . .] to each other, within each column and from one column to the other of *what remained* infinitely calculable'; 'Of the remain(s), after all, there are, always, overlapping each other, two functions.' [He goes on to say these two functions are the fall to the tomb and the simultaneous erection – JHM.] In the 'Blurb': 'What remains of absolute knowledge?' (*Que reste-t-il du savoir absolu?*) (*Glassary*, 28; 'Blurb', *verso*).

The meanings of *reste* are, as Derrida says, infinitely calculable. I could never have done with them. Nevertheless, I terminate, without really terminating, with a few final remarks. By the way, we have 'rest' in English, meaning 'the missing parts', as in 'Where is the rest of me?' or 'What did you do with the rest?' 'Rest' also means a period of relaxation, as in 'I think I'll take a rest now.' The French word *reste* is clearly an example of a 'double antithetical word'. It not only has many meanings, but those meanings contradict one another. *Reste* means 'remains' in the sense of dead body, as in 'The remains were laid to rest.' It means what is left over, perhaps something of great value, though now in fragments. It means both a fall to the tomb and the erection of something that is still there, even though in morsels. The mind goes back and forth between these two extremes. To initiate that oscillation is perhaps the most important feature of Derrida's use of *reste*. It is a key word in *Glas*.

I return in conclusion to my initial question about what actually happens in the act of reading. What takes place when I read Derrida's iterations of *reste*, in its various contexts in the insert and on page one of *Glas*, is that bit by bit there arises in my mind a composite image, a collage or montage, of a pile of debris such as you might find in the town dump or in a garbage can or in a waste basket; of faeces; of a Rembrandt torn into regular squares; of the works of Hegel similarly fragmented; of a dead body (Derrida's own: he was obsessed with the question of his own remains, in all senses, including his unpublished manuscripts); of a fragmented poster of an imperial German eagle; of debris falling and then rising again as a tower and simultaneously as a colossus.

I rest my case, in all senses of 'rest'.

NOTES

1. John Keats, 'On First Looking into Chapman's Homer', *Poetry Foundation*, available at <https://www.poetryfoundation.org/poems-and-poets/poems/detail/44481> (last accessed 15 December 2016).

2. The essays on Anthony Trollope's *Framley Parsonage* and Wallace Stevens's 'The Motive of Metaphor' are forthcoming in Ranjan Ghosh and J. Hillis Miller, *Thinking Literature Across Continents*, Durham, NC: Duke University Press, 2016; I discuss Yeats in 'Cold Heaven, Cold Comfort: Should We Read or Teach Literature Now?', in Paul Socken (ed.), *The Edge of the Precipice: Why Read Literature in the Digital Age?*, Montreal and Kingston: McGill-Queen's University Press, 2013, pp. 140–55; the essay on Derrida's *Otobiographies* appeared as 'How to Read the Derridas: Indexing *moi et moi*' in a special number on *A Decade after Derrida* of *Oxford Literary Review*, 36: 2 (2014), 269–73.

3. Jacques Derrida, *Glas*, Paris: Galilée, 1974.

4. Jacques Derrida, *De la grammatologie*, Paris: Minuit, 1967; Jacques Derrida, *Of Grammatology*, trans. Gayatri Chakravorty Spivak, Baltimore and London: Johns Hopkins University Press, 1976.

5. Jacques Derrida, *Glas*, trans. John P. Leavey, Jr. and Richard Rand, Lincoln, NE and London: University of Nebraska Press, 1986. Page references will henceforth be given in the text to this translation and to the Galilée edition preceded by E and G respectively.

6. John P. Leavey, Jr., *Glassary*, Lincoln, NE and London: University of Nebraska Press, 1986; henceforth *Glassary*.

7. See 'Galileo Galilei', *Wikipedia*, available at <https://en.wikipedia.org/wiki/Galileo_Galilei> (last accessed 15 December 2016).

8. An English translation of the 'Blurb' is given in *Glassary*, p. 28.

9. Jacques Derrida, 'Tympan', in *Marges de la philosophie*, Paris: Minuit, 1972, pp. i–xv; Jacques Derrida, 'Tympan', in *Margins of Philosophy*, trans. Alan Bass, Chicago: University of Chicago Press, 1986, pp. ix–xxix.

10. Paul Robert, *Dictionnaire alphabétique & analogique de la langue française*, ed. Alain Rey, Paris: Société du Nouveau Littré, 1976, p. 787.

11. See 'Aufheben', *Wikipedia*, available at <https://en.wikipedia.org/wiki/Aufheben> (last accessed 15 December 2016).

12. Paul de Man, 'Conclusions: Walter Benjamin's "The Task of the Translator"', in *The Resistance to Theory*, Minneapolis: University of Minnesota Press, 1986, p. 87.

13. See 'The Judas Window', *Wikipedia*, available at <https://en.wikipedia.org/wiki/The_Judas_Window> (last accessed 15 December 2016).

14. See 'Jalousie Window', *Wikipedia*, available at <https://en.wikipedia.org/wiki/Jalousie_window> (last accessed 15 December 2016).

15. L. 2. For the whole sonnet, see Percy Bysshe Shelley, 'Ozymandias', *The Literature Network*, available at <http://www.online-literature.com/shelley_percy/672/> (last accessed 15 December 2016).

16. Walter Benjamin, *The Arcades Project*, trans. Howard Eiland and Kevin McLaughlin, prepared on the basis of the German volume, ed. Rolf Tiedemann, Cambridge, MA and London: The Belknap Press of Harvard University Press, 1999.

17. Jean-Paul Sartre, *Saint Genet, comédien et martyr*, Paris: Gallimard, 1952; Jean-Paul Sartre, *Genet*, trans. Edmund White, corrected edn, London: Picador, 1994. I taught myself back in the 1950s good enough French to read this book before it was translated, so important did it seem to me then to learn what Sartre said about Genet.

18. See note 2 above.

19. See Jacques Derrida, 'La Loi du genre/The Law of Genre', trans. Avital Ronell, *Glyph*, 7 (1980), 176–232, especially 190–2, in French; 217–19, in English. See Simon Morgan Wortham, *The Derrida Dictionary*, London: Continuum, 2010, p. 76: 'an invaginated text is a narrative that folds upon itself, "endlessly swapping outside for inside and thereby producing a structure *en abyme*." [Derrida] applies the term to such texts as Immanuel Kant's *Critique of Judgment* and Maurice Blanchot's *La Folie du Jour*. Invagination is an aspect of différance, since according

to Derrida it opens the "inside" to the "other" and denies both inside and outside a stable identity.'

20. See Thomas Hardy, *The Return of the Native*, Book Six, ch. 1, available at <http://www.gutenberg.org/files/122/122-h/122-h.htm> (last accessed 15 December 2016).

21. See Derrida, 'La différance', in French, in *Marges de la philosophie*, pp. 1–29; Derrida, 'Différance', in English, in *Margins of Philosophy*, pp. 1–27.

22. 'This invention of doubling as a preservation against extinction has its counterpart in the language of dreams, which is fond of representing castration by a doubling or multiplication of a genital symbol' (Sigmund Freud, 'The Uncanny', trans. Alix Strachey, then considerably modified, in *The Standard Edition of the Complete Psychological Works*, under the general editorship of James Strachey, in collaboration with Anna Freud, assisted by Alix Strachey and Alan Tyson, London: Vintage; The Hogarth Press and the Institute of Psycho-Analysis, 2001, vol. XVII, p. 235).

23. Wallace Stevens, 'The Idea of a Colony', ll. 6–7, Part IV of 'The Comedian as the Letter C', in *The Collected Poems*, New York: Vintage Books, 1990, p. 37.

CHAPTER 12

'A very black and little Arab Jew': Experience and Experimentation or, Two Words for Jacques Derrida

Julian Wolfreys

I am trying to disinterest myself from myself to withdraw from death by making the 'I', to whom death is supposed to happen, gradually go away, no, be destroyed before death come to meet it, so that at the end already there should be no one left to be scared of losing the world in losing himself in it, and the last of the Jews that I still am doing nothing here other than destroying the world on the pretext of making truth, but just as well the intense relation to survival that writing is, is not driven by the desire that something remain after me, since I shall not be *there* to enjoy it in a word, *there* where the point is, rather in producing these remains and therefore the witnesses of my radical absence, to live today, here and now, this death of me, for example, the very counterexample which finally reveals the truth of the world such as it is, itself, i.e., without me, and all the more intensely to enjoy this light I am producing through the present experimentation of my possible survival, i.e., of absolute death, I tell myself this every time I am walking in the streets of a city in which I love . . .

Derrida, 'Circumfessions' (1993: 190–1)

Jacques Derrida.

I speak the proper name.[1] How do you hear this? What is your 'experience' of this word? What does memory conjure? What does it call to mind or banish? How are you called, by the name 'Jacques Derrida'? How are you called, in the name of Jacques Derrida? Before you rush to decide on an answer, before you decide, or believe you have already decided, in your response or non-response (presumed or otherwise) to the other, on your answer, pause. Hesitate before taking a step, before refusing to enter or refusing entrance, remaining on the side of the inhospitable. It may well be that you believe your response to be the affirmation of a non-response. Someone speaks up, saying, 'I am not called by this name.' 'This proper name has nothing to do with me.' 'I have nothing, I *want* nothing to do with this name.' I am, if you will allow, experimenting here with x number of voices, ventriloquising them, paraphrasing or translating from experience or memory – and perhaps from anticipation of what might be coming at my conclusion, or, more undecidably, from an act of telepathy in which I am engaging just at present. (How could you tell?) Or, more radically, these variations on a theme, being examples of a performative speech act underlying every response that affirms itself as a non-response, which affirms its response just as this despite all protestation to the contrary, in enacting the role of non-respondent; and refusing, as it were, all correspondence with the name, refusing to accept the name, returning, or seeking to return the name to sender (but wait a minute, one cannot refuse the summons, one cannot avoid being served); all such variations, so many riffs, play on the proper name, and in this, they are called. The subject who believes he or she refuses or has refused the name is deluding him- or herself – for every act of non-response is not the avoidance, the denial, it likes to delude itself that it is.

That said, allow me to reiterate these two words, the proper name:

Jacques Derrida.

Beyond the possible recognition of a proper name as such, I am saying nothing. For the moment, here, now, at this very moment. That's not saying a lot. And yet, it speaks volumes. Though saying nothing more, nothing as yet, nevertheless there are those of you for whom the name speaks volumes, or so you believe. You will supply your own contexts from experience or memory, even, and perhaps especially if your contexts are those bricks in a wall you employ to build a fortress that keeps the name, like the foreigner, the stranger, the immigrant, the 'little black and very Arab Jew' (Derrida 1993: 58) at bay, on a border, some limit of your own making. You will supply your own contexts, whether or not you believe yours is a refusal, a non-response, whether or not you think you accept the proper name. However you align yourselves, however and in whatever ways you recognise, accept, refuse, associate, disassociate, the proper name; even if you have never heard the name until today, the name calls on you. The name is given. That it is a name is, as we say in English, a given, though not necessarily a gift. The name is nothing. It delivers nothing, nothing is given, even though the idea of a proper name, of 'having' a proper name, is a 'given'. Yet something comes to be. The arrival of a name, the very principle of its arrival – and names always arrive, whether or not you recognise them; though you might not know the name, you apprehend in some fashion, on hearing or seeing, that this therefore will have been a proper name – produces in our cultures an effect, having to do with the following: singularity, property, propriety, alterity, the self and other, the subject, identity. So, the proper name, say it once more (I've written it again):

Jacques Derrida.

You may have noticed, some of you, that I have proposed a number of hypotheses, all of them connected in one way or another, each of them threaded through the matrix of the proper name. Even as those hypotheses begin to define without determining, the shape of the proper name, and our assumptions concerning the identity and function, the purpose or economy of the proper name; so too, the proper name, as idea, as presumed and shared concept across what we think of as 'our' cultures is, properly speaking, a matrix, it generates, it engenders. This is still not to speak of context, or at least the contexts I assume are already presumed, assumed, assembled, contrived, recovered. Yet, I have risked certain hypotheses, without indicating my intentions (supposing I know them myself), in order to begin carrying out a small experiment. The experiment, put simply, is to send the name, to deliver this name to you, to deliver that proper name, which, for a number of you (I cannot possibly know or guess, and do not intend to take a head or hand count, this has nothing to do with data, or the quantifiable) has already, as I've hypothesised, been delivered. It strikes me that at this very moment, I could abandon the keynote, give up my delivery, and invite you all for the rest of the time allotted to engage in a supplementary experiment: to write in brief, as if this were an exam as well as an experiment, about your experience of the proper name. Not simply the proper name in general, but the name I have re-delivered today, this morning. To recall just the first of my questions: how do you hear it? Thus, the experiment might begin. Were it not for the fact that it has already begun, that it has always already begun as soon as any of us is named, as soon as any of us receives our own proper names. To name is an experiment, it is an act of experimenting with the self, with identity. For to give the name is to introduce the animal to its subjectivity, a subjectivity it will only belatedly begin to reflect upon. We have language inflicted on us; we suffer under the sign, the signature, of the proper name; the proper name is ours on sufferance. This is a digression, however; having announced – confessed – my experiment, I will say unequivocally, nothing could interest me less than seeing the experiment through to some conclusion. The very idea of a conclusion is itself, for me, risible. For this matter of experimentation in the name, experimentation with, on, in the name of, the proper name, has more to do, as my questions, my provocations, my hypotheses and analyses of response and non-response, engagement and avoidance, might suggest, with experience. We experience the proper name, we experience proper names, as no other word.

Such experience (and I'm not done with this word just yet in relation to experiment), along with all the modalities that 'experience' implies, all those modalities I have just named (non/response, engagement/avoidance, and so forth) have to do with 'exappropriation'. Not expropriation, but *exappropriation*, a neologism invented by one Jacques Derrida for the purpose of continuing a career-long experiment with, and experience of the proper name, beginning at least with the essay 'Signature événement contexte', from his 1972 publication, *Marges de la philosophie*, and lasting beyond his death, in comments made in a posthumous translation, *For Strasbourg*. (A parenthesis: all translations are posthumous inasmuch as they take place in the structural absence of the author. This is the risk the translation takes, whether or not the author is 'actually' living or dead; every translation behaves *as if* the author were dead, this is its inescapable necessity and responsibility. The words translated are always remains; and however faithful the translation, there is always a remainder, even, and perhaps especially, because translation bears witness, taking place *in the name of the author*, exactly in order to seek to preserve the author's proper name. The proper name has its chance only in being no longer what it is but being, however lovingly, improperly reinscribed, in, or on, the tongue of another. Translators always know more about death than any author.) Here is Derrida on 'exappropriation' and the name, in response to a question from Jean-Luc Nancy concerning the difference between expropriation and exappropriation:

> What I wished to say with *exappropriation* is that in the gesture of appropriating something for oneself, and thus of being able to keep in one's name, to mark in one's name, to leave in one's name, as a testament or an inheritance, one must expropriate this thing, separate oneself from it. This is what one does when one writes, when one publishes, when one releases something into the public sphere. One separates oneself from it and it lives, so to speak, without us. And thus in order to be able to claim a work, a book, a work of art, or anything else, a political act, a piece of legislation, or any other initiative, in order to appropriate it for oneself, in order to assign it to someone, one has to lose it, abandon it, expropriate it. That is the condition of this terrible ruse: we have to lose what we want to keep and we can keep only on the condition of losing. It's very painful. The very fact of publishing is painful. It departs, one knows not where, it bears one's name, and – it's horrible – one is no longer even capable of reconstituting it oneself, not even of reading it. That's *exappropriation*, and it applies not only to those things we speak of with relative ease, that is, literary or philosophical works, but to everything, to capital, to the economy in general. (Derrida 2014: 24)

As soon as there is the proper name, there is exappropriation. The parent, the priest, loses the very thing it seeks to claim or to keep, the animal, on which it confers identity and subjectivity by the act of giving the proper name. As soon as there is the proper name, as soon as the fiction of singularity is inscribed, there takes place exappropriation. This is the experience. This is our experience in the name of the proper name. Allow me therefore, once again, to reiterate this particular proper name:

Jacques Derrida.

Thus far I have sought to let the name resonate unremarkably, leaving it for you to consider, reflect on, experience, and perhaps to experiment with a little, the experiment shifting as I have spoken and as you will now be reading. I cannot control any of this. I have sought, as part of my small and admittedly insignificant experiment – refusing to accept any methodological premises or theoretical models, and insisting instead on the primacy of experience, and, along with that, all that cannot be predicted, programmed, measured, ordered – to embody, if you will, or to perform that which hypothetically speaking the proper name makes possible. Of what it makes possible, I might say, in the name of Jacques Derrida. When I write, as I wrote 'in the name of Jacques Derrida' (last Tuesday shortly before 1 p.m.), and what I say, when I say 'in the name of Jacques Derrida', I hear this phrase two ways at least. On the one hand, in a wholly conventional way, I am speaking, I am writing in Derrida's name. That which I articulate – and we're not even talking about matters of style so-called, much less 'school of thought', 'literary theory', poststructuralism (sic), or any other -ism – is in Derrida's name, on behalf of 'Jacques Derrida'. On the other hand, to raise the stakes and risk a strong reading, I am excavating, experiment- ing with what takes place *in* Derrida's name, what comes to pass in the experi- ence of the name *Jacques Derrida*. A problem arises immediately though. When I say I am seeking to say something in Derrida's name or on behalf of Derrida, a confusion might emerge. Am I speaking for the man or the text signed in his name? The two are only homologous to a degree. The one signs the other, the other bears the name. Whenever I have said

Jacques Derrida,

which is it, do you imagine, I have been speaking of – citing, referring to, using, giving you? I have not said. I might be talking of the person (cultural identifi- cation, pronominal signifier, inscription of the biological entity), the person's ideas (synecdoche, metonymy), the person's texts, or a particular text, not even an entire essay or a book, a lecture or article, but a paragraph, a phrase, a passage, an extract. Indeed, my experiment has wagered in part on the hypoth- esis that, in stating the name, keeping citation and reference to a minimum, you would, to varying degrees, presume the individual, the human animal on which the name is inscribed, thereby providing a camouflage of individual- ity, selfhood, singularity, and that you would, of your own accord, conflate the name with the writing; this is to say, in part my trivial experiment was to imagine you inventing the figure that stands behind the texts and not wonder- ing whether I was in fact speaking of one or the other, as if there were an inevi- table economy, a modality of metonymic or synecdochic substitution taking place. And, I have to admit, I nudged you toward the self – albeit an estranged, perhaps defamiliarised figure of the self – rather than the text. Often, it must be said, the things we believe we understand are the result of that aspect of experiment that is akin to sleight of hand. When I spoke earlier of a 'little black and very Arab Jew' I called to mind an image, a representation conjured by Jacques Derrida, an auto-representation, the self as other, the self speaking on behalf of, bearing witness to the self as other, in a place where the other cannot speak, but stands as mute testimony to the experience of racism and anti-Semitism, in one of fifty-nine otherwise unpunctuated sentences or what are called, by the author who exappropriates himself knowingly, 'periphrases', small more or less cryptic, confessional and autobiographical traces of the self.

As early as *Marges de la philosophie* Derrida had observed how the proper name in Aristotle, specifically the *Rhetoric* (III, V) ('recourir aux noms propres, c'est éviter le détour de la périphrase . . .' / 'using proper names evades the periphrastic detour . . .' (1972: 328/1982: 247; translation modified)) served to control reception, which for Aristotle was the correct thing to do.

Before returning to periphrasis as experiment on the name and experience of the self, and looking at an extract from one of the periphrases in question, I wish though, to offer a short commentary on Derrida's understanding of the proper name. This is so as to offer an 'internal' parergon, an inner frame within which the proper name might be situated as that around which I have been writing, without identifying with any certainty to what or whom the proper name belongs. I can do no better than to cite John D. Caputo:

> The whole idea of a proper name, its very 'condition of possibility,'
> is to come up with a signifier that is just that particular person's own
> signifier, the sign of just that one person, of that singular one and of
> no one else, to be that singular one's own personal sign. In a proper
> name, only that person answers to that name and that sign picks out
> only that one person. That is what we desire, what we love, so that the
> proper name is a work of love. But that is impossible (which is why we
> love and desire it all the more), so that the very condition under which
> the proper name is possible makes it impossible. [Recall, if you will,
> Derrida, on exappropriation, and the horror of writing and publishing
> – JW.] For were the sign to be utterly proper, absolutely unique and
> idiomatic, no one would understand it, and we would not even know
> it was a sign rather than just a noise or a scratch on a surface. To be a
> name it must be a signifier, and to be a signifier it must be significant.
> And to be significant it must be repeatable. We must be able to sign
> this name again and again, call it or be called by it, use it again and
> again, including when its referent is absent [either structurally absent,
> not in the room, or in the country, for example, or as Derrida has
> it, radically absent, which is to say dead – JW.]. A signifier must be
> woven of repeatable stuff or be consigned to unintelligibility. But
> if this signifier is repeatable. It is assignable to others [or to books,
> works of art, and so forth – JW.] who can bear the same name, so that
> its propriety is compromised. It cannot be an absolutely *proper* name,
> not if it is to be a proper *name*. A proper name is an attempt to utter
> something repeatable about the unrepeatable. (Caputo 2000: 40)

Something takes place in the proper name, or, one is tempted to say in the name *of*: this one or that one, this or that text. Yet, as soon as the name is signed, supposed guarantor of some unique property, the signatory standing in for the subject whose proper name this is assumed to be, in order for that signature to operate in its singularity, it has to be capable of being spirited away; indeed, it is always already haunted from within by its own iterability, the paradoxical quality by which, in the name of which it might be added, the proper name is no longer proper to itself. We might just illustrate this in part with a proper name, a surname, such as *Wiewiórka*, which some of you will know means squirrel. *Červenka*, to take another proper name, a Czech example, means robin, which in Polish is *Rudzik*, also a proper name. (Names, like birds, have no borders.) The proper name very quickly slips away from itself, from any propriety or formal qualities. In names such as these, the human's individuality is partially erased, its animality the trace that haunts that illusion.

It is not necessary, however, in exploring what appears as an experiment in the proper name to dwell further. We need only return to the point almost of departure, and so start once more with the proper name, the two words that have insisted:

Jacques Derrida.

When I wrote this proper name, to what, to whom, was I referring? Was I in fact not referring but citing? Alluding? Acknowledging, perhaps, remembering, mourning, bearing witness. All of these, any of them, each iterable occurrence in a different register, another modality of representation, of presentation without representation. Of course, Jacques Derrida has, in his writings, played on his own name, as some will know; this is not the place to offer a recapitulation of such performative tropes, to suggest different headings. My small experiment, this gestural tic I have assumed, a prod, a provocation, an allergen it might just be; my experimental foray in speaking so as to make possible for you an experience that I can neither govern nor control, still insists on that which, in its revenance, refuses its proper status, its propriety – and so performs its own impropriety, enacting its own exappropriation, exappropriation as the haunting trace within the proper name itself (as though all proper names were suddenly betrayed, as though we found ourselves plagued by some restless spirit). It may be that I am speaking of, in the name of the man, the author; or it may be that I am speaking of a text – not merely a text on which this name is inscribed as its author, but a text that is named *Jacques Derrida*. Or, third possibility, I may be alluding to, signifying both, man and book, the former writing himself within, and against a book with such a title. And what a title! I have not yet let you in on what – or who – I am calling what or who calls when I write, when I say *Jacques Derrida*. The name not only is nothing, not

in any case . . . the 'thing' that it names, [it is] not the 'nameable' . . ., but also [it] risks to bind, to enslave or to engage the other, to link the called, to call him/her to respond, . . . even before any freedom. . . . And still, if the name never belongs originarily and rigorously to s/he who receives it, it also no longer belongs from the very first moment to s/he who gives it. . . . the gift of the name gives that which it does not have, that in which, prior to everything, may consist the essence, that is to say – beyond being – the nonessence of the gift. (Derrida 1995: 84–5)

As scrupulously as I have tried – and failed – neither to cite, refer, allude nor acknowledge in any but the most minimal manner (which is still the most violent, with the nudity of command or injunction) this or that or the other Jacques

Derrida, my experience of the proper name still insists on binding the other to me; my experiment has involved calling, demanding unreasonably a response. But this experiment has been engaged, in the name of Jacques Derrida, in order to announce that which escapes, or exceeds any 'economical formalization' (Derrida 1995: 85), any methodological systematisation – I have wagered everything on challenging, by experimenting with the minimal requirements of the proper name and all that comes to put in place the proper name in 'our cultures', in 'our traditions', so as to withdraw in the face of 'economical formalization', or theorisation so-called, so as to remain with, and allow to remain a certain 'reserve of language, almost inexhaustible' (Derrida 1995: 85) that the presumed propriety and containment of the 'proper name' serves most starkly to reveal, despite the intention with which it is given, despite the desire that accompanies this gift of nothing that calls, binds and enslaves.

Which returns me once more, returning to me as just the name

Jacques Derrida,

whether 'person' or 'book' (I will not say 'text', for both 'person' and 'book' are textual, textile, and for which the proper name merely serves as something 'elliptical, taciturn, cryptic . . .' (Derrida 1995: 85), thus:

Figure 12.1

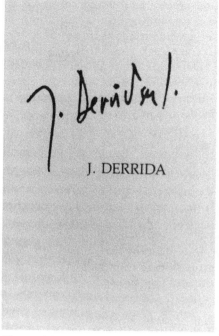

Figure 12.2

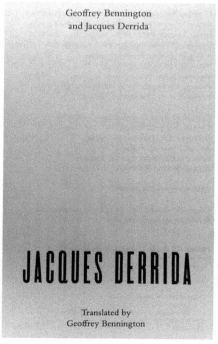

Figure 12.3

Taking these pages, the cover, on which the name appears twice on every occasion, and on two occasions the proper name 'improperly' escapes its purpose to give itself as other than itself, as title and, no longer, strictly speaking, 'author', I would like you to ask yourselves, to which – to book or person – have I been alluding, referring, citing, calling? To which have I bound myself? To one more than the other? Both? And what have I given away, giving something that *stricto sensu* is not mine to give, is nothing as such? Can you tell? Is this possible? Someone, not me, would need to wish to engage and so bind themselves to a more or less rigorous reading of the 'uses' of *Jacques Derrida* in this paper. Someone would have to try, having been called by the name, finding themselves addressed, called, as it were, in the name of *Jacques Derrida*. (Though which one, we will never know; even were I certain, I could not say for sure; this is my experience, this is why, in memory of my experience and the experiences of the proper name to come, I have experimented here, today, in the name of *Jacques Derrida*.) And this experiment would have to begin, once again with the experience, confronted all the while with that which is undecidable, and which therefore, haunting every iteration, would withdraw, even as it undoes all that is proper in the proper name.

However much a few of you, some, or even all of you may believe this so much frivolity, irresponsibility, mere word games, grant me the possibility that I am seeking to direct you to something in the experiment having to do with experience, an experience to which each of our proper names attests. This paper is an experiment inasmuch as it has sought from the outset to adopt a course without being sure of the outcome or destination. This is not an experiment in the sense of testing out hypotheses. I have put forward particular hypotheses, it is true. But this has been done in order for you to test them if you wish, leave them alone if you don't. The experience of that to which you are attending has at its heart the merest chance that you may wish to pursue the experiment in your own way.

I have, you may have noticed, used the word 'experience' repeatedly, alluded to experience, often in conjunction with or adjacent to 'experiment'. Both 'experiment' and 'experience' derive from the same Latin source, *experiri*, meaning, quite simply, 'to try'. In thinking about 'experiment' for this paper, this conference, in trying out various ideas, rejecting many, my experience was one that led me to consider, as the fiction of a starting point, an artificial 'origin', or what George Eliot calls 'the make believe of a beginning' (Eliot 2014: 3), which she insists all men need, I searched Derrida's texts, the texts that bear the name 'Jacques Derrida', for the word 'experiment'. It is used relatively infrequently. Experiments are tried in telepathy by the Russians and Americans, or by Freud, observes Derrida in 'Telepathy' (Derrida 1988: 236). It is used by Lacan, Derrida reminds us, in speaking of experimentation on humans and animals (Derrida 2009: 156–7). Or it is used to describe Hegel's hypotheses on sense-certainty (Derrida and Ferraris 2001: 112). It is rarely used by Derrida about his own writing. Experience, however, as experiment's other, its countersignature, is everywhere woven into the weft of the Derridean text, in the texts signed by this singular proper name.

Which brings me to that inaugural passage, from which I departed but which now returns, as if the experiment required that one start, again. As if one had never left, stepped over the threshold of the proper name.

The book that is named *Jacques Derrida*, which is written, first in French, then in English, by Geoffrey Bennington and Jacques Derrida, is first of all an experiment. It is an experiment concerning the possibility or impossibility of methodological systematisation. Put bluntly, this experiment, which the putative authors describe as presupposing a contract, 'itself established or stabilized on the basis of a friendly bet' (Bennington and Derrida 1993: 1) concerned the attempt on the part of Geoffrey Bennington to 'describe, according to . . . pedagogical and logical norms . . . if not the totality of J. D.'s thought, then at least the general system of that thought', without 'any quotation'. Bennington, the brief preface continues, 'would have liked to systematize J. D.'s thought' (Bennington and Derrida 1993: 1). You know the kind of thing. You must do, some of you at least. For there are some of you who assume, judge, prejudge or prejudice yourselves by speaking of some, or all, of the following: literary theory, theory, critical methodology, structuralism, poststructuralism (with or without the hyphen), or, raising the stakes just a little more, 'deconstruction', as if this named a theory, a system of thought, a methodology. However, given this experiment, this wager or contract, this is only half the story. For while Bennington's text, that which occupies in the book *Jacques Derrida* the upper two-thirds of most of the pages, is just this attempt to describe and so systematise, the bottom part of the page consists of those fifty-nine periphrases, to which I have already alluded. Derrida's stake in the work is 'to show how any such system must remain essentially open, [the] undertaking [of systematisation] . . . doomed to failure from the start . . . . In order to demonstrate the ineluctable necessity of the failure'. Derrida wrote something 'escaping the proposed systematization, surprising it' (Bennington and Derrida 1993: 1). This 'something' concerns, touches on, autobiography, the mother, the mother's illness, the sister, St Augustine (at one time, someone 'very black and little Arab'). A typical periphrasis focusing on his mother's illness begins: 'April 10, 1990, back in Laguna, not far from Santa Monica, one year after the first periphrasis, when for several days now I have been haunted by the word and image of mummification . . .' before shifting to the recollection of a dream: 'this does not stop me from walking out in the street, arm in arm with a young lady, under an umbrella, nor from seeing and avoiding, with a feeling of vague guilt, my Uncle Georges' (Derrida 1993: 260–1). The text by Jacques Derrida, to which he puts his name, exceeds that written by Geoffrey Bennington, that which is titled *Jacques Derrida*, whether in the French or the English edition (the proper name moves, its register different in each language, but it remains untranslatable). Indeed, both upper and lower parts of the text are titled *Jacques Derrida*, even though one is 'by' Jacques Derrida about a certain Jacques Derrida, and other is about the 'thought' of Jacques Derrida and not the life, the person of, Jacques Derrida. This is the experiment.

In this experiment comes the statement cited above. I will not repeat this aloud, but allow it to appear, for you, each and every one, to read, or not read, to experience or to seek to avoid the experience, to engage with, take up, or to believe you can ignore (rather like the graffito that reads 'Do not read this' [if you've read it, it's too late; if you haven't, it is impossible to obey]):

> I am trying to disinterest myself from myself to withdraw from death
> by making the 'I', to whom death is supposed to happen, gradually
> go away, no, be destroyed before death come to meet it, so that at
> the end already there should be no one left to be scared of losing the
> world in losing himself in it, and the last of the Jews that I still am
> doing nothing here other than destroying the world on the pretext
> of making truth, but just as well the intense relation to survival that
> writing is, is not driven by the desire that something remain after me,
> since I shall not be *there* to enjoy it in a word, *there* where the point
> is, rather in producing these remains and therefore the witnesses of
> my radical absence, to live today, here and now, this death of me,
> for example, the very counterexample which finally reveals the truth
> of the world such as it is, itself, i.e., without me, and all the more
> intensely to enjoy this light I am producing through the present
> experimentation of my possible survival, i.e., of absolute death, I tell
> myself this every time I am walking in the streets of a city in which I
> love . . . (Derrida 1993: 190–1)

I remarked earlier that Derrida rarely speaks or writes of experiment. Here is an exception. The passage exceeds the proper name by confronting the self's ownmost condition, the future memory, the memory to come of the self's death, the death, not of the author, but of the 'I', of saying 'I'. One of a possibly infinite, certainly uncountable number of selves, who may well happen to bear the name *Jacques Derrida*, but whose name could equally be any of ours, mine, yours, his or hers, seeks in anticipation of that death that is 'supposed to happen', to lose consciousness of selfhood, of the 'I'. Derrida writes 'supposed' because none of us knows; I may know that I am dying, I certainly know that I will die, as I know, one day, each and every one of you, and everyone you know, will die – this future is guaranteed, it is just the when and the how that remain to come, unknowable as such. The 'I' seeks to remove itself from the scenario it anticipates but cannot experience. But it does so by writing. For writing is what remains, it remains to come, the trace, not the presence. The trace is the remains of the self, what remains to come, to return, to be read, misread, not read. In a word, iterable; in another, revenance itself, a revenance that reminds the reader that the itself is not there, in the writing, in the signature, in the proper name, even though the proper name is of the order of writing, despite its apparent singularity.

For 'I' exceeds the singularity, the weight, the burden, of the proper name. 'I', more properly that which expresses the self, yet which is irreducible to any particular self, but which is the most naked affirmation of Being, escapes the proper name. Derrida's experimentation, the 'present experimentation of my possible survival', is just this writing of the self, an ongoing process, an experience of the self, the 'I', in writing, as the trace itself, anticipating itself as the not-self, the non-essential trace, remainder, revenant that lives on, surviving, 'living' beyond mere physical, corporeal, animal existence, beyond the death of the one who bears the proper name. Derrida erases the proper name in the name of 'I', *L'Innommable*, the unnameable. (It is as if, I like to imagine, another proper name were being called, came calling, was cited without being cited, cited indirectly; it is as if, imagine it, Beckett were cited, called, referred to, alluded to; as if Beckett had come calling here, had left in this word his calling card, and this were Derrida's response.) No proper name, no one chained to the name, yet in the face of death, 'I' presents itself even in the absence, the structural or radical absence of the one who writes, the 'I' continuing to arrive even post-mortem. 'I' survives absolute death. This is, to reduce it to its starkest element, what takes place as experiment and experience in the name of Jacques Derrida, in *Jacques Derrida*, exceeding and escaping systematisation, totalisation and even life. And because there is no proper name that can encompass, frame or enslave the 'I', there remains, as there remains to come for each and every 'I' who speaks, who reads the 'I' of an other, the singularity of experience in intimate relation to the world, at once singular and also universal; or, as a certain Jacques Derrida has it, thereby countersigning with his trace as the trace of a survival ahead of and beyond his death, though unnameable as such, 'I' bespeaks a 'universal pronoun, but of so singular a universality that it always remains, precisely, singular. The function of this source', writes Jacques Derrida, speaking to us from beyond the grave, 'which *names itself I* is indeed, within and without language, that of a singular universal' (1982: 281).

I can't go on.

I'll go on.

Or, in the words of Gloria Gaynor, I will survive.

NOTE

1. A version of this chapter was first delivered as a keynote address on 19 May 2016, at the Seventh Between.Pomiędzy Festival and Conference, Sopot-Gdynia-Gdańsk, Poland, 16–21 May 2016. I would like to thank the organisers, David Malcolm, Monika Szuba and Tomasz Wiśniewski, for all their hard work and for being such gracious hosts.

WORKS CITED

Bennington, Geoffrey and Jacques Derrida (1993), *Jacques Derrida*, trans. Geoffrey Bennington, Chicago: University of Chicago Press.

Caputo, John (2000), 'For the Love of the Things Themselves: Derrida's Phenomenology of the Hyper-Real', *Journal of Cultural and Religious Theory*, 1: 3 (July), 37–60.

Derrida, Jacques (1972), *Marges de la philosophie*, Paris: Minuit.

Derrida, Jacques (1982), *Margins of Philosophy*, trans. Alan Bass, Chicago: University of Chicago Press.

Derrida, Jacques (1988), 'Telepathy', trans. Nicholas Royle, *Oxford Literary Review*, 10, 3–41.

Derrida, Jacques (1993), 'Circumfessions', in Geoffrey Bennington and Jacques Derrida, *Jacques Derrida*, trans. Geoffrey Bennington, Chicago: University of Chicago Press, pp. 3–315.

Derrida, Jacques (1995), *On the Name*, trans. Thomas Dutoit, Stanford: Stanford University Press.

Derrida, Jacques (2009), *The Beast and the Sovereign, vol. I*, trans. Geoffrey Bennington, Chicago: University of Chicago Press.

Derrida, Jacques (2014), *For Strasbourg: Conversations of Friendship and Philosophy*, ed. and trans. Pascale-Anne Brault and Michael Naas, New York: Fordham University Press.

Derrida, Jacques and Maurizio Ferraris (2001), *A Taste for the Secret*, trans. Giacomo Donis, ed. Giacomo Donis and David Webb, Cambridge: Polity Press.

Eliot, George (2014), *Daniel Deronda*, ed. Grahame Handley, intro. K. M. Newton, Oxford: Oxford University Press.

Index